MEMORY, EDITED

Taking Liberties with History

ABBY SMITH RUMSEY

The MIT Press
Cambridge, Massachusetts
London, England

The MIT Press would like to thank the anonymous peer reviewers who provided comments on drafts of this book. The generous work of academic experts is essential for establishing the authority and quality of our publications. We acknowledge with gratitude the contributions of these otherwise uncredited readers.

This book was set in Adobe Garamond and Berthold Akzidenz Grotesk by Jen Jackowitz. Printed and bound in the United States of America.

Library of Congress Cataloging-in-Publication Data

Names: Rumsey, Abby Smith, author.
Title: Memory, edited : taking liberties with history / Abby Smith Rumsey.
Other titles: Taking liberties with history
Description: Cambridge, Massachusetts : The MIT Press, [2023] | Includes bibliographical references and index.
Identifiers: LCCN 2022052573 (print) | LCCN 2022052574 (ebook) | ISBN 9780262048477 (hardcover) | ISBN 9780262376167 (epub) | ISBN 9780262376150 (pdf)
Subjects: LCSH: Soviet Union—Historiography. | Russia—Historiography. | Collective memory—Soviet Union. | Collective memory—Russia. | Soviet Union—Intellectual life. | Russia—Intellectual life. | Soviet Union—In literature. | Russia—In literature. | Political culture—Soviet Union. | Political culture—Russia.
Classification: LCC DK38 .R86 2023 (print) | LCC DK38 (ebook) | DDC 947.084—dc23/eng/20221116
LC record available at https://lccn.loc.gov/2022052573
LC ebook record available at https://lccn.loc.gov/2022052574

10 9 8 7 6 5 4 3 2 1

For David and Izzy

Love of the fatherland is certainly a very beautiful thing,
but there is something better than that; it is the love of truth.
—Peter Chaadaev, "Apologia of a Madman"

CONTENTS

1 MAKING THE PAST MAKE SENSE

REVERSAL OF FORTUNE

The twenty-first century has gotten off to a rocky start. In the United States, people expected that after they won the Cold War, peace would reign and liberal democracies would go global. At home, social and political tensions would lessen as freedom and equality would gain ground. It would all be worth the high price of having waged war and lived under threat of nuclear attack for over four decades. Yet, after the Soviet Union came apart in 1991, the peace dividend failed to materialize. Instead, there were new shocks at home and unforeseen threats from abroad. The Y2K scare passed without incident, but that near-miss was followed by a cascade of crises: 9/11, the Great Recession, the dangerous acceleration of climate change, rising wealth inequality, foreign and domestic terrorism. The election of Barack Obama was seen as progress. At the same time it spurred the growth of right-wing cadres in reaction. Then Donald Trump became president. So, it turned out this wasn't really the post-racial era after all. What happened to the arc of moral history that bends toward justice?

The shocks continued. In 2020, a novel coronavirus became pandemic and killed over a million Americans in two years. Racial tensions exploded yet again. Mass murders and hate crimes proliferated. Trump lost the presidential election and refused to leave office. On January 6, 2021, his armed supporters stormed the Capitol in an attempted coup. The long, proud tradition of America's peaceful transfer of power was shattered. The eyes of the world were fixed on the increasing internal threats to the great superpower.

On the morning of February 24, 2022, the world woke up to learn that Russia had invaded Ukraine in an attempt to annex the nation. It seemed a final blow to the promise of peace after the Iron Curtain was breached in 1989. The post–World War II global order became a memory, and the new one is up for grabs.[1] Amid high-pitched media coverage of weakening democracies, decreasing institutional trust, polarizing populations, and apocalyptic movements from Al Qaeda in the Middle East to QAnon in the United States, people are struggling to understand where this turbulence is coming from.

Two decades into the century, the United States is in a full-blown identity crisis. For all intents and purposes, Americans are so polarized they do not even acknowledge each other as fellow citizens.[2] The divisions are so dramatic that Americans no longer refer casually to a collective *we* but specify which people think *our* way and which *their* way. The American people proclaim the values of freedom and equality to be self-evident, but they don't agree on what these values mean. Is America still what Madeleine Albright called "the indispensable nation," able to "see further than other countries into the future"?[3] She said this confidently in 1998, before the nation was taken by surprise on September 11, 2001. Some experts had warned about Islamic terrorism, just as they warned about easy credit and mortgage-backed securities, growing alt-right militias, and Russian aggression. Despite this, neither the US government nor the media prepared the public for these crises. Perhaps it was because the idea of progress was so deeply ingrained that it was impossible to imagine regression—or if imagined, too unpopular for approval-ratings-sensitive administrations and media to report. The history taught in schools also inculcated in the US public an expectation of continued progress. This is not a history that serves people well in times of crises and reversed expectations. It is time for a new American history, one that meets the moment.

But which history? Looking in the rearview mirror, some Americans date the founding of the nation to Philadelphia in 1776. Others, looking in the same mirror, see deeper in time and argue that the arrival of enslaved Africans on the continent in 1619 is the true beginning. In these debates, the past is always prophetic. Accordingly, national origins have significance because they fix the character and destiny of a people. Therefore, either

Americans are born free and equal, which makes the nation a noble experiment in democracy and a model for the world, or they are born in sin, and the guilt of that ancestral crime passes from generation to generation, not fully acknowledged, not fully atoned for. These two versions of the American genesis are offered as an either/or proposition and deemed irreconcilable. This attitude is both a symptom of the polarization now paralyzing democratic governance and a primary cause. At least adherents of both ideas agree that a reckoning with the past is necessary before Americans can move on, wherever they're going.

The present moment raises the critical question: Does a nation need a shared past to have a shared future?

This book addresses the question by examining the price paid when the answer has to be *yes*. Harmonizing views of the past seldom creates a shared vision for the future. Nor is it desirable. The twentieth century spawned utopian experiments in creating a more perfect world in which one and only one future was available to people. In the Soviet Union, the Third Reich, Communist China, and Cambodia (Kampuchea), there was a single vision of the good society, and how to build it was predetermined by the laws of history. What's characterized today as the history wars in the United States is a battle about who owns the future. Neither tale of US genesis can be correct because neither takes into account the nature of historical change and the starring roles that chance and contingency play.[4] When we discount the power of chance events and underestimate our ability to adapt to adversity, history is reduced to a fairytale and humans to perpetual childhood. The philosopher Leszek Kołakowski said that "we learn history not in order to know how to behave or how to succeed, but to know who we are."[5] The value of history, then, is neither to predict the future nor to teach lessons about how to live; it is to gain a truer sense of ourselves and of the world.

It is not a shared past that nations need, but a shared sense of reality. Especially in a nation of immigrants that nurtures a pluralism of values and beliefs as essential to true freedom, a pluralism of facts courts disaster. In this book, we will look at the consequences of regimes that treat history not as an archive of self-knowledge but as mere prologue to the future. Such regimes weave information—true or false—into a fabric of fables with the power to control the mind and soul of the population. We will see what happens when generations grow up ignorant of their true history, therefore not knowing who they are.

By necessity, narratives are selective in their recitation of events. Fiction has the license to ignore or depart from the facts of the case in an effort to get at a deeper truth. Not history. Imagine meeting a stranger at a party and, to break the ice, you ask where they come from. The stranger you chat up may exaggerate some details and leave out others that reflect badly on them. But little harm is done because experience tells us this is common. We may even have done it ourselves on occasion and so are prepared to discount small departures from the facts. People seldom intentionally embroider facts designed to deceive. Besides, nowadays it's easy to google a person and check the veracity of what they say.

Here's the rub: search engines and social media platforms don't test the truth of their search results. In 2016, it became starkly evident that the internet can be easily used by bad actors to deliberately circulate stories they know to be untrue, especially about the American past and present—all to seize control of the future. The bizarre barrage of fake facts and elaborate conspiracies surprised many people. It shouldn't have. The real surprise is how many people believed these stories, defended them, and identified those who didn't believe them not as misguided fellow citizens, but as enemies.

This nefarious way of doing politics is all too familiar to me. I am a historian of Russia.

In 1982–1983, I was a Fulbright fellow in Moscow and Leningrad, where I conducted archival research for my doctoral dissertation. Despite the fact that my topic was the ruling elite of the late seventeenth century, I was still denied access to many files I requested. Sometimes I was told they didn't exist. I knew better because a Russian colleague was working on them. This was a fact I couldn't mention without getting him in trouble. That said, the logic of denial was impeccable. The way the Soviets constructed their history, there was absolutely nothing in the Russian past that was truly past. Their historical record was carefully edited to be a narrative leading in a predetermined fashion to the end of class struggle and the ultimate triumph of the proletariat. I knew this going into the archives. The denials were infuriating but not surprising. What I had not fully grasped were the everyday consequences of imposing that narrative on hundreds of millions of people.

That epiphany happened one day when my Soviet roommate, who was from the closed military city of Vladivostok on the Pacific, returned from a four-hour scour of food markets across Leningrad and showed me her prize purchase: a kilo of butter. Butter was a scarce commodity, even in well-provisioned cities such as Leningrad, Moscow, and Vladivostok. She beamed with the pride of someone who had just won the lottery, and she had every right to gloat. She asked me how often butter was available in our markets. I answered, "Always." (I had just read *The International Herald-Tribune*'s story about Midwestern dairy farmers dumping tons of cheese to protest the farm subsidy bill just passed in Congress, but I spared her that news.) *Always* was so far from what she could even imagine that she had to take a beat. Then, pulling herself up in all her dignified skepticism, she said in a tone somewhere between pity and condescension that she understood I naturally was patriotic and quick to defend my motherland, but I did not need to lie. When I protested that I wasn't lying, she grew indignant. I had just confirmed everything she heard about capitalists.

It may not surprise many in the West that authoritarian countries are cavalier with the facts. We assume this is simply part of the regimes' intrinsic moral corruption. Surely we in democratic nations—in particular the United States, the oldest continuous democracy—are immune to such abuses. We do not take such liberties with our history.

Sadly, we now know this is not the case. It is increasingly clear what happens when the human need for certainty and stability finds an ideology that gives people what they're looking for. It's happening before our eyes in the United States. In extreme cases, that ideology, whether leaning left or right, is staked on a vision of a future that uses the past as a required backstory to the (inevitable) realization of the future. It becomes necessary to burnish the past so that it's a compelling story of heroes and villains. Then make that version official to ensure that it—and it alone—is taught in schools, written in history books, propagandized through films and television, embodied in memorials, statues, and history-themed amusement parks. It goes unchallenged and is so ubiquitous, it is scarcely noticed on a conscious level. It works its magic subliminally.

The experience of Soviet and post–Soviet Bloc nations has urgent relevance for understanding the ongoing competition over whose history is told. My roommate was only one of hundreds of millions behind the Iron Curtain whose entire grasp of reality was controlled by the regime down to every detail and reaching even into their dream life. This manufactured reality lodged itself deep in the psychology of individuals. Its effect was so crippling on the population that when the Iron Curtain lifted and these lies were exposed, they had little capacity to deal with the radically new reality they faced. If the reality they had known all their life was in fact not real, maybe they were not real either.

What did my Leningrad roommate think when the Berlin Wall came down in 1989? What did she make of the end of the Soviet Union two years later? What was it like when the world she knew and cherished was unmasked? For millions of former Soviet Bloc citizens, it was all too painful to see, let alone acknowledge, the lies that robbed them of true self-knowledge. Their psychic shock is compounded by the sudden revelation of horrific crimes committed by the regime *in their name* and that in many cases they were party to, willingly or not. Their experience reveals what happens when people are forced to reexamine and even abandon long-held ideas of the past in light of newly revealed facts. Not all nations and not all people react the same. There is a stark contrast between those former Soviet Bloc countries willing and able to confront their past, such as East Germany, and Russia, whose early efforts to excavate long-buried facts were quickly shut down by a new regime led by a former KGB official, Vladimir Putin. From that perspective, the cognitive dissonance experienced by many Americans trying to reconcile the facts and consequences of slavery with the dominant narrative of freedom and equality is understandable.

Leo Tolstoy believed that "a historian has to do with the results of the event, the artist with the fact of the event."[6] It is the task equally of historians and artists to find the truth and validate it as the key to moral freedom. By examining the reckoning with a painful past through the prism of Eastern European experience, we can see the contours of the American impasse from an oblique angle. (I use the collective term "Eastern Europe" to designate countries that were part of the Soviet Bloc, including Russia, and "Russia" when I refer specifically to that country.) From that angle it becomes clear that the Americans' struggle to know and acknowledge their history will succeed if and when the values of equality and liberty regain equilibrium.

The small lies my Leningrad roommate believed and the big lies told by Putin are of a piece. In justification of his invasion of Ukraine, Putin claims Ukraine is not and never has been a sovereign nation: "Russians and Ukrainians were one people—a single whole."[7] Therefore he is compelled to "reunite" Ukraine with Russia. Foreign Secretary Sergei Lavrov warned the West in his chilling baritone that "we will define Ukraine's destiny by ourselves."[8] These claims are based on fabricated history. Despite Putin's efforts to restore Russia's imperial power and prestige, he cannot put the Russian Empire back together again.

For individuals and their larger society, history is a precious source of self-knowledge. Of special value is the knowledge gained only through personal experience. The depth of an experience can be so profound and intimate that at times only subjective descriptions, a bearing of witness, can do it justice. For this reason, artists and writers are best positioned to speak to all dimensions of a life dominated by lies. I give priority to the voices of writers and artists who lived with liberally edited histories, fanciful facts, and propaganda about their glorious future. They convey exactly what is at stake when the truth is fungible and their own history becomes whatever some regime or ego-driven leader chooses to make of it. I focus more on *earned* knowledge and less on theoretical. I provide relevant background that the reader may need to understand the context of key events. Sources are cited in English translation to make it easier for curious readers to pursue topics of interest to them. Above all, I emphasize what these writers and artists reveal about how abuse of history robs people of the ability to know themselves and make informed moral choices. And so, while I write about the influence of Marxism on Russian intellectuals, it is not what Marx wrote that matters but what Lenin and his fellow Bolsheviks made of it. I write not about how Stalin turned Marxism-Leninism into totalitarianism, but about the effect of totalitarianism on those subject to it and the role that lies about the past played in the party's grip on power. Its crippling effect still exerts power over post-Soviet populations.

It is equally important to understand how people can be so susceptible to a regime of lies. Why embrace an ideology founded on absolute certainties when the world provides abundant evidence of the unpredictability of all things human? In the present age, dominated by social media, buying into lies has more than personal consequences. One deluded person has a mental health condition and deserves our compassion. But a society that's lost its sense of reality poses a threat to itself and to the world.

The similarities between the United States and the Russian Empire and its successor, the Union of Soviet Socialist Republics, are striking. They are easy enough to overlook, though, because the lingering effects of Cold War rhetoric play up existential antagonisms and the renewed alienation between the nations. Both nations lie on the periphery of Western Europe and, until the Second World War, they measured themselves against European culture. Both nations built their super-scaled economic and military powers on an abundance of natural resources made productive through centuries of unfree labor. Both nations believe themselves to be endowed with a destiny of world-historical importance. Both believe they have a unique moral mission to serve as a beacon of light to other nations. In 2000, US president George W. Bush told his audience at the Simon Wiesenthal Center, "I believe our nation is chosen by God and commissioned by history to be a model to the world."[9] This statement could have been said by Tsar Nicholas I or Vladimir Putin. If we did not have so much in common with the Russians, Trump could never have aligned himself as co-equal with Putin. It is true that some of Trump's affinity with strongmen is due to quirks of his personality. But the portion of Americans who found nothing disturbing about the sitting president of the United States saying he preferred the intelligence of Russian state security sources to America's intelligence sources is what matters.

Some of the writers and artists in our investigation of memory edited are well known in the West. Others are not but should be. Anton Chekhov illuminates the ways that memory works to endow a life with meaning. Fyodor Dostoevsky's account of his time imprisoned in Siberia as a political prisoner was the crucible from which he emerged with profound insight into how personal memory and identity are constrained by community. In the nineteenth century, a widening division between the educated classes and the mass of illiterate peasants sparked a heated debate between those among the educated who desired to emulate the West and those who rejected Western identity in favor of a Slavic, pointedly non-Western sense of self and national destiny. This debate is memorably articulated by Peter Chaadaev in the 1830s. That identity crisis has never been resolved. It casts a long shadow over Putin's 2022 invasion of Ukraine, a direct result of his antipathy to the West. Putin justifies violation of Ukraine's sovereign territory as a necessary righting of a grave historical wrong. *History tells us*, he says, that Ukraine is Russia. The West (that is, the United States and the European Union it dominates) must be stopped from annexing Ukraine into its sphere of influence.

Communism promised to accelerate modernity and destroy the oppressive Russian imperial order, sweeping it into the dustbin of history. The Bolsheviks mapped a path to the utopian future, and many artists and writers eagerly set off to help build that human paradise. We can see the influence of that radical utopian vision of history in Kazimir Malevich's invention of nonobjective art. The same vision inspired the writer Yevgeny Zamyatin, a committed Communist, who by 1919 understood that the Bolshevik mode of revolution would create a dystopia rather than a utopia. It moved the memoirist Nadezhda Mandelstam to record how millions survived under the regime that controlled information and propagated a fictional past. Together these men and women prove the continuous assault on reality led not to the withering away of the state, but to the withering away of society.[10]

In the conclusion, I address the challenge of emerging from behind the Iron Curtain to reckon with an ugly past, newly revealed. For this, I turn to the contemporary artist Gerhard Richter. Well known today as a German artist, he grew up not in the West but in Communist East Germany. He was twenty-nine when he moved to the West. By his own account, he was profoundly shaped by growing up in a totalitarian country. The past that Richter's art confronts belongs to a Germany that was first in thrall to Nazism and then subordinated to Soviet communism. These multiple layers of personal and collective past are the red thread running throughout his work. I chose an East German rather than Russian artist for the simple reason that the Russian government, unlike that of the united Germany, has refused to reckon with its own past. In fact, through a series of laws controlling the media and limiting access to state archives, the Putin regime has made it illegal to do so once again.

HISTORY AS PROPHECY

Do we create history, or does it create us? Historical narratives implicitly embed one assumption or the other. Memory—personal and collective—weaves a sense of continuity between past and future. But it is narrative that orders time. Historical narrative is a structure whose power of persuasion rests on three pillars:

—causation, which defines the shape and mechanism of change over time, be it linear or cyclical, goal-directed (teleological) or open-ended, controlled by a higher power or subject to the whims of chance;
—agency, which specifies the capacities of humans to affect their fate as either free historical actors or mere instruments of historical processes; and
—a vision of a moral universe, which accounts for a world rife with human suffering, injustice, and conflict—in short, evil—and that same world infinitely rich with goodness and grace.

The difference between one version of origins and another is not necessarily the facts cited, but intuitions of reality itself, the universe of human affairs. A model of history that envisions an end-state—whether it be the determinism of Marxism, the march of technological progress, or the apocalyptic extinction of Homo sapiens following anthropogenic climate change—is flawed because it discounts both human adaptability to change and contingency as a factor in change over time. Such narratives will frame the past and present in terms of their ultimate goal or final purpose—in short, its teleology. (To avoid this technical term as much as possible, I refer to these as goal-directed, end-state, or closed narratives; their opposites are open-ended or undetermined.) Closed narratives follow a through line, "the arc of history," as if human affairs were like a rainbow that had a beginning you could not quite see, and an end, also invisible. (In a utopian arc, when you reach the end you'll find a pot of gold.) Proponents of closed narratives have trouble with facts that don't fit into the scripted ending. Magical thinking is substituted for evidence-based history.

At the core of the clashing narratives of American origins are civic values inherited from the Enlightenment that shaped the early republic's ideals of governance. The values written into America's founding documents are often spoken of confidently as timeless and immutable. These notions are not unique to the Enlightenment by any means, but the role liberty and equality play in the American imagination does derive from a specific time and place. What if they are as obsolete as other now-discredited notions inherited from the Enlightenment? Is the idea of freedom and liberty's compatibility as dated as the belief in a universal human nature that is essentially perfectible, or the gradual triumph of reason over superstition, or the virtue of spreading Western civilization across the globe to enlighten those living in darkness? By no means did all Enlightenment thinkers hold such beliefs. But over time, these ideas were taught in classrooms and passed into common parlance. They have become the stuff of campaign promises and partisan sloganeering.

The present isn't a puzzle that a careful reading of the past can fully explain. It's tempting to conclude that things turned out the way they did because they had to. Our intuition of cause-and-effect should be tempered by the knowledge that if there is great uncertainty today, there was equally great uncertainty in all our yesterdays. In the past, people felt as flummoxed and fretful about current affairs as we do. Confusion, coincidence, and pure luck all played parts in things that happened unexpectedly, and things that did not happen, though they were expected. The future of past generations was the great unknown to them, just as our future is shrouded from us.

The trick is that imposing a narrative on the past requires a complicated adjudication between facts and storytelling, contingency and coherence.[11] Historical narrative's job is to create a coherent tale from an undifferentiated mass of details. It edits the known facts to sort events and people that are significant from those that are not. In a story, nothing "just happens." There are causes and effects, actors with motivations and actions with consequences. The literary critic Frank Kermode argues that stories are satisfying only to the degree that the beginning harmonizes with the end.[12] Facts alone cannot make a satisfying account of the past, no matter how deftly arranged. Historical truth is antithetical to narrative satisfaction.

Trying for a comprehensive sense of the past can spin a narrative that tells people little more than what they are inclined to believe. That's when knowledge of the past is taken to be prophetic. The prophecy can be nostalgic—the South will rise again. We can make America great again. Or it can focus on the future as progress toward a happy ending because history tells us that "by walking straight ahead one would rise into the air."[13] Faith in continuous progress is likewise the tenet of the techno-optimists of the digital age. They believe that significant social problems should be understood as technical problems: engineers can solve these problems by creating more technology, only newer and better. That mentality has driven the globalization of communication, trade, and education in the name of universal good, which in reality has benefited chiefly the few.

The crises of this century are among the results of multiple technical "fixes"—Google for search of burgeoning databases, Facebook for connecting and sharing content with others, Amazon for one-stop shopping and instant consumer gratification. But searches can be skewed to generate company profits; social media can promote propaganda and lies; and a centralized online market can become a juggernaut that eliminates valuable local or small-scale businesses. The problems created by powerful technology enterprises will not be resolved by forging ahead with more technical innovation. As for the fallout from these largely unregulated industries, especially in undermining trustworthy civic discourse, the accounting has barely begun. So while today's social, political, and economic problems don't appear to have much to do with a closed narrative, in reality such a narrative constrains our choices and drastically limits the kinds of solutions we can imagine and implement.

The proximate cause of Americans' dangerous ignorance of the past is the failure of the public education system. But the proximate cause, which can be addressed, is itself only a symptom of a larger disregard for the past. There is a long tradition of seeing America as a place to welcome the new and leave behind the old. This view is foundational to both conservative and liberal convictions. Neither the technology nor news industries created this trope. They capitalize on it.

James Baldwin homed in on the difficult truths in the American past that trouble the nation to this day. He believed that, when unrecognized, those truths poison the present and future. Baldwin articulated those truths without demonizing *them* or deifying *us*. He resolutely steered clear of ideologies that offered false comfort in unambiguous answers, writing:

> The great force of history comes from the fact that we carry it within us, are unconsciously controlled by it in many ways, and history is literally *present* in all that we do. It could scarcely be otherwise, since it is to history that we owe our frames of reference, our identities, and our aspirations. And it is with great pain and terror that one begins to realize this. In great pain and terror one begins to assess the history which has placed one where one is, and formed one's point of view. In great pain and terror because, thereafter, one enters into battle with that historical creation, Oneself, and attempts to re-create oneself according to a principle more humane and more liberating: one begins the attempt to achieve a level of personal maturity and freedom which robs history of its tyrannical power, and also changes history.[14]

If Americans take the premises of the Declaration of Independence seriously today, they are doing so in an era that entertains conflicting views about humanity's perfectibility, the compatibility of personal freedom and social equality, and material and moral progress marching hand-in-hand. Among many there persists an expectation that Western civilization will expand over the globe because it is the apex of a linear cultural development. This assumption in the Bush White House justified the shock and awe of America's invasion of Iraq. It undergirds the conviction that economic globalization is a universal good, as well as the belief in digital technology and social media. Such zeal to spread the good word of modern life and technological innovation is today's form of the crusade to save souls or spread enlightenment. Seeing the consequences of these views in the degradation of the physical environment and the nihilism of "what-about-ism" in civic discourse has spawned a reaction against technology, capitalism, and democracy here and abroad.

The facts of the past don't change, but they are often inaccessible to us—censored, permanently erased by the destruction of records, buried with those who bore witness to the truth. Tracing the lives and work of Eastern Europeans allows us to see that the meaning of the past as determined by the model of history—open or closed—frames the narrative. So if the meaning of the past is not absolute, what possible good is history to us?

History doesn't teach lessons, but if we consider it as an instrument of self-knowledge, we see the hidden dangers of taking liberties with history. If history tells lies, then the foundation we build our lives on is no more stable than quicksand. If we don't know our true origins, we live in ignorance of our true character and capabilities. History is not a court of law, and pleading ignorance cannot protect us. In other words, what we don't know will kill us. We cannot always anticipate what the past holds in store for us. But if we choose to ignore it, we stumble blindly into the future and encounter the past there, waiting for us.

2 THE WORK OF MEMORY

MAKING MEANING

The peculiar nature of human consciousness allows us to reflect on ourselves. We can see ourselves in the moment, as we read this page or walk down the aisle of the grocery store, or see ourselves in the mirror washing our face in the morning. But we can also picture ourselves retrospectively when we think back on our childhood, and prospectively when we anticipate lying on the beach next month, giving birth in three months, or finding a new job in the new year. Nothing is more certain than that *I exist*, unique from all others who live, have lived, and ever will live. How are these separate selves all recognizable as "me," given how much "I" change over the course of a lifetime? The neuroscientist Anil Seth proposes that the apparent continuity of selfhood is to some extent a fine and useful trick that keeps us alive. The body knows itself through a continuous communication between brain, gut, limbs, and the senses. Seth explains that the biological functions of this misperception are critical to self-preservation. The continuity of self doesn't require conscious effort. It just requires memory.[1] Our ability to keep our multiple selves integrated is the bedrock of our resilience in a world that constantly changes.

In his stories and plays, Anton Chekhov depicted memory as the vital link that not only keeps people physically and mentally whole, but at a deeper level is the source of having hope not despair, knowledge not ignorance, and kindness not cruelty. Memory is the great sifter of human values. Chekhov was a physician who began writing when young to earn money for his tuition, and then to support his large family—his despotic, bankrupt father, long-suffering mother, devoted sisters, and importunate, feckless brothers. He frequently complained about needing money but on occasion would turn down a commission. While in Nice in the winter of 1897, Chekhov received a request from his editor at *Cosmopolis* for a story taken from his life abroad. He declined. "I can write only from memory," he replied, "and have never written directly from nature. I must have my memory process a subject, like a filter that leaves only what is important and characteristic."[2] That winter, instead of writing about the sunlit pleasures of life on the Mediterranean, he turned out stories about young women and men living deep in the Russian provinces with little prospect of escaping from the tedium of their lives—all this from memory.

At first, this insistence on letting time do its work seems paradoxical, given how vividly Chekhov's stories incorporate extremely precise, well-observed details that come from everyday life—the way a farm smells of hay, warm manure, and steaming milk in June; that moment of transformation when a singer goes to the top of her range and sounds more birdlike than human; the violet glow of the sea at sunset in the Crimea. These details are not bits of journalistic color, nor are they mere word-count padding (Chekhov got his start by cranking out comic stories and gags for newspapers that paid by the word). These details were elements of the world that bound his characters in time and place and from which they could not escape.

Chekhov made his observation about memory when he was thirty-seven years old. He wintered in the south of France to give his tubercular lungs a rest from the dry frigid air of Moscow. Chekhov was born in 1860, when life expectancy was somewhere in the mid-forties. Atul Gawande has remarked that in 1900, "old age was not seen as something that increased your risk of dying, as it is today, but rather as a measure of good fortune."[3] Chekhov was not apportioned that measure of good fortune. He died of tuberculosis when he was forty-four, after years of suffering symptoms of weakness, insomnia, irregular heartbeat, chills, and fevers. He first noticed ruby-red sputum coughed up from his lungs when he was only twenty-five.[4] There was no cure for his disease, but his symptoms could be somewhat relieved by spending time in the south, so he wintered in the Riviera or Crimea.

Chekhov read deeply in Darwin, Herbert Spencer, and others who articulated a revolutionary view of human nature. In this view, humans are thoroughly naturalized, subject to the large-scale evolutionary forces that respond to random events in the environment—a fire that destroys a thriving habitat, a new bacterium that infects a population, a decade of drought. The fate of humanity is no different from the fate of other species. There is no special destiny set out for it. Chekhov was a thoroughgoing Darwinian who spoke with equanimity about outbreaks of cholera as the way that nature culls the weak, even as he was working twenty-hour days in his clinic to alleviate the pain and suffering of those affected by the disease. His task as a writer was identical to his task as a doctor and man of science. A writer is

> a person with an obligation, bound by his awareness of his duty and by his conscience; once he has taken up the pen, there's no turning back, and no matter how terrible something seems, he is obligated to overcome his squeamishness and sully his imagination with the filth of life. . . .
>
> To a chemist, nothing on earth is unclean. A writer must be as objective as a chemist; he must renounce ordinary subjectivity and understand that the dung heaps on the landscape play a venerable role, and that evil impulses are as much a part of life as the good ones.[5]

That said, his great subject as a writer was not the dung heaps on the landscape. It was memory itself, with its power to endow a life, no matter how humble, with meaning and, on occasion, states of pure bliss. In his plays and short stories, memory becomes more than a noun. It is a verb, an action fleeting and ephemeral, that makes sense of the otherwise random and senseless lives people lead.

Chekhov is said to have been tender, kind, compassionate. As a man, he may have been these things to his friends and patients, but never as a writer. In his stories and plays he depicted people without flattery. Given his acumen as a physician and diagnostician, he made observations that were precise and unsparing. This frankness was not intended to shock, dismay, or dishearten his readers. "The artist is not meant to be a judge of his characters and what they say; his only job is to be an impartial witness."[6] Few of his characters are masters of their own fate, and even fewer are eager to take responsibility for themselves, let alone others. Chekhov had a dim view of humans' capacity for self-understanding. Time and again, his characters meet misfortune and are degraded by it. They cheat and are cheated. They lie to themselves and they lie to others. Angry and despairing, they drink to excess. Or they live in indolence, out of cowardice, and keep quiet when they should speak up. We read of people who are offered a chance at happiness and don't notice it. Or if they do notice it, they turn it down, out of vanity or a passing spasm of spite, or they fret and grow anxious about change and take to their beds. Above all, they succumb to self-pity. They dwell in the past, enumerating their regrets. They worry about the future, paralyzed by anxiety. They stand still and life passes them by.

Yet his stories are studded with moments of gratuitous grace, fleeting as meteors in the moonless night sky, leaving traces long on the retina and even longer in memory. Where do these moments of grace come from? They are always the fruit of a memory stimulated haphazardly and appearing full-blown as a feeling and a vision. The character time-travels to a happier moment, is suffused with contentment, and catches a glimpse of paradise lost, perhaps, but nonetheless real in the moment. It reminds the reader (though seldom the character) how mysteriously, ineluctably, events in the present are linked to the past. Hopes crushed by life, buried beneath layers of disappointment and bitter experience, can return to us in a flash as emeralds or sapphires hardened into crystalline perfection under the tectonic pressures of the earth. For Chekhov, only with the passage of time can we grasp the meaning of an event or a feeling. But we must be patient and bear much pain before anything becomes clear to us.

Among Chekhov's most affecting works are those that walk right up to the mystery of life's bitter unfairness and stand still to let us gaze at it. We know it intimately through the unadorned imagery of his prose and unexplained behaviors of his characters. Then, depending upon Chekhov's mood, he either slaps us in the face (thus making it a comedy) or he steps away and leaves us in a state of wonderment, looking through the door he leaves open for us as he disappears.

In "The Lady with the Little Dog," the married protagonist Gurov casually starts an affair while on vacation in the Crimea. It wasn't out of boredom or restlessness, but just his habit of checking out the women wherever he happened to be and making one the target of his seduction. He chose someone he spotted walking on the seaside promenade with her dog. Anna Sergeevna was no more interesting and certainly no more beautiful than any other woman he had dallied with. But for some reason he couldn't account for, when they parted, he couldn't forget her. After he returned to his habitual life in Moscow, her image "would be covered in mist in his memory." Over time, "the memories burned brighter and brighter." Then they would "turn to reveries, and *in his imagination the past would mingle with what was still to be*. Anna Sergeevna was not a dream, she followed him everywhere like a shadow and watched him."[7]

What does the filter of memory reveal to Gurov that he could not otherwise know? As time did its work, sifting through the moments of his life, it left behind the one thing that meant anything to him—the strange, unprepossessing woman without whom he could not live. "Closing his eyes, he saw her as if alive, and she seemed younger, more beautiful, more tender than she was; and he also seemed better to himself than he had been then, in Yalta."[8] Perhaps these images were a trick of memory, but they revealed the truth to him. There was no escape in the end; his fate was attached to hers. He came to the tormented realization that he loved her. He had never expected to love, he never wanted to love, he didn't know how to love. Through no power of his own, he became attached to her, and through her, he became attached to the world, something he had never looked for, never wanted, and that he knew was only going to make his life more complicated: "And it seemed that, just a little more—and the solution would be found, and then a new, beautiful life would begin; and it was clear to both of them that the end was still far, far off, and the most complicated and difficult part was just beginning."[9]

Only in Chekhov can we read that lovers are finally united and that is when the difficulties begin. Only in his tales about the vanity of human ambition and the emptiness of people's promises can we find so much happiness overtaking a poor soul that he feels it almost as an affliction. What does this mean? It was through the work of memory that Gurov found his place in the world. That place was with Anna Sergeevna.

THE SCIENCE OF MEMORY

People call on memory to make sense of things and fashion order out of chaos. But memory isn't unique to humans; nor is its primary purpose to serve the needs of human consciousness. On the contrary, memory is intrinsic to all life and its purpose is entirely pragmatic—survival and procreation. This understanding of memory in its purely biological context is relatively recent, a product of scientific investigations into evolution, genetic coding, and neurobiology, all things that were in their earliest stages of development during Chekhov's lifetime.

While Chekhov was in Nice, occupied in writing "from memory," an anatomist in Madrid labored patiently to isolate, stain, and record nerve cells in meticulous and dramatically beautiful drawings (see figure 2.1). Santiago Ramón y Cajal (1852–1934) grew up wanting to be a painter, but that ambition was thwarted by his father. Instead, he devoted his considerable artistic gift to drawing the nerve cells he saw under the microscope, a feat he accomplished by devising a way to stain the neurons. What he saw contradicted the prevailing view of the nervous system, including the brain, as a continuous web of connected cells. Instead, he demonstrated that neurons, oddly shaped attenuated cells, though packed tightly together, were separated by small gaps called synapses. He was the first to articulate what is now a foundational theory of neuroscience: that neurons receive signals from other neurons at one end and pass them on to neurons at the other end. The one-way direction of this flow creates a communication vector. Cajal even hypothesized, correctly, that the ability to make multiple connections across synapses facilitates learning.

Ramón y Cajal is today recognized as the founder of neuroscience. He developed the neuron doctrine, stating that "the nerve cell, or neuron, is the fundamental building block and elementary signaling unit of the brain."[10] In

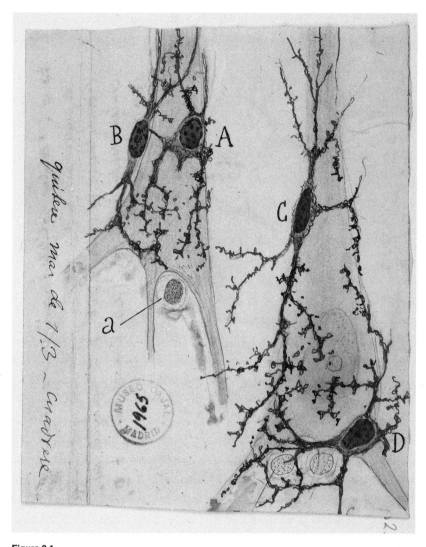

Figure 2.1

Santiago Ramón y Cajal drew neurons from the hippocampus, the seat of memory and "the oldest center of association in the brain" (quoted in *Beautiful Brain*, ed. Newman, Araque, and Dubinsky, 140). They receive signals at one end and transmit them at the other, thus creating and changing associations and memories. Ramón y Cajal, *Glial Cells Surrounding Pyramidal Neurons in the Human Hippocampus.*

his autobiography, *Recollections of My Life*, Cajal concludes that "intellectual power, and its most noble expressions, talent and genius, do not depend on the size or number of cerebral neurons, but all the richness of their connective processes, or in other words on *the complexity of the association pathways to short and long distances*."[11] He goes on to explain why repetition strengthens neuronal pathways and practice makes perfect: "Adaptation and professional dexterity, or rather the perfecting of function by exercise (physical education, speech, writing, piano-playing, mastery in fencing, and other activities) were explained by either a progressive thickening of the nerve pathways . . . excited by the passage of the impulse or the formulation of new cell processes . . . capable of improving the suitability and extension of the contacts, and even of making entirely new connections between neurons primitively independent." This hypothesis has "considerable probability . . . which lends itself, as the reader will imagine, to interesting rhetorical and psychological developments." His neuron doctrine, fruitful as it was, could not be confirmed until the electron microscope became available in the 1950s.[12]

Cajal's contemporary Sigmund Freud (1856–1939) was simultaneously developing his theories of memory as an archive of human experiences that exerts profound influence on a person's psyche. Freud hypothesized that psychological disorders stemmed from the suppression of conflicting emotions and thoughts. These emotions and thoughts were impossible to access directly because they lived beyond the reach of our conscious minds in what Freud called the unconscious. These repressed emotions forced their way to the surface through somatic symptoms such as tics, stutters, phobias, hysteria, even physical paralysis. The greater the repression, the greater the power of the unacknowledged past to dominate a person's will. For Freud, his patients were, in essence, *effects*, and his job was to unearth the *causes*. At the time, genteel society was shocked by the doctor's claim that neuroses were fueled by the libido—that is, sex. But over time what came to the fore was the power the past has to rob an individual of reason, control, and ultimately free will. Memory and history itself were seen as forces that determined not only a person's present state of mind but also the future. Long-stifled memories could exert their power by limiting a person's imagination and freedom of thought. The only way to gain leverage over an individual's future was to excavate the past and, in essence, rewrite their autobiography. Through the editing of memory, the repressed memory would be dissected, probed, and its energy released.

Today we take this idea for granted, as we do the physiology of the brain that Cajal pioneered. We tend to sideline Freud's psychotherapeutic techniques in favor of pharmaceutical interventions for mental illness, but the central idea that the workings of the mind are only partially accessible to consciousness is uncontested. So is Freud's idea that excavating long-buried parts of our past and confronting them can rob them of their power to haunt us. From there, incorporating these facts into a revised narrative of our lives creates a more healthy and integrated sense of self. The past acts on us whether we acknowledge it or ignore it. Cajal describes mechanisms in the brain by which people can loosen the bonds of existing memories and create new connections, thus expanding the possibilities of freedom through learning.

At this point in scientific understanding, the body itself looks like a mega memory machine. It operates from the instruction manual encoded in the genome, which transmits legacy information not only from one's parents but from the entire history of life on earth. In addition to genetic memory, the body acquires memory as it learns from each encounter with the world. Living organisms memorize their environment, and as the environment changes, memory is emended. Creatures learn, unlearn, and relearn. Just as Cajal imagined, the nervous system is able to make new or stronger connections to better adapt to a changing environment. The immune system likewise recognizes pathogens through innate immunity, which is genetically endowed, and through immunity acquired upon exposure. Memory of an encounter with a pathogen allows the body to be prepared to activate a targeted immune response for that specific pathogen should it encounter it again. This is how vaccines work, as the general population learned in 2020. Scientists are able to create molecules that mimic the COVID-19 pathogen enough to initiate an immune response that teaches the body how to fight off the real thing. In 2022 the world watched as the Delta variant of the virus succumbed to the vaccine and opened the field for yet more variants better able to elude the vaccine's protections.

As a man of science, Chekhov would marvel at the progress his peers have made since his day in understanding the physiology of memory. Neuroscientists in turn would agree with Chekhov that memory is the great sifter of value. No matter how much information a person takes in each day, only what is of long-term value sticks in memory. The rest, either redundant or irrelevant, is eventually flushed from our minds. This act of forgetting isn't to be mistaken for a weak memory that can't retain much information for long. On the contrary, forgetting is a crucial part of remembering. Forgetting is one of the ways the mind refuses distraction in order to pay attention. In terms of our mental software, forgetting is a feature, not a bug.

The biological work of memory is to keep us alive. By remembering something, experience is transformed into learning. In turn, learning enables us to anticipate what is about to happen by projecting past experience onto the future. To stay current in a dynamic environment, memory is labile, subject to constant updating. The mind disposes old, useless, or misleading information and organizes new information into useful knowledge. A healthy mind is always open to changing and adapting to new information and new environments. It's adept at distinguishing between the news that is signal and the news that is irrelevant or redundant. This is true as well of cultural memory; it's only with the passage of time that we come to understand the significance of cultural events. Particularly now, when digital networks flood all communication channels with too much information, people can't expect to be certain about what's important and what's mere noise. Uncertainty can be very uncomfortable, though, and anxiety-provoking. This unease makes people vulnerable to trusting sources that may or may not be credible, but that project certainty. From a biological point of view, unease is an important signal to a person that they may be facing a threat. Living in a war zone, unease is the natural state and prompts a person to protect themself. But in peacetime, an environment that overstimulates the brain can create anxiety that clouds a person's judgment. The common advice to take time out from the data deluge may be sound, but it ignores the fact that a person can then fear missing out on what's going on. This in turn can cause social anxiety. So instead of a timeout, people opt for certainty. They may continue seeking more information that confirms their views and thus lessens their anxiety.

Unrestrained production and unrestrained consumption of information, especially on social media, can harm our ability to learn and adapt. Other kinds of problems arise with learning abilities, including the growing diagnosis of being on the autism spectrum. The characteristic "behavioral inflexibility" of autism spectrum disorder might result from specific kinds of learning and adaptation being stymied. In such cases, experience doesn't work on the mind as it should; instead, it interferes with the process by which learning changes the way a person with autism reacts.[13] In the brain, this looks like a reversion to the pattern of connections among neurons set long before, which fails to incorporate the new information. An unbridgeable gap opens between a new situation, which demands adaptation, and the brain's autistic response, which defaults to an old reaction. Something prevents new information from taking its rightful place in the mind's hierarchies of knowledge. This is why change can be acutely distressing to someone on the autistic spectrum. But all people have some degree of negative response to change.

The same pattern occurs in the cognitive dissonance created by exposure to facts that contradict what a person thought to be true. People have a tendency, called confirmation bias, to give greater credence to evidence that confirms their view of things rather than flies in its face. The need to resolve mental conflict can override normal standards of evidence. The search for consistency and coherence drives storytelling, pattern recognition, and poetic discourse. It also drives conspiracy theories and paranoid interpretations that characteristically appear at junctures of rapid change, economic hardship and anxiety, and human-caused catastrophes. Conspiracy theories have a sweeping grandeur to them, a comprehensiveness that appears to explain and integrate miscellaneous contradictory or inexplicable events. Above all, their advantage is that they deny the randomness of everyday life. Their baroque theories arm believers with a plot line, contorted and incredible as it may be, that predicts the future. Marry that to a certain cognitive and affective disposition with low tolerance for ambiguity and, like magic, there is a population of conspiracy theorists ready to resort to political violence.[14]

The resistance to learning and adapting to change has multiple causes—some biological, some psychological, some autobiographical, and some a matter of circumstance. (The implications of these causes for individuals are vast and are subject to research, treatments, and therapies.) The way communities and nations adapt to change—or not—is influenced by a sense of whether human fates are open-ended and respond to a number of factors at any given time, or whether humanity is subject to a greater law or power that moves humans through time toward an end point. In both open and closed narratives, memory filters the important from the insignificant.

THE PARADOX OF AMNESIA

Memory copes with information overload by discerning patterns, consolidating memories, and embedding them in neural networks that generate meaning and coherence. This bit of mental housekeeping maximizes the overall health of the mind and reduces the entropy inherent in all the energy-intensive tasks the nervous system performs. Over time, meanings emerge and forge an integrated sense of self.

Memory holds us together; without it, all sense breaks apart into bits and pieces, like a jigsaw puzzle dumped helter-skelter on the floor. Cases of amnesia are dramatic and frightening demonstrations that we are what we remember. When memory decays, our grasp of the chain holding us together is lost. A person with amnesia can clutch a link or two in the chain, but the chain itself is broken. Content is unmoored from its natural context and confusion ensues. In severe cases of dementia, a person can't make out where they are or why. The unified self disappears as consciousness is reduced to the body. The tragedy of amnesia is that the fate of consciousness—of the self—is decided by the fate of the body.

Amnesia entails more than a loss of self. It poses a difficult question about the nature of humanity itself. If dementia destroys the higher, self-reflecting consciousness that we think is unique to humans, does this loss mean a person's claim to basic humanity is lost as well? Failures of memory can engender anxiety and self-doubt even among the most brilliant and accomplished. This question haunted two of the most acclaimed mathematicians of the last century, John von Neumann and Stanislaw Ulam.

Mathematicians usually grow into their powers when quite young. The confidence endowed by these powers, including memory, becomes intrinsic to their personality. As the notably gifted mathematician Stanislaw Ulam (1909–1984) said, "Good memory—at least for mathematicians and physicists—forms a large part of their talent. And what we call talent or perhaps genius itself depends to a large extent on *the ability to use one's memory properly to define the analogies, past, present and future, which . . . are central to the development of new ideas*."[15] He and his good friend John von Neumann (1903–1957) were Eastern European Jews who fled to the United States in the 1930s to escape fascism. Both were beloved, precocious firstborn sons. During the Second World War, they went to work combating fascism and played critical roles in the Manhattan Project. Between the two of them, von Neumann and Ulam were responsible for major contributions to game theory, probabilistic thinking, the Monte Carlo method, the atomic and hydrogen bombs, programmable computing, advances in combinatorics and set theory, and how modern states conduct war and negotiate peace.

Shortly after the war, Ulam was stricken by what was most likely viral encephalitis—no conclusive diagnosis was ever reached. The pressure on his brain from inflammation came close to killing him. Emergency surgery saved his life, but he consequently lost some physical and mental functions and struggled hard to recover them. In particular, his memory was compromised. During his long convalescence, Ulam repeatedly tested his memory to calculate the degree of deterioration and eventual recovery of his faculties. Was he the same person? It was at this time that he began thinking about the mathematics of memory. (How else would a mathematician think about memory?) He describes memory as a layered, self-referential entity that operates with a logic apart from what might serve as the original impulse for recollection: "There must be a trick to the train of thought, a recursive formula. A group of neurons starts working automatically, sometimes without external impulse. It is a kind of iterative process with a growing pattern. It wanders about in the brain, and the way it happens must depend on the memory of similar patterns."[16] Ulam speculates that unconscious thought works not in a linear way but according to associational or networked maps. He's thrilled by this notion because it presents a series of mathematically challenging questions: "Something goes on in our heads in processes which are not simply strung out on one line. In the future, there may be a theory of a memory search, not by one sensor going around, perhaps more like several searchers looking for someone lost in a forest. It is a problem of pursuit and of search—one of the greatest areas of combinatorics."[17]

Several years after Ulam's brain surgery, John von Neumann developed a disease that compromised his own sense of self. He had cancer that spread to his bones, causing extraordinary pain and creeping paralysis. Eventually it metastasized to his brain. He died prematurely at the age of fifty-three, when, by his own calculations, he had done only half or at most five-eighths of his life's work. From his youth on, von Neumann had been recognized by mentors and peers as a mathematical genius, and so he was treated. He was a man with charming, at times overweening, self-confidence, until the day his brain betrayed him. The cruelest aspect of his fate was the deterioration of his mental acuity and spectacular memory. His daughter, Marina von Neumann Whitman, who grew up to be an eminent economist, was in her early twenties when her father got sick. In her memoir, she relates the harrowing experience of visiting him in Walter Reed Hospital, where he lay dying. He was in the high-security wing of the hospital because of his work on nuclear weapons. There was concern that in his delirium, he might spill state secrets. (He expressed his hallucinations in his native Hungarian, which, it's safe to say, no one understood.)[18] The man many spoke of as the brightest mathematician of his time instructed his daughter to give him simple numbers,

> like seven and six or ten and three, and ask him to tell me their sum. For as long as I could remember, I had always known that my father's major source of self-regard, what he felt to be the very essence of his being, was his incredible mental capacity. In this late stage of his illness, he must have been aware that this capacity was deteriorating rapidly, and the panic that caused was worse than any physical pain. In demanding that I test him on these elementary sums, he was seeking reassurance that at least a small fragment of his intellectual powers remained.[19]

The physicist Eugene Wigner, his friend and fellow Hungarian, recalled that von Neumann "spoke five languages and also read Latin and Greek. He had done important work in economics: the role of profits, the benefits of competition, and the best methods of developing national economies.

He read widely and remembered it all, whether technical or literary. Large chunks of world history he knew thoroughly, especially Greek history. The history of the Renaissance he knew as thoroughly as a professional historian."[20] Ulam would visit his friend in the hospital and found his memory, while sporadic, still uncanny in its recall. Just days before von Neumann died, Ulam recalls "reading to [von Neumann] in Greek from his worn copy of Thucydides a story he liked especially about the Athenians' attack on Melos, and also the speech of Pericles. He remembered enough to correct an occasional mistake or mispronunciation on my part."[21] Thucydides's text had lived inside von Neumann since he was a child. It was a memory laid down in the deepest core of his being. The fact that he could remember the text so exquisitely was proof positive to Ulam that his friend was still there.

Nietzsche may or may not have been serious when he quipped that "God made forgetfulness the guard he placed at the threshold of human dignity."[22] But God did make forgetfulness of a specific kind crucial to the building up of culture. Source amnesia, whereby a person cannot remember when or where they first read or heard of something, is a common trick of memory. It is probably due to the way the brain generalizes the content of memories so that it can be used in different contexts. Memories can be stripped of their episodic particulars and allow for analogies and patterns to present themselves, to pop up as an association, metaphor, or heuristic. This exfoliation of details is an intentional form of forgetting, intentional though unconscious. Maybe this is similar to the "wander[ing] about in the brain" that Ulam mentions. The more richly associated one memory is with others, the more likely it is to shed its association with its original source along the way.

Exfoliation of source details and absorption into a large network of associations is how culture builds up over time. Culture requires the constant recycling of the past. Each generation takes what it needs from the past and repurposes it for present needs. Over time, the loss of ties to its original context can result in content changing its meaning 180 degrees. For example, the concept of America as "a city on a hill" is taken from a lay sermon by John Winthrop, written in 1630.[23] In its original context, it was used as an admonition to Winthrop's fellow immigrants that they were setting themselves up to be under the constant watch of a judgmental God. It was an anxious warning against self-satisfaction. Now, the phrase has been turned inside out to mean the opposite. It doesn't convey anxiety over imminent judgment, but is a self-satisfied, if not self-congratulatory, boast that America is a shining beacon for the world.

Cultural memory operates much like personal memory. It grows stronger every time it is recalled. If never used, it fades away. And like physical memories, cultural memories are imperceptibly modified with each use as we deploy the remembered fragments of the human past in new contexts and attach new associations to them. Thus the paradox of why we restate the obvious: unless we say what we already know in new ways, we will lose what we know.

Source amnesia accounts for the persistence to this day of Christian morality and the Christian sense of history, with its expectations of an end-of-time fulfillment. The linear, goal-directed history of salvation permeates modern cultures that are completely secular. People subscribe to this model of history because it's part of the natural landscape. Most have no idea where it comes from or think its origins bear scrutiny. Especially in secular cultures, this lack of curiosity can foist upon mere mortals expectations and demands that used to be made of an omniscient and eternal divinity. The human race can't compete with that. Even ideas seen as authentically modern and secular can be rooted firmly in the soil of religious convictions. Francis Fukuyama argues that the contemporary ideal of becoming our true, authentic self is in fact a Christian aspiration to achieve an authentic and unmediated relationship with God, dressed in secular clothing. What was once a soul in need of God for salvation is transformed into an innately perfectible individual who needs not divine love and mercy but a good liberal education.[24]

Before the rise of secularism, people in the West lived in what would be called today a unipolar world. It didn't matter whether someone believed in God or not. Time was kept by the church calendar, the days and seasons marked by liturgical hours, holy days, the calendar of saints, and all of it worked up to the end of time and the Last Judgment to come. All realms of human life, from cosmology and history to art and philosophy, were unified under the divine providence of an omniscient and merciful God. That unity was lost during the Protestant Reformation, and over time the realms of science, philosophy, and art became independent of one another, developing distinct and often competing epistemologies and standards of truth. We are the inheritors of this epistemological pluralism, which has spawned and supports a pluralism of values.

The twenty-first century began with fearless attacks on Western democracies by terrorists who used religious rhetoric to proselytize their cause. It is safe to say that many people in the West were shocked, even offended, to be accused of what these terrorists claimed. They characterized the terrorists as fanatics from a backward culture, wholly alien to the secular West. By the second decade and increasingly in the third, American domestic terrorists and political extremists resort to similar religious rhetoric. They aren't galvanized by foreign ideas or actors. The Americans who want to "take back our country" operate from a vision of "the real America," which they imagine traces back to that mythic founding of the country as a city on a hill. The fact that many others in the country denounce these violent actions and claim, "This is not who we are," betrays a lamentable ignorance of the country's long history of antigovernment, racialized violence. The concept of the city on a hill in its original context was a warning, anxious and riddled with self-doubt, about how these early immigrants would be judged by God should they stray from the straight and narrow path. That such a vision could be used so self-confidently, with braggadocio, illustrates what can happen when ideas move forward through time, lose connection with their origins, and attach themselves to contemporary needs.

The principles of liberty and equality are likewise born of a different age. They once signified meanings orthogonal to current understandings of these terms and existed in an utterly different time and context. In America, these words have been repurposed over the course of over two hundred years to encompass women and nonwhites, with or without property. The principles of liberty and equality live today in a culture that is urban, not rural; industrial, not agrarian; and embedded in an international superpower, not a scarcely self-sufficient cluster of colonies turning their back on Europe and looking westward for so-called virgin—though not unoccupied—lands. They sit uncomfortably alongside the contemporary understandings of human nature: that we are primates whose sociality is hardwired and organized hierarchically when groups exceed one or two hundred. Yet these principles persist with even greater power than before as more people claim freedom and equality as rights. Over time, they have been liberated from their original context and used freely—sometimes too freely. On March 14, 2020, Representative Alexandria Ocasio-Cortez of the Bronx, a district especially hard-hit by the first wave of COVID-19 infections, tweeted a plea to fellow New Yorkers to "stop crowding bars, restaurants, and public spaces right now. Eat your meals at home." In reply, Katie Williams, one-time Ms. Nevada State, shot back with a message for Ocasio-Cortez to mind her own business: "I just went to a crowded Red Robin [restaurant]. . . . It was delicious and I took my sweet time eating my meal. Because this is America. And I'll do what I want."[25]

At the beginning of the twentieth century, Marcel Duchamp committed acts of appropriation that have since become a highly generative standard in art. He took everyday objects—a bicycle wheel, a snow shovel, and most infamously, a porcelain urinal, displayed them as he would a sculpture, and declared them art. They were readymades. The act of creation was not in crafting the object, he said, but in the feat of imagination. A urinal, for example, was no longer a magnificently crafted invention for personal hygiene; it was transformed into a fountain, a decorative, useless object to be admired for its form and shiny enamel texture. Also to be admired is the audacity of the man who declared that a piece of plumbing is a work of art. Duchamp's act vividly demonstrated that context creates meaning.

Ideas, then, are simply readymades as well, cultural assets in general circulation belonging to everyone and no one in particular. Their value increases with use and decreases with neglect. Complaining about cultural appropriation is most times misguided. If it were true that a metaphor, a story, the cut of a dress, or the style of a song once used should remain the property solely of the first to use it, we would be forced to say that Shakespeare was a second-rate playwright at best, a plagiarist at worst. He took his plots either from history books or from other plays and stories. Instead, we have canonized him as the greatest writer in the English language. We no longer read Holinshed's *Chronicles of Scotland*, the source of *Macbeth*, or the play *The True Chronicle History of King Leir*, a likely source for Lear. But we know these stories because we know Shakespeare.

The hoarding of ideas impoverishes us all. James Baldwin wrote that "what one has to do as a black American is to take white history, or history as written by whites, and claim it all—including Shakespeare."[26] This was not avarice on his part; Baldwin was a generous man. It was a claim of shared humanity.

The anthropologist Joseph Henrich identifies the sharing of cultural heritage as key to the success of our species. Through sharing we grow the collective brain that has given us the unique and possibly only advantage we have over all other species. He writes: "Once we understand the importance of collective brains, we begin to see why modern societies vary in their innovativeness. It's not the smartness of individuals or the formal incentives. It's the willingness and ability of large numbers of individuals at the knowledge frontier to freely interact, exchange views, disagree, learn from each other, build collaborations, trust strangers, and be wrong. Innovation does not take a genius or a village; it takes a big network of freely interacting minds."[27]

Rather than think of using pieces of exogenous cultural expression as appropriation, we would be more accurate to see it as rescuing and recycling what is valuable. It is additive. To return to John von Neumann as an example, he was renowned for his prolific work in a number of fields, including early computer science. He was the first to write about the computer and its resemblance to the mind. He was at work on a series of lectures about the computer and the brain when he died. (His notes were turned into a book, *The Computer and the Brain*.) For this, von Neumann was criticized by some of his colleagues at Princeton who felt he should stick with pure mathematics, by their lights a higher order of knowledge than any applied discipline. There were others who criticized him invidiously for not having particularly original ideas. For his part, von Neumann was dismayed by the intellectual culture he found in America that discouraged conversation and collaboration among scholars. His biographer, Norman Macrae, reported that von Neumann "was worried from the first both at the way practical Americans worked with patents in mind and with the way unpractical Americans got cross with each other on the irrelevant matter of who had thought or said something first. He believed the only way science could progress was by scholars picking up each other's work and improving it."[28] While von Neumann was criticized for freely taking the ideas of others, he made something of the thoughts that they could not. He added to the sum of knowledge while subtracting nothing. He understood ideas to be readymades, waiting to be discovered, plucked out of their original context and placed in a new one in which they could be fruitful and multiply.

The work of memory is fragile enough without being subjected to punitive scorekeeping by overeager virtue police. Curious about the length of time that cultures retain different types of collective memory, scientists have derived an algorithm of oblivion. Cristian Candia and his lab claim to have found a mathematical law that governs the rate of collective memory decay.[29] Analyzing attention as a proxy for memory, they discovered that memories (that is, online mentions and citations) of pop music drop off fastest (about six years) and sports stars stick the longest (twenty to thirty years). The difference between short-term and long-term forgetting is that the former rests on oral communication between individuals and groups; the latter on cultural memory, the great crucible of long-term value. Twenty to thirty years is a generation. From Candia's evidence, it is reasonable to infer that because sports create metrics of excellence—number of home runs, Super Bowl wins, goalie saves—comparisons between individuals across time is a common and pleasurable indulgence of fandom. A pop song, on the other hand, lives past the first generation only if covered by later artists in a completely different context. Then it becomes a song for the ages.

CANCEL-HISTORY CULTURE

There is only one thing more injurious to cultural growth than the hoarding of ideas, and that is the declaration that there is one truth, one fate, one future for all humanity. All other ideas and truths are thereby deemed to be errors, and the thought police are unleashed to protect the vulnerable from nonconforming notions and expressions. There is always an impeccable logic to their vigilantism. That is why the more zealously the acolytes devote themselves to righting the wrongs of society, the more dangerous they become. Freedom of speech is the right that protects freedom of thought. If a given society cannot tolerate a pluralism of views, religions, political persuasions, and values, the regulation of speech is the first step taken to regulate thought. Though the United States touts its laws protecting freedom of speech, it paradoxically finds itself in the throes of a "cancel culture" that heaps abuse on people who violate an unwritten code. Anxious monitoring of the self for the true intentions behind actions or inactions can be traced back to Calvinism and the particular strain that landed in New England with the Puritans. If expressing ideas that run counter to cultural consensus is punished by law or public shaming, most people will regulate their own speech. They internalize that legal or cultural censor and spare themselves the very real pain of social ostracism.

Joseph Stalin is reputed to have said that self-doubt is the greatest waste of time in all human history. Whether he said it or not, the thought perfectly fits the mindset of a totalitarian mass-murderer. Stalin was an extraordinarily successful politician, but doubt and fear played a role in his systematic elimination of anyone he fancied was or conceivably could become a foe. After eliminating these enemies, Stalin would summon up new ones to suspect, triangulate, and annihilate. This cycle went on in the late 1920s, then repeated itself at least twice in the 1930s, then again in the late 1940s. A new round of persecution and murder was gaining momentum when he died in 1953, under suitably suspicious circumstances. (He suffered something like a stroke at his country house and was left untreated and unattended by his body guards for hours.)

Stalin was from the Caucasus and, to the end of his days, spoke with a detectable Georgian accent. (There's one good reason for self-doubt. The second was the smallpox scars on his face.) He was a man of fierce discipline and self-control. Yet Stalin was an anarchist, too, in his own way. He loved to sow discord among his colleagues—he saw them all as rivals—and create chaos where he saw order. What else can account for his inducing a famine that killed between seven million and ten million Ukrainians in 1932–1933 and imagining that was an effective and altogether acceptable political strategy for subduing the region?

Is self-doubt a motivation to harm others? Do we try to allay doubt and find certainty in the self by proving we're able to inflict pain on someone else? Or is it compensatory—the infliction of pain to dispel the pain that dwells within us? These are questions that come up whenever there is extreme cruelty in the home, the marketplace, or on the battlefield. Possibly Hitler, Pol Pot, Mao, and Idi Amin were all pathological self-doubters. These are matters of speculation that cannot be answered in retrospect. But the doubt and anxiety these leaders engendered in their people is a matter of historical fact. Each one preached a messianic vision of a purified society they alone could lead their people to. They could create a world in which there would be no doubt about what is good and what is evil, who should live and who should die, and in which anything and everything that had to be done to arrive at that ideal state sooner rather than later became state policy. If you feel compelled for whatever reason to slaughter your fellow humans, you must do everything you can to push uncertainty about your legitimate hold on power out of your mind and the minds of others. Self-doubt can be stilled by passionate, blinding belief.

As for the ghosts of the dead—well, what is to be done? You cannot kill the dead. But Soviet leaders could and did write them out of history in the hopes of purging them from memory. The pattern of cultural amnesia was predictable. As Stalin gained power, he eliminated all rivals but needed collaborators to carry out the work. Certain Party members (commonly referred to as "henchmen") were promoted into his inner circle, executed his orders, and found themselves soon enough at the other end of Party justice. The head of the NKVD (the precursor of the KGB), Nikolai Yezhov (1895–1940), was in charge of the secret police during the time of the Great Purge in the 1930s. He and his colleagues were extremely effective in eliminating saboteurs and traitors, many of whom were in reality neither. When expedient for Stalin, Yezhov and his colleagues fell victim to the very mechanisms of the Great Purge that they had developed. The man who was once portrayed as the confidante of the Great Leader became persona non grata. All positive references and images of him were erased. One example of his disappearance from the record is a photograph of Stalin and Yezhov walking on the Moscow–Volga Canal embankment (figure 2.2). On the top

Figure 2.2

Photographs both create and edit collective memory. At the height of the purges (*top*), the head of the NKVD Yezhov (*right*) strolls with Stalin. After Yezhov was purged, he became a nonperson, so evidence of their relationship was erased (*bottom*). Anonymous artist, *Stalin, Ezhov, Molotov, and Voroshilov at the Moscow–Volga Canal Embankment, 1937.*

we see one moment in time in the 1930s, one version of the past in which Comrade Stalin and Comrade Yezhov stride together toward the camera. In the bottom photograph, dating from the 1940s, we see a revised version of the past, a past in which Nikolai Yezhov is not Stalin's confidante and never was. He has been airbrushed out of the picture and in his stead looms a tenuous gray spot that looks strangely empty. It was easy to be un-remembered and written out of history even before Photoshop.

When you have a narrative that tells you what the future will be—communism, democratic liberalism, the apocalypse, whatever—you need to rearrange the past to create the history that best suits that future. Rearranging history kept Soviet citizens fully occupied, such was the speed at which the Soviets raced into the future. In her memoirs of the Stalin years, Nadezhda Mandelstam recalls the time she lived with the Shklovsky family. She writes of Varia Shklovsky, who was the family custodian of history as it changed:

> She showed us her school textbooks where the portraits of Party leaders had thick pieces of paper pasted over them as one by one they fell into disgrace—this the children had to do on instructions from their teacher. Varia said how much she would like to cover up [Nikolai] Semashko [the People's Commissar of Health]—"We'll have to sooner or later, so why not now?" At the same time the editors of encyclopedias and reference books were sending subscribers—most such works were bought on subscription—lists of articles that had to be pasted over or cut out. . . . With every new arrest, people went through their books and burned the works of disgraced leaders in their stoves. In new apartment buildings, which had central heating instead of stoves, forbidden books, personal diaries, correspondence and other "subversive literature" had to be cut up into pieces with scissors and thrown down the toilet. People were kept very busy.[30]

The question arises of how present-day archivists and librarians are to deal with the evidence they take in that, like Varia's textbook, has been tampered with, modified, "updated"? How are present-day archivists to handle the flood of data coming from social media that carry extremist, seditious, or offensive views and are rife with fabricated stories? Altered photos, falsified texts, tapes with suspicious blank spots in them—these phenomena are hardly new. Librarians and archivists have protocols for dealing with records that contain false information. Their task is to document all historical actions and actors faithfully, not just the evidence sanctioned by today's victors. Archivists do not choose the correct picture to preserve and discard the rest. They must preserve the textbook with all of the thick pieces of paper pasted over the photographs of the disgraced. The textbook as it was published is evidence. The censored textbook is evidence as well. Archives do not warrant the truth value of what they have, only the chain of custody that guarantees authenticity—it is what it purports to be. If we live in a time of lies, archivists must document it as a time of lies.

Gaps in memory are a chronic anxiety for the aging. Every little hiccup in recall is anxiously scrutinized for signs of Alzheimer's, though the average person has little idea how normal memory decay differs from that caused by disease. It is also the chronic anxiety of our age, as we create more and more digital content and toggle from one task to another. (We avidly consume journalism quoting scientists that multitasking is bad for memory retention.) There is a global anxiety about having so much of our knowledge stored in digital memory by private companies that have no obligation to the public commons.

There's anxiety about having too much as well as too little information. We rue our inability to get rid of things that we don't wish to remember or be remembered by. Social media engenders this anxiety early in life. As one teenager put it, "We all do cringey things and make dumb mistakes and whatever. But social media's existence has brought that into a place where people can take something you did back then and make it who you are now."[31] Even young people fear being haunted by the "cringey things" and "dumb mistakes" of their youth. Digital technologies flood the present with too much information, but over time, as we better understand the values and dynamics involved, we will create public policies that help control it. In the meantime, caution is advised and parental guidance needed.

On the other hand, digital technologies provide a distinct advantage by retrieving traces of the past that have left few or no written records. Laser technology can reveal traces of past cultures by "seeing" evidence lying just below the surface of the ground but invisible to the naked eye. For example, laser technology points to the existence of extensive trading networks among cities in precolonial Africa. These data force historians to reassess the history of the continent. What is revealed is not simply evidence of a past long obscured from view; the colonists' strategies to promulgate a version of history justifying their colonization are also illuminated. (They are like the pieces of paper pasted into Soviet textbooks.) In South Africa, for example, "The history of the trading city of Mapungubwe, which was capable of manufacturing magnificent gold objects 800 years ago, was deliberately obscured by racist officials during the apartheid era." The thrust of the obfuscation went beyond claiming that the land the occupiers held had been "wild"; it allowed them to claim that "local populations they dismissed as fit only for manual labor were not capable of sophisticated artistic production."[32]

The narrative the colonists had created was not only about the landscape but also about the humans they encountered there. According to the archaeologist John Giblin, the white South African government claimed that the land "was not populated when Europeans began to settle there in the 16th century and that black South Africans only arrived at the same time and only occupied a relatively small area of the country, leaving the remainder ripe for white settlement and ownership."[33] Evidence from before European settlement, now in the hands of the post-apartheid government, is used to tell a different history, one "about the importance of Mapungubwe, the precolonial past, the crimes of colonialism and apartheid—and the ambitions of a contemporary South Africa."[34]

Both the colonizers and the colonized deploy historical evidence as critical instruments of nation-building. The post-apartheid nation-builders are working with the same set of facts, some of which had been ignored by the apartheid nation-builders. It is the same evidence, but it tells a different story because it is told by a different storyteller. In both cases, the goal is to create an origins story that justifies the storytellers' claims to be the legitimate people of this legitimate nation. At the direction of the post-apartheid government, the treasures unearthed at Mapungubwe, including a gold-clad rhinoceros figurine, have been described, catalogued, preserved, and reborn as museum objects that have been exhibited in museums to further the Black South Africans' claim to their place among global civilizations. They have won their freedom to self-rule. Freedom from the legacy of subjugation is harder to achieve.

DR. CHEKHOV AND MR. HYDE

Chekhov himself struggled with the legacy of bondage that cast shade on the humanity of serfs. Chekhov was only two generations removed from serfdom. His grandfather started life as a serf, and Chekhov's father deeded to his children the serf's legacy of servile fear. He was a pious, bitter, cruel man who "educated" his children, as Chekhov said, by beating them, then making them kiss his hand in gratitude for the lesson received. It was an education in the mentality of a slave who endures beatings because he cannot defend himself; and who then must express gratitude for his punishment in recognition that this is the order of the world, as it is, has been, and ever shall be. Chekhov struggled all his life to escape that mentality, just as his grandfather had escaped serfdom when he bought his way out of it. Psychological enslavement differs from the legal kind, though. You cannot buy your way out of psychological slavery. There is no document that confers manumission from protective habits of self-abasement and abnegation. Chekhov engaged all his life in the battle best described by James Baldwin as the attempt to achieve personal freedom and thereby rob history of its tyrannical hold on the psyche. Long after his father died and he had reached acclaim as a playwright, Chekhov admitted, "I have never been able to forgive [my father] for whipping me."[35]

Today we might call Chekhov an abused child and diagnose anger as the subtext of his writing and the psychic force fueling his work. He refused to comfort the reader. He wrote to his brother that in his plays, "I finish every act as I do my stories; I keep the action calm and quiet to the end, then I punch the audience in the face."[36] A cold fury runs through all of Chekhov's work. He was angry about the conditions of dire poverty, lack of basic hygiene, safe drinking water, clean bandages, and the pollution of air, water, and soil already visible as environmental degradation. This anger is fully voiced in the jeremiad given to Dr. Astrov in *Uncle Vanya*: "[The devastation around us] is a result of an uncontrolled struggle for survival. A man is freezing, hungry, sick, trying to save what was left of his life, trying to take care of his children, so what does he do? He lets instincts take over; he grabs whatever he thinks will feed him and keep him warm, he destroys everything around him without a thought for the future. It's almost all gone already, and there's nothing to replace it."[37]

Chekhov was angry about the horrific famines and subsequent outbreaks of typhus, diphtheria, and cholera that coursed through the countryside with frightening regularity. His correspondence reveals a stark contrast between Chekhov the doctor and man of science, who knew the limits that disease and mortality place on the promise of humankind, and Chekhov the writer, ruthless in his honesty and frequently lapsing into cruelty. The healer and man of science was Dr. Chekhov; the writer who returned over and over to the ways hopelessness works its destruction, Mr. Hyde.

It wasn't just Chekhov's father who was censorious and cruel. In imperial Russia, learned professionals such as historians, lawyers, and academics were expected to uphold and even glorify the existing regime and the underlying traditions that endowed them with moral authority. Writers, on the other hand, were not, strictly speaking, servants of the regime. The most potent political voices belonged to artists, writers, and critics, as long as they avoided the subjects of politics, the emperor, and the Russian Orthodox Church, as well as the rights of Russia's subjugated peoples: the Poles, Ukrainians, Balts, Estonians, Crimeans, Georgians, Armenians, Finns, Muslims, and Jews.

A far more draconian censorship was practiced by Chekhov's fellow writers and readers. The literati and intelligentsia expected literature to be politically committed and morally uplifting. According to Isaiah Berlin, the intelligentsia were "the small minority of persons who had access to the civilization of the West and freely read foreign languages [who] felt relatively cut off from the mass of the people; they felt they were almost foreigners in their own land—what is nowadays called 'alienated' from society. Those among them with sensitive consciences were acutely aware of a natural obligation to help their fellows who were less happy or less advanced than themselves."[38] Chekhov faced an array of people on the left and the right eagerly policing his words, raising a clamor of condemnation for every utterance they deemed politically incorrect. He was judged both too political and not political enough. The reading public demanded that novelists write edifying works. They would edify through their searing criticism of the world as it existed, and would uplift readers by featuring positive figures in starring roles. Ideas that were not discussed openly in public life were smuggled into literature in the form of characters who would give disquisitions on the pressing issues of the day. Writers such as Lenin's favorite, Nikolai Chernyshevsky, saw literature not as a way of speaking the truth, but as a way to espouse opinions. That, too, made Chekhov angry. A writer should confess that "he understands nothing of what he sees." The rest is cant.

Readers are free to read whatever nonsense they wish into Chekhov's writing—dead writers are defenseless against our ignorance—and for a long time the nonsense that people read was a prophetic vision of the Russian Empire's collapse. Chekhov rejected utopian demands. Deferring to the promise of a better future was always done at the cost of living fully in the present. While his characters could never free themselves entirely from the past, they suffered the most when they dreamt of the future and neglected the present. It is only in the present that they can grasp one end of life's long chain and feel it tremble at the other.

Chekhov's most profound meditation on memory as the link between past, present, and future is "The Student," a four-page story the writer called his favorite. It is the tale of a restless young seminary student walking home after a day of hunting. It was Good Friday, a day of fasting and repentance in the Orthodox faith, a day gravid with the gloom that fell upon the world when Jesus was crucified. "Desolation was everywhere, and it was somehow particularly gloomy."[39] The student is filled with inchoate longing for something different, some fresh horizon that would offer opportunities to do great things. But where is that horizon? The young man is weighed down by the knowledge that "the same emptiness everywhere and darkness and oppressive grief, and all these horrors have been and were and would be and even the passing of a thousand years would make life no better. And he had no desire to go home." The story is all of four pages long, but at this point, with three more to go, the reader thinks the shorter, the better: We're in for a dreary time.

As the student crosses the field, he comes upon two widows, mother and daughter, sitting by the fire after they had cooked dinner. He stops to warm up—to pass the time, really, and delay his return to the cheerlessness of his home. He recites the Gospel tale of Peter waiting outside Pilate's palace after Jesus has been arrested. Peter sits near a group gathered around a fire, like the one they gathered around here. "He loved him passionately, to distraction, and could now see them beating him," the student recounts. Jesus had warned his disciple that before the night was over and the cock crowed, Peter would deny him three times. Utterly horrified, his pride wounded, Peter vigorously denies this. But there it is. The student goes on to tell how Peter denied Jesus on three distinct occasions, denied he even knew him, let alone was his disciple.

A cock crows. In a flash, Peter recognizes what he has done. He walks off into the dark dawn and weeps bitter tears.

The student, rapt by the sound of his own voice projecting far through the cold, thin air, pauses. He notices that the mother, tall, plump, wearing a man's sheepskin coat, is moved to tears. The daughter, a small, pock-marked woman with "a slightly stupid face," stared at the student, and "the look on her face grew heavy and tense like that of a person holding back great pain." He gets up and continues his journey homeward. It is dark, the wintry wind numbs his hands. Spring retreats. A few minutes later, remembering the widow's tears, it occurs to him that she was moved not because he told the story movingly, but because "Peter was close to her and her whole being was concerned with what was going on in Peter's soul." The student is so taken with this realization that he has to stop and catch his breath. The young man has seen the unbroken chain of events uniting all of humanity through time, all feelings flowing from one into another, "and he felt he had just seen both ends of the chain: he had touched one and the other had moved." As he nears home and climbs the hill, he looks around and sees that the truth and beauty of that biblical time is still present, even here in the village that is wretched, cold, full of misery, and damned to be that way forever. So here we are, on the last page of the very short story, to learn that all people in all times and in all places are connected:

He kept thinking of how the truth and beauty guiding human life back there in the garden and the high priest's courtyard carried on unceasingly to this day and had in all likelihood and at all times been the essence of human life and everything on earth, and a feeling of youth, health, strength—he was only twenty-two—and an ineffably sweet anticipation of happiness, unknown and mysterious, gradually took possession of him, and life appeared wondrous, marvelous, and filled with lofty meaning.[40]

This chance encounter opens a hidden door in the impenetrable ramparts of the world, the unscalable wall that keeps us trapped down here in the dreary stasis of worldly existence. For a moment, we grasp the soft, pliable chain that connects each of us with one another.

Chekhov's world is populated by people caught in tangled nets of vanity or sloth, feelings of hopelessness or weakness of will. Our therapeutic culture, ever eager for retrospective diagnoses, may recognize symptoms of low self-esteem in some, of narcissism in others, and of the sense of entitlement that comes with rank and wealth. Chekhov never passes judgment on the people he depicts, even when he picks the most unflattering shades with which to color them. Some are lucky, some are unlucky, and in the end, we all die.

And so, too, with the student. He glimpses how everything is connected through time, that under the tedium of the everyday lies deep meaning, and that it is always there, silent and abiding. How long does this young man have to live? If he is lucky enough to see old age, will he still know and feel that all is connected? The hard truth of mortality had to be remote in the student's mind. The women might as well have been living on the other side of an invisible gulf. Unlike the student, they were old, poor, illiterate, with no prospects of changing their position in life. Yet they knew what he did not know and may never live long enough to find out.

Today scientists can track some of the physiological processes by which one set of memories can overlap and share content with another set of memories—be they olfactory, aural, visual, textual, or spatial—to become a larger memory that connects heterogeneous content. This is how one thing can remind us of something seemingly unrelated. At the same time, a context of associations is created, and within that context emerges a sense of meaning—not in the logical sense of meaning that this equals that, but the atemporal sense that there is a depth to the moments in our lives. The moments extend backward and forward through time and space so that we ourselves are connected with something larger than the space we are in and the fleeting moment of the present. That is what the student has seen. This is what tragically happy Gurov and his lover see. That is what Chekhov makes us feel.

Our brain may be, as Anil Seth says, a prediction machine, but it makes those predictions by constantly consulting its bank of memories gleaned over a lifetime. It sheds episodic information and memories that are no longer called upon. It filters for what is "important and characteristic." Active recollection edits facts into a narrative, and moments of the story are time-stamped. The narrative activates our subconscious associations and suggests meaning. This makes it both seductive and necessary. It doesn't need to be true to be powerful; it needs merely to reveal patterns muffled by the noise of random events. The same editing features cause memory to be unreliable and tricky. Pursuit of the truth requires something else—a strong grounding in the present and a clarity of thought. The continuity between generations and the sense of a shared human fate is what makes each life consequential, even those lived in obscurity. It is what makes tradition worth preserving and defending—not for its own sake, but so that someone can see themself against the backdrop of time deeper than any one person can know.

3 SELF AND SOCIETY

ENTERING THE HOUSE OF THE DEAD

Everyone has a story, and the story always has a beginning. When you asked the stranger at the party where they came from, chances are they didn't rattle off all the events of their life, one thing after another, without any attempt to sort the significant from the commonplace. They may highlight the struggles they've overcome or the role luck played, the examples their parents set, or the disappointments and failures that proved pivotal. What matters are the moments that are seen in retrospect as consequential. And nothing is more consequential than the beginning. It time-stamps a person for all their life.

For Leszek Kołakowski, identifiable beginnings are important because "people who are uncertain about their origins, . . . who, although they know they must have been born somewhere, some time, do not know who their parents were or where and when they were born—must have a seriously damaged sense of identity."[1] Such people feel something is missing and hanker after that precious key they think will unlock an essential truth about themselves. That's why adoptees will track down their birth parents. It's why people map their genealogies as far back as records go. It's why they pay commercial enterprises to tell them what their DNA says about who they descend from and which inherited traits may affect their future. Like a latter-day astrological chart, genetic information is thought to lay out the possibilities and parameters of a life. Kołakowski concludes that few people, except "Buddhists at a very advanced stage in their path to enlightenment and an even smaller number of philosophers, can cast any real doubt on the validity of the 'I' as such."[2] (He isn't that kind of philosopher.) Psychotics and schizophrenics suffer from the delusion that their private thoughts belong to somebody outside themselves.[3] They suffer precisely because they do have a sense of self and know that it's broken.

Humans are social animals and need more than the certainty that we exist. We need to know we exist in the world, not just in our heads. Koła-kowski explains that belonging to "various collective entities is also part of what makes me a person (although this does not entail that I am no more than a part of these collective entities, nor that I am literally nothing if I do not belong to them)."[4] Private and public selves can be so entangled they are indistinguishable.

In December 2019, the Harvard University admissions office became the scene of spirited protest by Black, Latinx, and Asian American students. They claimed the university was happy to use them as tokens of Harvard's invest-ment in diversity but would not invest in academic programs that taught them their own history. "I am tired of Harvard using my story without giving me [a department of] ethnic studies so I can fully understand what my story even means," the *New York Times* quoted a Vietnamese-American student. "Harvard, stop using our stories when you won't listen to us."[5] (The students kept referring to history as a "story.") There were multiple reasons for their anger. A professor of ethnic studies had recently been denied tenure, and the reasons that the university president overruled the tenure committee's vote to offer tenure were not revealed. The administration said it was a matter of confidentiality, as all personnel matters are. But the lack of transparency only deepened existing doubt, distrust, and anxiety—combustible ingredients leading to an eruption of anger.

For the Harvard students, their task is to find evidence in the archives that tells them who they are and where their place in the world is. Today's sensibility defines "finding our place in the world" as seeing ourselves fully empowered to shape the world we live in. This is a characteristically Western perspective. It prizes the autonomy of individuals and attributes to them the power to change the world and thus make their mark. But there are many traps that lie in wait for them as they look for their place in the larger world. The one easiest to fall into is seduction by a narrative that appears to make the greatest sense of their past and hints at their greatest future. The music we love, movies we commit to memory, cultural figures we admire, and media influencers we follow—all feel deeply personal. Our allegiance to them creates a bond with others who treasure them as we do. Group affiliations and elective affinities meld our inward sense of self with who we are in the eyes of others. In other words, the world is in us as much as we are in it.

This duality of identity as an individual and as a member of a collective poses a fundamental question about how much or how little individual agency is constrained by the world. The membrane between the private and public self is like skin: it protects us from the aggressions of the world. If we know and trust the world, we can be at ease in our own skin. But once our skin grows thick in order to protect ourselves, our ability to feel the outside world attenuates. We give less of ourselves to others. Once the world changes—or worse, betrays us—we feel uneasy in ourselves and no longer trust others. The crises we faced in 2020 rapidly and dramatically eroded our trust in the world and others. We began to see people as vectors of disease, or enemies of "Real America," or deplorable threats to democracy. These crises have forced us to reexamine what freedom and equality look like in action. How we'll understand those values in ten years isn't clear, and that lack of certainty in itself is profoundly destabilizing. We've begun to examine our origins so that we can ground ourselves, but we don't know exactly where to stand and are sometimes afraid of what we will find.

This was exactly the fate Fyodor Dostoevsky (1821–1881) faced when he lost the world he knew. He emerged from the purgatory of a decade-long crisis of identity with a new understanding of himself and the world he lived in, an understanding we recognize as modern. His concept of a moral society, of the relationship between the individual and the community, and of the meaning of freedom and equality was turned upside down and inside out.

At the age of twenty-eight, Dostoevsky was already acclaimed for his novel *Poor Folk*. Though his subsequent stories and novellas met with decidedly mixed reviews, he had every reason to expect that he was on his way to a successful life as a writer.[6] That expectation was scotched at 4 a.m., April 23, 1849, when he was awoken by security police, arrested, and charged with being a member of a secret society of utopian socialists. For ten months, Dostoevsky was kept in solitary confinement in St. Petersburg's notorious Peter and Paul Fortress, awaiting charges to be filed. On December 22, he and his alleged fellow conspirators were taken to a city square, where they learned they were to be summarily executed.

None of the twenty-three arrested had an inkling of their fate when they arrived at Semenovsky Square. On their arrival, they saw a raised platform and what some took to be coffins ready to receive their corpses. The men were given thin peasant shirts to don in the sub-zero weather, then were hooded and separated into groups of three to be shot. Awaiting his imminent death, Dostoevsky felt "a mystic terror" at the thought that in a minute or two, this life would end and some other, unknown life, would begin.[7] He experienced past, present, and future collapsing into an eternal present, a terrifying and blissful experience of time suspended, of his body and his time of consciousness in perfect synchrony.[8]

Suddenly, before the first volley began, the condemned (still blinded by their hoods) could hear the troops' muffled retreat. Instead of death, the accused were given varying years' sentences in Siberian hard-labor prisons, to be followed by years of exile. Dostoevsky was sentenced to four years of hard labor, followed by four years of military service in Siberia.

Dostoevsky did enter some other, unknown life, but it was not *there* but *here on earth*, in a Siberian prison.[9] The meaning of that experience took time to ripen and bear fruit in his consciousness. A decade of prison, exile, and desperate attempts to re-establish his place in Russia's literary life were necessary for the significance of *not dying* to gel into the intuition of rebirth. In making sense of his misfortune, he gave up his ardent belief in humanity's progress toward the socialist utopia he had viewed as the purest realization of moral society. In its place, he gained what his biographer Joseph Frank memorably calls an "eschatological consciousness," the knowledge that at any moment, life could end and therefore every moment was pregnant with meaning. Frank explains: "Eschatology is a theological term meaning the doctrine of last things—death, immortality, resurrection, etc. Such preoccupations moved into the foreground for Dostoevsky because, it seems, after his experience in facing death, he could never again portray human life except in relation to these ultimate values and the ultimate choices that one becomes aware of in such moments of crisis."[10] The term is now used more broadly to connote anything touching the ultimate fate of humankind, such as the expectation of mass extinctions (including humans) due to climate change, or the anticipation of trans-humanism and a point of singularity when humans are superseded by artificial intelligence.

Awareness of a time "when time will be no more" is what Dostoevsky experienced when he thought he was about to die. It was also the feeling he experienced during the aura preceding the epileptic seizures that began sometime after his arrest and plagued him mercilessly for the rest of his life.[11] The pervasive atmosphere in which *everything is at stake in every moment* is what makes his mature work—*Crime and Punishment, The Idiot, The Devils, The Brothers Karamazov*—full of dramatic existential tension. Frank calls Dostoevsky's literary technique dramatization by "ideological eschatology, that is, carrying 'the logical presuppositions and possibilities of ideas to their consistent conclusion.'"[12]

In Siberia, Dostoevsky lost his conviction that history moves toward a harmonious state for all humanity. He rejected the corollary that the living are called upon to sacrifice their own lives in the present for that future time of ultimate human fulfillment. Either the possibility of realizing one's full humanity exists for each and every person, or it exists for none. This was a radical shift from believing that human fate is essentially destined to end in a good place, to knowing that this cannot be. It's not in human nature to suffer being merely a midwife to the future. He had discovered that when forced to do so, a person will rebel against the tyranny of destiny even unto death. Dostoevsky's mature work dramatizes the struggle against that kind of ideological enslavement. His pivot from utopianism to the first full-blown articulation of eschatological consciousness in *Crime and Punishment* (1866) is detailed in two radically different works he wrote after returning to St. Petersburg from exile in 1859. In these two works, he explores the trade-offs that must be made between the individual and the community and the dire consequences of refusing to take responsibility for those trade-offs.

The first book is a lightly fictionalized memoir, *Notes from a House of the Dead* (hereafter *House of the Dead*), published serially in 1860–1861.

It was an unprecedented eyewitness account of the Russian penal system and met with great acclaim, praised by both Tolstoy and Turgenev. It has the lamentable distinction of being the first in a long line of Russian prison memoirs. The second work, *Notes from Underground*, appeared in 1864.[13] It is a meditation on the human will to freedom—though stylistically, it is grimly satirical, at times hysterical in tone, and has little of the meditative mood about it. Unlike *House of the Dead*, *Notes from Underground* was little noticed at the time. In the twentieth century, it gained renown as a prescient diagnosis of modernity's crises and is routinely cited as a founding text of existentialism.

As different as these works are, both take up the same subject of humanity's contradictory nature at war with itself. True personal freedom exists only in the absence of certainty. The protagonists of both books are plagued by a yearning for certainty yet put their need for freedom above that. The works use the same strategy of a first-person narrator who finds himself in an extreme situation. Readers are inside their heads as they try to find their way out. One succeeds. The other fails ignominiously. In both narrators, the reader encounters a wholly new perception of reason and rationality as an antagonist to freedom rather than its handmaiden. It took Dostoevsky some time to grasp the full consequences of this new consciousness. Once he did, he renounced his utopian convictions and devoted himself to agitating against the very ideas he had been imprisoned for.

Dostoevsky's alleged crime against the state was to frequent the home of Mikhail Petrashevsky, where the socialist utopian ideas of Fourier and others were debated. The failed European revolutions of 1848 caused Tsar Nicholas I to order increased vigilance against any political activity (political discussion was considered a political activity). The group, known now as the Petrashevsky circle, had no concrete plan for antigovernmental action. They developed no political theory per se and few of them agreed on the solutions to the problems they discussed. They were united in their opposition to serfdom, of course, as any self-respecting liberal thinker would be. In fact, according to eyewitnesses, serfdom was the only subject that galvanized Dostoevsky. It has come to light recently that Dostoevsky was also a member of a secret group which was persuaded that in the wake of the intransigent government reaction, violent overthrow of the regime in the name of the people was necessary. This wasn't known by the authorities or other members of the Petrashevsky circle, so Dostoevsky's punishment, severe as it was, was light in comparison with what the facts warranted, had they been known.[14]

Shortly after getting out of prison, Dostoevsky wrote his brother Andrei that "I consider those four years as a time during which I was buried alive and shut up in a coffin. Just how horrible that time was I have not the strength to tell you . . . it was an indescribable, unending agony, because each hour, each minute weighed upon my soul like a stone."[15] He was lost. He never abandoned his ambition to be a writer, but that seemed increasingly hopeless. In retrospect, he saw his years of suffering in Siberia as a necessary crucible for his "rebirth of convictions." *House of the Dead* is the tale of that regeneration.

To tell the story, Dostoevsky had to "disappear from view."[16] He used a frame narrative and writes as Alexander Petrovich Goryanchikov, a young nobleman stripped of his status and rights because he killed his wife in a fit of jealousy. A fictional editor says that he knew the man when he was out of prison and living in exile in Siberia, that these notes were found among his papers when he died, and that he, the editor, put them into some kind of order and published them, thinking they would be of interest to the public. One reason for the frame structure and calling the crime murder, a civil crime, was to put the censors off the scent by avoiding any mention of political crime. That said, readers would have known the story of Dostoevsky's arrest and imprisonment. They read the book with avidity, believing it to be an authentic account of his time in prison.

The narrative is told chronologically in vignettes, in the style of a reporter or an anthropologist recording details of individuals living in the dynamic of an anthropologically interesting collective. The style is uncharacteristically sober and straightforward. (Tolstoy, known for his aversion to Dostoevsky's melodramatic plots and hyperbolic prose style, considered this book among the finest literary works of its time.) What emerges is a microcosm of Russian society and an anatomy of the Russian personality.

The book begins with the narrator's first year of deep disillusionment and painful adjustment to his new life. A tale of regeneration must begin with a death, real or metaphorical, and here we see what killed Dostoevsky's utopian socialism. His socialism was grounded in an idealization of the peasant, derived from ideas circulating among his friends and written about in journals and French novels by George Sand, Victor Hugo, and others in vogue at the time. Frank explains: "Such works were steeped in 'a divinization of the people' and took for granted that 'they are good, they are moral; better than the wealthy, more moral than the wealthy.'"[17] Dostoevsky spent most of his youth in cities and had minimal direct exposure to serfs. Being strangers to the lived experience of serfs, he and his fellow urbanites fell prey to essentialism. In prison, Dostoevsky had his first close encounter with the people on whose behalf he had plotted revolution, and he did not like what he saw. The narrator was one of a handful of "gentlemen" among the prisoners; the other 250 were "chance murderers and professional murderers, robbers and gang leaders. There were petty thieves, and tramps who lived by holdups or by breaking and entering."[18] He was horrified by the casual violence, obscene language, brazen pilfering, and shocking depravity he found among his fellow convicts. Most of the details Dostoevsky could only hint at because of the censors:

> They were coarse, ill-natured, cross-grained people. Their hatred for the gentry knew no bounds, and therefore they received us, the gentlemen, with hostility and malicious joy in our troubles. They would have eaten us alive, given the chance. Judge, moreover, how much protection we had, having to live, eat and drink and sleep with these men for several years, without even a chance of complaining of the innumerable affronts of every possible kind. "You are noblemen, iron beaks that used to peck us to death. Before, the master used to torment the people, but now he is lower than the lowest, has become one of us."[19]

It was impossible for Dostoevsky to maintain hope for a utopian socialism founded on the simple, irenic communitarianism of the Russian peasants. They were a profane and hostile group, unrepentant for their crimes, and in all ways alien to his sensibilities. Coming to know them *on their own terms*, he abandoned his belief that the peasants would willingly play the role the ideological intelligentsia cast them in as the revolutionary masses. (Lenin didn't make the same mistake.)

Dostoevsky entered the hard-labor camp believing that the injustices of the world do not arise in the hearts and minds of humanity, but are products of the despotic organization of society. He discovered he was entirely wrong. To his surprise, the power hierarchies of autocratic Russia were punctiliously re-created by the prisoners and strictly enforced. It was the same world, turned upside down: those on top on the outside were now on the bottom. Fellow convicts demanded that the few dozen gentry among them behave as they expected gentry to. Dostoevsky was distraught that he was now defined by his gentry origins, further isolating him from the comforts of human companionship. If he made any effort to be friendly with other prisoners, be on equal footing with them, or act in any way ingratiatingly or sympathetically, the convicts rebuffed him with contempt and abuse: "I still had to maintain and even show respect for my noble origin before them, that is, to pamper myself, put on airs, disdain them, turn up my nose at everything, and keep my hands clean. That was precisely how they understood a nobleman to be. Naturally, they would abuse me for it, but deep down they would still respect me."[20] Convicts insisted that the nobility behave in the ways they expected from their time before imprisonment, in part for the sake of stability and predictability, and in part for the pleasure of denying them the freedom to do otherwise. Dostoevsky felt the depth of class hatred ingrained in the peasants, the vengeful hatred ("they loved to watch our sufferings") that would show its full force decades later in the savagery of revolution and civil war.[21]

These encounters early in his imprisonment ripened into a profound crisis of identity. He could not bear estrangement from his fellow Russians, though they provoked feelings of disgust in him. He had banked on the idea that the intelligentsia understood the peasants and, being superior in education and access to power, would act on their behalf to bring about the end of serfdom. He was devastated to discover that the prisoners who were peasants not only despised him; they didn't even see him as an individual but viewed him as a type: the nobleman who had oppressed them all of their lives. (Dostoevsky was, however, not of the nobility, but a member of the middling gentry.) It is no coincidence that the one truly evil person in the book is the nobleman Aristov, who is described as "the most repulsive example of the baseness and vileness a man can sink to, and how far he can go in killing all moral feeling in himself, with no effort and with no regret. . . . He was cunning and intelligent, good-looking, even somewhat educated, and not without abilities." Aristov faithfully reported everything that happened in the barracks to the sadistic major in charge and brought greater misery to the men already living in degradation. Nonetheless, the convicts "were all very friendly with A—v and treated him much more amicably than they did us. Our drunken major's favor towards him lent him importance and weight in their eyes."[22]

Hierarchies emerged spontaneously within the large group of strangers because of their dependence on one another. No one could subsist on the food and clothing provided by the prison. It was crucial to have money to buy food, warm clothing, tea, sugar, tobacco, vodka, or sex: "Money is minted freedom, and therefore, for a man completely deprived of freedom, it is ten times dearer. Just to have it jingling in his pocket half comforts him, even if he cannot spend it. But money can be spent always and everywhere, the more so as forbidden fruit is twice sweeter."[23] At first Dostoevsky was puzzled to see prisoners who had scraped and saved and even sold their most treasured possessions throw it all away in one extravagant gesture:

> A prisoner is greedy for money to the point of convulsions, to a darkening of the mind, and if he does indeed throw it away like woodchips when he carouses, he does it for something he considers on a higher level than money. What is higher than money for a prisoner? Freedom, or at least the dream of freedom. . . . The whole meaning of the word "prisoner" is a man with no will; but in wasting money, he is acting by *his own will*. . . . and even persuades himself, *at least for a time*, that he has much more freedom and power than it may seem—in short, he can carouse, brawl, reduce somebody to dust, and prove to him that he can do all this, that it is all "in our hands."[24]

Hard labor was not as hard as Dostoevsky expected. The real punishment was in it "being *forced*, imposed, under the lash." To inflict the worst possible punishment, "so that the most dreadful murderer would shudder at this punishment and be frightened of it beforehand, they would only need to give the labor a character of complete, total uselessness and meaninglessness."[25]

The greatest affront to even the most hardened criminal was to rob him of his dignity. To be robbed of dignity by someone in a position of power was so dreaded that the prisoners would resort to acts of self-abasement. If they were to be degraded, they would not let *one of the prison guards* do it. They would do it to themselves, as a negative expression of their free will: "The prisoner himself knows that he is a prisoner, an outcast, and he knows his place before his superior; but no brands, no fetters will make him forget that he is a human being. And since he is in fact a human being, it follows that he must be treated as a human being."[26]

The extravagant examples of human irrationality Dostoevsky witnessed persuaded him that people are not fundamentally rational and do not act in their rational self-interest. Some prisoners, forced to run the gauntlet when they arrive or were recently convicted of a crime they committed in prison, become so terrified of the punishment that they would do anything they could to postpone it. They committed new crimes knowing that the trial would delay the punishment for the first: "Naturally, [the prisoner] knew very well that by such an act he would greatly increase his sentence and his term of hard labor. But he was precisely counting on putting off the terrible moment of punishment for at least a few days, a few hours!"[27] Dostoevsky's dreams of a better future were revealed as incoherent, even delusional. In prison, there is only the present. Repeated demonstrations of prisoners acting in defiance of what a rational person would call their self-interest seared themselves into Dostoevsky's brain. His fiction from then on is populated by characters who willfully harm themselves or others and do things blatantly against their supposed self-interest in defiance of all reason—all in the name of freedom.

LEAVING THE HOUSE OF THE DEAD

Late in life, Dostoevsky recounted a memory he had while in prison which he claims was the beginning of his spiritual and artistic regeneration: "During all my four years in prison, I was constantly remembering my whole past and, it seems, living through all my former life again in memories. These memories arose of themselves; I rarely called them up by my own will."[28] Lying on his bunk one day, he suddenly remembered an encounter with a peasant on his family estate when he was nine. He had completely forgotten about the incident until that day over the Easter holiday, the commemoration of Christ's death and resurrection and the most sacred holiday in the Russian Orthodox Church.

Because of the holiday, the guards left the convicts alone for a few days to indulge in unrestrained drinking and brawling. One convict, a giant of a man named Gazin, became violently drunk. Six beefy peasants "set about beating him so as to quiet him down; they beat him absurdly, such blows could have killed a camel; but they knew that this Hercules was hard to kill, and so they beat him without second thoughts." Then they laid him down on a bed. The man showed almost no signs of life: "Everyone passed him by silently: though they firmly hoped he would come to the next morning, still 'who knows, after such a beating, a man might just up and die.'"[29] The writer made his way past Gazin to his own bunk and lay there, sunk deep in a dark mood, silently staring at the ceiling and hoping nobody would bother him. At that moment, he remembered something.

It was an August afternoon on his family's estate. He was out wandering in the woods, collecting bugs, picking mushrooms, and gathering wild berries. "Suddenly, amid the deep silence, I clearly and distinctly heard a cry: 'A wolf's coming!' I screamed and, beside myself with fear, shouting at the top of my voice, rushed out to the clearing, straight to the plowing peasant."[30] He had spotted the serf Marey on his walk earlier. They had never spoken before, but now the boy clutched the peasant, desperately seeking safety. Marey calmed him down: "'I'll keep an eye on you. I won't let the wolf get you!' he added with the same motherly smile. 'Well, off you go, and Christ be with you'—and he made the sign of the cross over me and over himself."[31]

Dostoevsky arrived home safely and the encounter was forgotten, until that day in prison as he lay on his bed—three planks of wood on a bunk, a thin layer of straw, and nothing to serve for a blanket except the short sheepskin coats issued to the convicts: "And now suddenly, twenty years later, in Siberia, I remember this whole encounter with such clarity, to the very last detail. Which means that it had embedded itself in my soul imperceptibly, *on its own and without my will*, and *I suddenly remembered it when it was needed*; I remember that tender, motherly smile of the poor serf, the signs of the cross, the way he shook his head: 'You're really frightened, lad!' And especially that thick, dirt-covered finger of his, with which he had touched my quivering lips gently and with such timid tenderness."[32]

To Dostoevsky, the wonder of the incident was the kindness freely given by a serf to his "little master." No one would know of his kindness, no one would reward him for it: "This had been a solitary encounter, in an empty field, and maybe only God above had seen what deep and enlightened human feeling, what refined, almost feminine tenderness could fill the heart of a coarse, brutishly ignorant Russian serf, who back then was not yet expecting or even dreaming of his freedom."[33] (By 1876, when Dostoevsky wrote this, serfs had been free for fifteen years, but this encounter had happened in 1830.) His description of the memory sums up the moment the scales fell from his eyes and he came to see the peasant he had idealized pre-Siberia, then feared and despised in prison, as the paradigm of one who suffers and retains his humanity.

In his narrative, Dostoevsky returned to the present, climbed down from his rude pallet, and looked about the barracks: "I remember suddenly feeling that I could look at those unfortunate men with totally different eyes, and that suddenly, by some miracle, all the hatred and anger in my heart [against them] had vanished completely. I went about peering into the faces I met. This shaved and disgraced [peasant], drunk and with a branded face, bellowing out his hoarse, drunken song, why, he also could be that same Marey: I could not look into his heart."[34]

The repetition of the word "suddenly" (*vdrug*) is not sloppy writing or negligent editing, but a deliberate choice to emphasize the feel of time when it stops. It stops *suddenly*—that is, unexpectedly—and in that suspension of time, anything could happen. Days, months, even years can telescope to an instant of singular transformation. In Dostoevsky's hands, this anecdote becomes a conversion tale, analogous to Saul of Tarsus on the road to Damascus. Dostoevsky makes a point of telling us that his memory of the peasant Marey saving him from an imaginary wolf lost salience almost immediately after the incident. It is probably fair to say that as a writer, Dostoevsky discovered—if not created—its meaning as a pivot point in his life only by writing about it, in recollection and sentimentally, after a lapse of fifty-five years. (This is the maudlin Dostoevsky tone that Tolstoy couldn't bear.) The incident is never mentioned in *House of the Dead*. Internal evidence from the book casts doubt on the memory coming to him during the first year of confinement. On the contrary, the first year is depicted as a year of total blindness. His anguish was so unbearable that "among my malicious, hateful fellow convicts, I did not notice the good people, capable of thinking and feeling, despite all the revolting crust that covered them outside. Amidst the biting words, I sometimes did not notice a friendly and affectionate word, which was the dearer for being uttered without any purpose, and often straight from a heart that had perhaps suffered and endured more than mine."[35]

After his experience on the scaffold awaiting death, followed by long and bitter years of confinement in the hell of prison and exile, Dostoevsky concluded that his former belief that the fulfillment of human aspirations happens only later, not now, is wrong. In prison, every second counts. The past is gone. The future doesn't exist. People live in a kind of waking coma. The vision of a utopian future has no meaning; it gives no hope or consolation. Dostoevsky returned time and again to the perils posed by those who commit crimes in the name of a more perfect world, such the murderer Raskolnikov in *Crime and Punishment*, and the revolutionary nihilist Peter Verkhovensky in *The Devils*. He now understood that all that mattered was freedom, and freedom exists *now* or it doesn't exist at all.

To survive, Dostoevsky had to accept the most painful condition of all—to live among those who saw him only by an identity that did not grant him his full humanity. He had the choice as an artist to deal with that alienation in writing, but his fellow convicts rebelled against their bondage in other ways. They harmed themselves, even to the point of effectively committing suicide by perpetrating crimes guaranteed to warrant a punishment they could not survive—hundreds, even a thousand lashes. Dostoevsky retreated into himself to avoid exposure to others, but over time found this, too, was not sustainable. He could regain a sense of his place in the world not through introspection, but only through engagement and reconciliation with others.

It seems natural that the memoirs of someone living in forced confinement are full of meditations on the joys of freedom, and *House of the Dead* is no exception. The entire story works artfully toward the moment when the narrator leaves prison. On the closing page of the book, he recounts how the irons he wore since his arrival were at last cut off by the prison blacksmith:

> The fetters fell off. I picked them up . . . I wanted to hold them in my hand, to look them over for the last time. It was as if I marveled now that they had just been on my legs.
>
> "Well, go with God, go with God!" the prisoners said, their voices abrupt, coarse, but as if pleased at something.
>
> Yes, with God! Freedom, a new life, resurrection from the dead . . . What a glorious moment![36]

This hour of exaltation stands in stark contrast to the acts of self-harm as the negative expression of freedom that is the heart of the book.

THE VIEW FROM UNDERGROUND

After Dostoevsky was released from prison and settled into exile in Siberia, he devoured books on history, religion, and philosophy. He was trying to make sense of his suffering and that of his fellow convicts. The nature and value of suffering became an idée fixe in his work. What justified suffering, especially that of the innocent? How free are individuals to choose their own fate, and how do their choices affect the freedom of others? Above all, he wondered about the role of his own nation in world history, located as it was on the periphery of Europe and deeply influenced by Europe's intellectual and artistic life. Notably, his reading included the work of Georg Hegel, whose highly influential philosophy of history defined the world-historical process as the necessary realization of the spirit (*Geist*, often translated as *mind*). The movement of history was a turbulent and dialectical progress toward achieving the full potential of humanity. The philosopher László F. Földényi provocatively speculates that in his reading, Dostoevsky came across Hegel's notion that Siberia, like Africa, was excluded from history as such. It was only within history that meaning could exist. "The whole character of Siberia," wrote Hegel, "rules it out as a setting for historical culture and prevents it from attaining a distinct form in the world-historical process."[37] Siberia was thus no more significant than Africa. What was Dostoevsky to make of this, given that Siberia was the very place where he had experienced the greatest suffering? Did his suffering have no meaning?

This thought inflicted a psychic wound akin to the one James Baldwin lamented in his 1965 Cambridge Union debate with William F. Buckley, Jr. Baldwin says that he "was taught in American history books, that Africa had no history, and neither did I."[38] Dostoevsky hints at what it means to face this conundrum when he says in *House of the Dead* that many released from prison or forced into exile choose not to return to European Russia. "Those who are able *to solve the riddle of life* almost always stay in Siberia and delight in taking root there. Later on they bear sweet and abundant fruit. But others, *light-minded folk, unable to solve the riddle of life*, soon weary of Siberia and ask themselves in anguish why on earth they ended up there."[39]

Dostoevsky returned to St. Petersburg in December 1859 to a world he barely recognized. The very reason for his political radicalism, his opposition to serfdom, evaporated with the news that the recently installed Emperor Alexander II would abolish serfdom. At the same time, a new generation of politically engaged intelligentsia arrived on the scene, "the men of the [18]60s," quite distinct from his own generation of "men from the 40s." They scorned idealism and romanticism, and instead aggressively embraced what they took to be scientifically rigorous thought—unsentimental, utilitarian, and purely instrumental. Dostoevsky's generation, with its benign sense that life could get better incrementally, had been replaced by men who professed a kind of egoistic utilitarianism, an urgent sense of end-state expectation, and a call for immediate revolutionary change.

In *Notes from Underground* (hereafter *Notes*), Dostoevsky picks up the theme of the riddle of life that, when solved, will "bear sweet and abundant fruit." He never tells us what the riddle of life is, let alone its solution. But in *Notes*, he comes very close to letting us glimpse it. The novella is a bitter satire on the fate of a man who denies there is a riddle of life because, as a materialist, he knows that all human actions are determined by the laws of nature. The underground man has signed on to the creed of "rational egoism" in vogue in the 1860s. It says that history is essentially an open-and-shut case of humanity's progress toward its full rationality. As any rational person can see, the concept of free will is a delusion, like thinking 2+2=4 might once in a while become 2+2=5 because we will it to be so. Once people recognize this is a delusion, they will act in their own rational self-interest, and that self-interest will align with what is best for all. What is best for all is best for each.

The leading ideologist of this movement was Nikolai Chernyshevsky (1828–1889), the son of a priest who received his education in a seminary and grew up to be a militant atheist. Other notable acolytes were typically the offspring of priests, government clerks, and well-to-do peasants. They were far removed from the world of the gentlemen intelligentsia that nurtured Dostoevsky. *Notes* has many complex layers, but its origins lay in Dostoevsky's reaction to Chernyshevsky's ideological novel *What Is to Be Done?*, published in 1863. (This novel became the bible of revolutionary radicals and continued to influence subsequent generations, most notably Lenin.) The underground man sums up Chernyshevsky's utilitarian ethics accurately but mockingly:

> Oh, tell me who was the first to announce, first to proclaim that man does nasty things simply because he doesn't know his own true interest; and that if he were to be enlightened, if his eyes were to be opened to his true, normal interests, he would stop doing nasty things at once and would immediately become good and noble, because, being so enlightened and understanding his real advantage, he would realize that his own advantage really did lie in the good; and that it's well known that there's not a single man capable of acting knowingly against his own interest; consequently he would, so to speak, begin to do good out of necessity.[40]

This is a fantasy world in which facts alone are persuasive because all decisions are made on a purely rational basis. Dostoevsky saw this naivete as common to liberals. Ultimately it would prove fateful, he prophesied, because it came from a willful disregard of the full scope of human needs.

In *House of the Dead*, the bondage Dostoevsky portrays was physical but inevitably had psychological effects. The convicts didn't accept despotic control over their bodies, nor did they accept "necessity"; they rebelled to the limits of their abilities and beyond. In *Notes*, the bondage originates in the mind, not the body. Dostoevsky wrote that "I conceived of it during my years of imprisonment, lying on a bunk bed, at a painful moment of *grief and disintegration*."[41] The prison experience is transposed to the psychological realm, with the narrator imprisoned by historical determinism and its denial of freedom. In Siberia, Dostoevsky saw humans as a compound of contrary parts: reason and emotion; egoism and altruism; virulent hatred and transcendent love. This was the fundamental human condition and it would not change. Later in the same passage as above, the underground man asks:

> What does one do with the millions of facts bearing witness to the one fact that people knowingly, that is possessing full knowledge of their own true interests, have relegated them to the background and have rushed down a different path, that of risk and chance, compelled by no one and nothing, but merely as if they didn't want to follow the beaten track, and so they stubbornly, willfully forged another way, a difficult and absurd one, searching for it almost in the darkness? Why, then, this means that stubbornness and willfulness were really more pleasing to them than any kind of advantage.[42]

The underground man tells us that his reason accepts the logic of determinism. But his spirit rebels against it.

"I am a sick man. . . . I am a spiteful man. I am an unattractive man."[43] The text infamously begins with this bold confession. (The original title of the work was *Confession*.) In the same paragraph he begins to contradict himself, as he does throughout his story: "I think my liver is diseased. Then again, I don't know a thing about my illness; I'm not even sure what hurts. I'm not being treated and never have been, though I respect both medicine and doctors. I'm extremely superstitious—well at least enough to respect medicine. (I'm sufficiently educated not to be superstitious, but I am, anyway.) No, gentlemen, it's out of spite that I don't wish to be treated."[44] Spite is the feeble, self-defeating action of thwarted freedom. The confessional parts of this work dwell on the multiple times that the narrator inflicts pain on others and on himself out of sheer spite. The worst thing is that he is plagued by memories of the times when he hurt people or humiliated himself out of spite. The pain is not in the memory, but in the ever-present recognition that he was not doing any of this of his own will. He had no free will and his actions were all done automatically, as it were, without his exerting any will or being able to resist it. But while he recognizes this logically, the feelings of guilt torment him precisely because he cannot take responsibility for his actions. He feels guilty but he knows he cannot logically be guilty. Because, logically, he can't be guilty so he shouldn't feel guilt.

Dostoevsky does an interesting thing with the structure of the novella. It is a frame narrative, like *House of the Dead*, put together by a fictional editor. In that book, the chronology is straightforward—he tells the tale from the time the narrator arrives to the time he leaves. It is psychologically accurate, the first year being told at great length, when everything is new and he is completely disoriented. But the following years are compressed in time because they are all familiar. The psychiatrist Veronica O'Keane describes the acquisition of this kind of knowledge as a "pattern of initial over-elaboration of new information . . . familiar to anyone who has tackled a new area of knowledge, and not just lifted information from the internet. There is an initial period of being lost and overgeneralizing in the sea of novel information, before emerging with an organized, contextual understanding of the new subject: knowledge expansion followed by knowledge discrimination."[45]

In *Notes*, the chronology is inverted and there is no knowledge discrimination. The first part takes place in the present, when we find the underground man living in a tiny room—a mouse hole, as it were, "under the floorboards."[46] We are trapped with him in the confined space of his mind as it loops through contradictory and self-incriminating trains of thought. The second, longer part is a series of memories of encounters that happened two decades earlier. The memories are of interactions with people—his boss, friends from school, his servant, a prostitute—that were deeply unsatisfying because he cannot connect with people. He feels an overwhelming need to impress some people, and when he cannot, he seeks to avenge himself either by attempting to humiliate them or, failing that, by humiliating himself. He plays chicken with an oncoming pedestrian to get him to give way. But the pedestrian doesn't because the underground man dodges out of the way at the last minute. He challenges an acquaintance to a duel, and the man ignores him.

The most wrenching of these memories involves his visit to a prostitute, Liza, whom he both taunts for her moral degradation and seeks to console for her fallen state. He insults her one minute and then, suddenly, plays the hero (something he insists came to him because of his consumption of Romantic literature) and offers her his friendship and aid. She visits him at his invitation, seeking to better her situation. Mortified by the shabby state of his quarters, he draws her out, expresses empathy, and then, *suddenly*, begins tormenting her. In a startling turn of events, Liza recognizes that he, too, suffers deeply and offers to console him. He is stunned by her candor and compassion. *Suddenly*, he hates her for it.

In his final act of spiteful vengeance, he gives her money. She leaves it behind when she goes. "But here's what I can say for sure: although I did this cruel thing deliberately, it was not from my heart, but from my stupid head. This cruelty of mine was so artificial, cerebral, intentionally invented, *bookish*, that I couldn't stand it myself even for one minute. . . . Out of shame and in despair, I rushed after Liza . . ."[47] But she was gone.

"A great deal comes back to me now as very unpleasant, but . . . Perhaps I should end these *Notes* here? I think that I made a mistake in beginning to write them. At least, I was ashamed all the time I was writing this *tale*: consequently, it's not really literature but corrective punishment."[48] Despite punishing himself by writing this down, he gets no relief. Nor does he stop. The editor mercifully interrupts the text, commenting: "However, the 'notes' of this paradoxalist don't end here. He couldn't resist and kept on writing. But it also seems to us that we might as well stop here."[49]

In *House of the Dead*, the reader traces a man's coming into a new consciousness through suffering. There is a transformation and the beginning of something new. Not in *Notes*. And there's the rub. The reader expects that the underground man revisits the past to explain the present and deliver himself from its torment. But in fact, the effect is the opposite. Nothing is resolved. He remains a sick, spiteful man. There is no catharsis. The underground man has no will of his own, makes no real decisions, and can undergo no transformation. Even when he lashes out to express his desire for freedom, even then he backtracks and says that of course it must be that he was acting according to some law. He is like an animal who, when its foot is caught in a trap, will try to gnaw it off but cannot succeed.

The underground man insists there is nothing special about his situation. He behaves like everyone else, though perhaps to an extreme others are too cowardly to approach. No one acts "in accordance with his own desire, but in and of itself, according to the laws of nature. Consequently, we need only discover those laws of nature, and man will no longer have to answer for his own actions and will find it extremely easy to live."[50] Then why does he find it all so hard? He cannot accept responsibility for his transgressions and therefore can never atone. He will be haunted by guilt and knows at the same time that it is irrational to feel guilty. He feels queasy at the idea that he has these feelings only because he may not be enlightened yet—for a truly enlightened person would not and could not experience guilt.

The censors butchered Dostoevsky's text by taking out an oblique reference in the first part to the possibility of finding his way out of the underground: "I know myself as surely as two times two, that it isn't really the underground that's better, but something different, altogether different, something that I long for, but I'll never be able to find! . . . I swear to you, gentlemen, that I don't believe one word, not one little word of all that I've scribbled. That is, I do believe it, perhaps, but at the very same time, I don't know why, I feel and suspect that I'm lying like a trooper."[51] Dostoevsky complained to his brother that the "something altogether different" that was excised was faith: "The censors are swine—those places where I mocked everything and sometimes blasphemed *for appearance's sake*—they let pass, but where I deduced from all this the necessity of faith and Christ—they deleted it. What's the matter with these censors of ours, are they in a conspiracy against the government, or what?"[52]

Christ fascinated Dostoevsky as an exemplar of humanity that approached divinity because he suffered intensely yet maintained the sublime ability to love. By contrast, the underground man complains about the least bit of pain because it seems unjustified. When a toothache causes him to groan, "these moans express all the aimlessness of the pain which consciousness finds so humiliating, the whole system of natural laws about which you really don't give a damn, but as a result of which you're suffering nonetheless, while nature isn't. They express the consciousness that while there is no real enemy to be identified, the pain exists nonetheless, the awareness that, in spite of all possible [dentists], you're still a complete slave to your teeth." Pain is a torment because it is caused by nature and nature itself lacks agency. It is just "bloody insults [and] jeers *coming from nowhere*."[53]

Suffering wrenches a person out of their everyday existence and thrusts them into a world cut off from their fellow man. Intense isolation is the real source of pain for the underground man, for humans are social creatures and need one another to survive. According to Kołakowski,

> On the one hand there is the need to ground one's existence in something outside oneself—a need which seems to spring from a fear of the idea that we are isolated entities responsible for our own decisions; we want to leave ourselves behind, as it were, escape our selfhood, shed our individuality. And on the other hand there is the fear that our actions and decisions are somehow not real: that some alien force resides in us which is not only the effective executor of our intentions but also the will which decides what those intentions are. This conflict—between the drive to affirm the self and the drive to destroy it, or rather between fear of losing oneself and fear of one's self—is the most general way of describing the content of philosophical thought.[54]

It is also the most general way of describing the content of *Notes from Underground*.

SELF VERSUS SOCIETY

Not surprisingly, Anton Chekhov found Dostoevsky's books uncongenial. They were "much too long and lacking in modesty. Too pretentious."[55] He was not alone. Dostoevsky's reputation experienced a steep decline after he died. Few appreciated his writing until the symbolists came along at the beginning of the twentieth century. They discovered in Dostoevsky the spiritual depths they were looking for in literature. From then on, his reputation has grown, along with a startling variety of interpretations.[56] In a strange way, the reception of *Notes from Underground* bears similarities to that of *Moby-Dick*, published in 1851. The former is short, the latter prodigiously long, but they are both utterly novel in their prose style. They are full of extreme opinions and tangled digressions into psychology, theology, history, natural law, and philosophy. At the time of publication, the books had little resonance with contemporaries, even those who liked the authors' previous works. Only with years did they emerge from obscurity and assume the mantle of prophecy: Melville about the depredations of capitalism and the mindless exploitation of nature; Dostoevsky about the pernicious effects of historical determinism and utopian dreams of human perfectibility at the cost of freedom.

The incongruous pair of Chekhov and Dostoevsky also makes strange company, but they did have much in common. They were both acute moral psychologists who focused not on what constitutes the good life but on what makes life worth living. Life loses its meaning when people dwell on the past or place too many hopes on the future. On the extreme end of the melodrama spectrum that Dostoevsky occupies, the thwarted desire for meaning leads to suicide. Those who reject God, such as Svidrigailov in *Crime and Punishment* and Stavrogin in *The Devils*, despair of meaning and, after falling into the abyss of moral nihilism, commit suicide. In Chekhov, ever the soul of moderation, hopelessness also leads to deaths of despair—due to depression, alcoholism, and random acts of violence, which can all be seen as slow forms of suicide. Throughout Chekhov's work there runs an iron streak of cold fury. In Dostoevsky, the fury is hot. Everyone gets scorched. Both authors trace the legacy of serfdom and the moral corruption inherent in the master-slave relationship that infects not just the slave and not just the master, but all of society.

Dostoevsky feared for the future of his country because its centuries of "unlimited lordship over the body, blood, and spirit of a man just like himself, created in the same way," have made a habit of tyranny: "A generation does not tear itself away so quickly from the inheritance sitting in it; a man does not renounce so quickly what has entered his blood, and what was passed on to him, so to speak, with his mother's milk. Such precocious revolutions do not happen. To acknowledge one's guilt and ancestral sin is little, very little; it is necessary to break with them completely. And that cannot be done so quickly."[57]

Dostoevsky knew that a nation's origins are not destiny, but a point of departure. What path Russia was to take depended more on processes of growth and change than on any starting place. But change could not happen unless there was an acknowledgment of guilt and a desire to atone. This did not happen. Instead, the spirit of historical determinism prevailed, denying personal agency and responsibility. In 1914, empires went to war with the expectation that the victors would emerge with a powerful advantage over the defeated. By the time the war ended and the terms of peace were settled, it became clear that everyone had lost, even the victors. What happened next in the scramble to make order out of the ensuing chaos depended very much on how each nation envisioned the future. The successor state to the Russian Empire did exactly what Dostoevsky most feared: it dedicated itself to building a just and moral society for the future at the expense of the living.

4 HISTORY AS JUDGE, JURY, AND EXECUTIONER

FROM REARGUARD TO AVANT-GARDE

If the future is generated from the past, does that mean it is determined by the past? This was the question facing the generation that survived the death of Europe's empires in 1914. If the world order they had built over centuries broke down in just four years, at the cost of tens of millions of lives, how could they begin again? Yet in those same years, a new world was already being born, as war spawned new visions of a moral society. In Russia, revolutionaries founded their utopia on the idea that the future is indeed determined by the past. The triumph of the proletariat over the capitalists was inevitable. The Great War was just the start of the transition to the new order of things.

In July 1914, the Austro-Hungarian Empire declared war on Serbia. Within a few weeks, a domino fall of alliances that bound nations to mutual defense forced all European powers—the Russian Empire, the Austro-Hungarian Empire, the German Empire, the British Empire, and the French Republic—to go to war with and against one another. That summer, military and civilians alike expected the conflict to be over by Christmas. The war would be like a storm that erupts after a summer's day of heat, humidity, and heavy clouds. It would dissipate the tensions building among the empires as they jostled for control over foreign lands rich with the natural resources and labor they lacked at home. Instead, when it was over, the Ottoman, Russian, and Austro-Hungarian empires had disappeared from maps of the world. The British Empire was fatally wounded and the French Republic weakened. The Japanese joined the conflict to pursue their own ambitions on mainland Asia. The United States sent troops to fight far away across the Atlantic and emerged with new power and prestige. For the rest, their precedence was gone.

The catastrophic scale of loss from combat and the 1918 influenza pandemic—40 million dead and wounded in the war, upward of 50 million dead from the flu—made restoration of the old order inconceivable.[1] Empires that once proudly bore the burden of history—the spread of civilization and enlightenment—lapsed into incoherence. For the multitudes who longed for change in Europe and its colonies, the end of the war was a moment of great expectations. Now at last there was a chance to build a better world, as envisioned by the utopian thinkers of the nineteenth century—Robert Owen, comte de Saint-Simon, Charles Fourier, Pierre-Joseph Proudhon, Mikhail Bakunin, and Karl Marx, among many others. Transformation was upon the world.

The boldest, most radical, and longest-lasting experiment in historical reinvention was staged in the most backward of nations, the Russian Empire. Over the course of the nineteenth century, Russians had developed a theory of history to account for the divergence between European and Russian political cultures. It was honed by the small but influential group of Western-educated, politically engaged intelligentsia who were deeply pained by Russia's backwardness. They were angry and ashamed that serfdom kept the majority of the population tied to the land and subject to forced labor. Above all, they felt the sting of their own political impotence. In autocratic Russia, the emperor's subjects didn't operate with the sense of political autonomy and agency that characterized the Western Europeans. The intelligentsia felt themselves to be in a false position, humiliated and powerless to effect political reform and create a moral society.

Through an improbable combination of French Enlightenment rationalism and German Romantic theories of history and nationality, the intelligentsia convinced themselves that it was Russia's very backwardness that made its future glory possible. They could raise Russia to the level of economic, political, and cultural achievement reached by the Europeans they admired and envied. Being backward, the country could avoid the centuries of turbulent growth and bloody internecine wars Europe had experienced. With millenarian fervor, they dreamt of a glorious future and set about figuring out how to get there. This required a heroic feat of imagination in addition to a giant leap of faith. Previous attempts at reform had routinely met with reaction and retrenchment, even when the reforms came from the top down, as they did under Peter the Great, Catherine the Great, Alexander I, and Alexander II.

The elites of the Russian Empire were European by education, taught either by foreign-born tutors at home or in boarding schools.[2] They naturally came to see themselves through the eyes of the West, and what they saw was not flattering—a legacy of appalling backwardness and the barbaric, inhumane exploitation of the great majority, who were impoverished and illiterate. The elites believed Europe had developed culture to the highest degree, while the Russians were pulling up the rear.

The Russian elites' unsparing measurement of themselves against Europeans was both invidious and inspiring. The result was a "schizophrenia of the educated Russians in relation to European culture, which they both admired and resented."[3] It spawned a pair of opposing views of Russia's future, accompanied by a pair of diametrically opposed interpretations of its past. One view, espoused by the Westernizers, advocated liberal reforms so that Russia could be counted a full-fledged member of the civilized nations. The other, promoted by the Slavophiles, urged Russians to turn away from corrupt, materialistic Europe. They envisioned a return to Russia's Orthodox traditions with renewed dedication and purity of heart.

These divergent views of past and future were articulated first and most vividly by Peter Chaadaev (1794–1856), a brilliant and singular figure among the Russian intelligentsia. He wrote a series of letters addressed to a friend who was in the throes of a spiritual crisis. The letters are like essays in which Chaadaev expressed, among many things, his views on Orthodoxy versus Catholicism and Russia versus the West. Like his friends Alexander Pushkin and Alexander Herzen, Chaadaev was steeped in European culture. As was typical of his class, he spoke French as easily as Russian. (The correspondence he was famed for was written to a fellow Russian in French.[4]) His letters attempt a historical explanation of why Russia pulled up the rear. He concluded that Russia's backwardness, while tainted by the moral pollution of serfdom, was nonetheless a providential exceptionalism. Russia was destined to play a special role in world history.

Though written as private correspondence, the letters were semi-clandestinely circulated among the intellectual salons of Moscow and St. Petersburg. In 1836, the journal *The Telescope* published the first letter (which was written in 1829). It so outraged Emperor Nicholas I that he ordered the confiscation of all copies of the journal. The editor was arrested and exiled to Siberia. Chaadaev was spared the most severe punishment. Instead, he was declared insane and put under house arrest. Chaadaev became an official non-person, never to be mentioned in public. The emperor's harsh treatment was understood as an acknowledgement of the raw power of ideas in a nation lacking independent institutions, private property, and individual rights. Naturally, as a consequence, the letter was copied and circulated even more widely. Chaadaev was the first dissenter declared insane for his views—a technique for handling dissidents that the Soviets favored after de-Stalinization—and his clandestinely circulated writings became a prototype of Soviet samizdat.

What exactly did Chaadaev say? That Russia was backward and unenlightened, its moral fiber weak, and its mentality barbarous. More scandalously, he compared Russian Orthodoxy unfavorably with Roman Catholicism, in effect saying that Orthodoxy was ritualistic, obscurantist, and spiritually impoverished. The Russians had been untouched by the Renaissance that had widened the intellectual horizons of Europeans. Nor did Russians experience the Reformation, which engendered a religious seriousness and spiritual inwardness among Protestants and Catholics alike. The one time the Russian Orthodox Church undertook reform, in the mid-seventeenth century, it was not in response to the laity's spiritual needs, but came from the top down, instituted by the patriarch himself and focused on liturgy and rites. A third or more of the lay population rejected the reforms and became schismatics (known as Old Believers) who clung tenaciously to the old rituals and anathematized state authority. Finally, Russia lacked the Enlightenment values that made possible Europeans' sense of personal freedom, vibrant civic life, and a measure of political autonomy. This, above all, held Russia back.

Chaadaev argued that as a result of being cut off from European culture for centuries, the Russians had contributed nothing to civilization—nothing to science, nothing to art, nothing to philosophy: "Glance over all the centuries through which we have lived, all the land which we cover, you will not find one endearing object of remembrance, not one venerable monument which might evoke powerfully bygone eras. . . . *We live only in the most narrow kind of present without a past and without a future in the midst of a shallow calm.*"[5] Chaadaev hit a nerve. His fear that Russia would be left behind in the one civilization "which is the ultimate destiny of mankind" was widely shared.[6] "We are not related to any of the great human families," he wrote; "we belong neither to the West nor to the East, and we possess the traditions of neither. Placed, as it were, outside of the times, we have not been affected by the universal education of mankind."[7] Like Dostoevsky after him, he was haunted by the specter of exclusion from history. If Russia were marooned on some vast continent out of time, then all the souls living there were outside of time, too. They could contribute nothing to the world, and the cultural riches of the world could never enrich them.

It may strike some as strange that Chaadaev's long disquisition on Russia's backwardness is the subject of a correspondence about spiritual matters. But such was the ethos of the times. Ivan Kireevsky, a leading spokesman of the nationalistic Slavophiles, wrote that "few questions nowadays are more important than this question—of the relationship of Russian to Western culture. How we resolve it in our minds may determine not only the dominant trend of our literature, but the entire orientation of our intellectual activity, *the meaning of our private lives*, and the nature of our social relationships."[8]

The relationship between the individual and the community constituted the through line of all Russian thought, whether political, religious, aesthetic, or philosophical. This is the direct result of there being no civic institutions that gave the autocrat's subjects even a moiety of political autonomy. The state didn't recognize the rights of individuals as such; the inhabitants of the realm were subjects, not citizens. There was no parliament or representative body until 1905. The church was under the authority of the tsar. Private associations, such as Freemason lodges, were deemed hotbeds of revolution and banned. (This is why Dostoevsky was arrested for his participation in a discussion club.) All publications and works of art were vetted by state censors before seeing the light of day. This is why Dostoevsky's *Notes from Underground* had references to Christ excised from his text, bowdlerizing its meaning. Kireevsky's statement that "the meaning of our private lives" will be shaped by the choice Russians make between Western individualism and Russian communitarianism, self and society, is why Dostoevsky's change in political beliefs was experienced as an existential crisis.

Raymond T. McNally, translator and editor of Chaadaev's work in English, warns readers that "too many writers have tried to see more in Chaadaev's work than was actually there. [He] was simply a religious, social, and cultural utopian thinker."[9] McNally is right. Yet, in a culture that did not permit free political discussion, it was a matter of course for people to read too much into literature, art, and journalism. Who's to say they were wrong? That's where discussions that would not pass the censors were nevertheless accessible in encrypted form. People spoke their minds in code, which Russians called "Aesopian language." This coded language was designed to make anodyne sense on the surface while carrying hidden messages with deeper meaning. Thus, writers and artists could maintain "plausible deniability" for their politically unpalatable ideas. What's striking and even historic about Chaadaev's correspondence is that he wrote bluntly, not using Aesopian language, about the failures of the Orthodox Church, the backwardness and ignorance of the people, and the moral stain of serfdom.

Chaadaev was not idle during his house arrest. He wrote an essay, "Apologia of a Madman" (1837), in which he reveals that his thinking about the future of Russia had changed by 180 degrees. Chastising the Slavophiles and conservative nationalists who turn their back on Europe and seek greater isolation from the West, Chaadaev voices his longing for a better world and his conviction that it will be realized in Russia. The country could leapfrog the West and avoid all the slow-rolling stages of organic development. This idea surfaced in Russia but has been embraced time and again in developing nations, first with respect to Marxist political revolution, and today with respect to technology and renewable energy infrastructure.

Chaadaev argues that the leading role that Russia will play on the world stage means it can join the March of Progress at the head of the parade:

> I love my country in the way that Peter the Great taught me to love it. I do not possess, I admit, this sanctimonious patriotism, this lazy patriotism which manages to see everything as beautiful, which slumbers upon its illusions, and which has unfortunately afflicted many of our good minds today. I think that if we have come after the others, it is in order to do better than the others, in order not to fall into their superstitions, into their blindnesses, into their infatuations. To reduce us to repeating the long series of follies and calamities which nations less favored than our own had to undergo would be, in my opinion, a strange misunderstanding of the role which has been allotted to us. . . . I have the inner conviction that we are called upon to resolve most of the problems in the social order, to accomplish most of the ideas which arose in the old societies [i.e., Europe], to make a pronouncement about those very grave questions which preoccupy humanity. . . . *By the very force of circumstances* we have been constituted as a genuine jury for countless trials being handled before the great tribunals of the world.[10]

Whether Chaadaev's diagnosis of Russia's problem was right or wrong, it was an influential explanation of the country's stultifying culture, coupled with an impassioned, morally inflected argument for Russia's exceptionalism. The following decade, Chaadaev's ideas were elaborated by the Westernizers who advocated following the path of the West. Abolishing serfdom, promoting educational and economic reforms, and developing robust independent civic institutions with genuine political power were prescribed as the path Russia must pursue. They did not advocate imitating the West for its own sake, for they were fiercely patriotic. Instead, the Westernizers were driven by a vision that would lift all Russians out of the grinding poverty and ignorance that were seen as a moral blight as well as an obstacle to reform. Neither Westernizers Alexander Herzen nor Mikhail Bakunin were naive worshippers of the West. They had spent long years living abroad in exile, and decried the monstrous inequities and injustices that industrialization and capitalism created. Chastened by the failed revolutions of 1848, they sought a different way for Russia.

Herzen came to see the Russian peasant commune as the foundational institution with the potential to advance equality and justice. The commune (*obshchina*) administered land held in common and periodically redistributed plots according to the changing demographics and needs of its members. The commune had collective responsibility to the state for taxes, military recruitment, and other state obligations. Because the intelligentsia possessed little firsthand experience of peasant life, it was easier for them to idealize the commune as a uniquely Russian phenomenon that always placed the good of the collective above the ego-centered interests of the individual. The intelligentsia attributed a moral quality to the periodic redistribution of common lands and collective decision-making, failing to perceive these practices as survival techniques that stifled innovation, individualism, and dissent. (The commune was rare in parts of the country with abundant arable lands, where individual households prevailed.) The vast peasant population was freed from serfdom in 1861, only to be saddled with mandatory redemption fees for forty-nine years that forced them into greater and greater debt.

The intelligentsia's idealized notions of the peasantry found its apotheosis in Russian Populism, the sometimes violent faction of the intelligentsia who took up the cause of the ex-serfs in the 1860s and '70s. The Populists held a romantic view of the commune, as if they could not see what should have been obvious—communes were rigidly patriarchal and risk-averse. Famine and disease haunted the Russian countryside year in, year out. Like other agrarian populations, Russian peasants viewed "the world as zero-sum. This means that if some individuals get more—a better harvest or a beautiful child—it comes at a cost for everyone else, which leads to envy, anger, and so has strong social pressures for redistribution."[11] When revolution arrived in 1917, the peasants were quick to make demands for bread, land, and peace—and then to be left alone. Lenin considered them to be reactionaries who posed the gravest threat to the revolution.

Like the Westernizers, Slavophiles also identified the Russian commune as the fundamental societal unit of Russia with exemplary moral integrity, but for completely different reasons. They present a fascinating case of radical reaction, as conservatives whose ideas were even more extreme in many cases than the liberal Westernizers. The Slavophiles looked at Europe and saw people who had lost their spiritual integrity by placing abstract philosophical principles above the intuitions of the heart and soul. In their view, Europe was intellectually bankrupt, materialistic, and self-centered, and thus Russian attempts to emulate Europe were wrongheaded and dangerous. Ivan Kireevsky resolutely rejected the notion that "the difference between European and Russian culture was merely a difference of degree, and not of kind, and still less a difference of spirit and basic principles of civilization. We (it was then said) previously had only barbarism; our civilization began only when we started to imitate Europe, which had outdistanced us immeasurably in intellectual development."[12] To the Slavophiles, this was a spurious reading of history. They believed Russia's virtue lay in its rejection of egoistic individualism and the degradation of materialism. Russia comprised a multitude of small communities (the peasant communes) that were bound together into "one shared, vast community of the entire Russian land under the Grand Prince of All the Russias, serving as the support for the entire roof of the social edifice, the foundation for all the ties of its supreme structure."[13] There was nothing legalistic or formal about these ties between people and tsar. They were free of the corruption of Roman law, pursuit of capital, and the glorification of the individual at the expense of the collective. If for the Westernizers autocracy was incompatible with liberty, for the Slavophiles, liberal democracy was incompatible with social equality.

Theirs was a tendentious, fanciful, and internally contradictory rendition of the past. For example, Kireevsky claimed that Russia's virtue was intrinsic, and its backwardness was easily explained as the fault of bad foreigners imposing themselves on Russia. Primary oppressors were the Mongol hordes who descended upon Russia in the Middle Ages and kept it under their thumb for centuries. By contrast, he wrote, "in Russia, there were neither conquerors nor conquered. It knew neither an ironclad demarcation of static social estates, nor privileges granted to one estate at the expense of another, nor the resulting political and moral struggle, nor contempt, hatred, or envy between the estates."[14] This is not true. The Muscovite state was assembled precisely by conquering neighboring principalities, co-opting the ruling elite, and executing a sufficient number of luminaries to demonstrate their capacity for pitiless cruelty, the very trait Kireevsky attributed to the Mongols. The empire of Peter the Great and his successors conquered

Finland, Poland, the Baltic states, the Caucasus, Siberia—the list goes on. In other words, the Slavophiles advocated for a rebirth of a Russia that had never existed, based solely on the native institutions of peasant communes and quasi-religious devotion to the tsar. They touted a society that was patriarchal and piously submissive, forged from an imaginary past populated by humble souls who bowed as one to a benevolent autocratic ruler. This was a moral and religious vision of the nation that was not based on the compact between the ruler and the ruled. Slavophiles rejected the logical rigor and pursuit of individual goals, preferring a collective body bound in devotion of God and elevating intuition above reason. They attached themselves to tradition because, by their logic, the endurance of traditions proved that they were the true and right sifter of value. The Slavophiles did not develop a clear political agenda. Instead, the compelling logic of their movement was as simple as "make Russia great again." Like the exhortation to "make America great again," it relied on a mythical Golden Age that had been corrupted by educated elites, radical leftists, moneygrubbing capitalists, Jews, Freemasons, and any number of other malefactors. Their ideas suited the times and permeated the culture. Paradoxically, they were picked up in the following decades by radical revolutionaries who for their own reasons envisioned the peasant commune as the foundation of the new society. In both cases, their impetus was moral.

The unselfconscious substitution of fiction for fact was not unique to Slavophilism, nor was its unapologetic conflation of the ideal and the real. The conservative Slavophiles and the liberal Westernizers sought to create a more perfect moral society. Liberals favored a world with greater individual liberty, while conservatives believed in the primacy of a well-integrated community over the individual. In both cases, they worked up versions of the past that could serve as a blueprint for the future.

The Russian intelligentsia used fiction, belletristic literature, and theater, as well as painting and music, as primary modes of articulating suppressed longings for equality, freedom, and human dignity. The lack of well-worked-out policy programs in no way weakened their appeal. On the contrary, the purest, most radical ideas were the ones with the greatest charisma. Direct political speech had to support the autocratic regime. If it did not, it would be butchered by the censors or simply shelved. What would normally be aesthetic expression in Western Europe carried in Russia the heavy freight of religious, spiritual, and political thought. Artistic expression was the sole channel of communication for developing alternative political thought.

Time and again, ideas that began by addressing a concrete social, economic, or political problem failed to find a natural outlet in constructive and sustained action. It didn't take long for ideas that began in moderation to morph into maximalism because civic institutions, such as they were, lacked standing. Ideas behaved like free radicals circulating in the air, looking to attach themselves to anything that could serve as a vector. Particularly in an environment in which action always led to reaction, ideas often became extreme because they could never be more than a reflection on the moral purity of those who held them. To seek compromise—in other words, to engage in the real-life politics of give-and-take—could be read by fellow intelligentsia as weakness of will or failure of faith.

The Westernizers and Slavophiles, though they arrived at opposing visions of the future and the past, were united in their conviction that Russia had a world-historical mission, a conviction that was deep, unquestioned, and required no proof. Russian messianism grew out of facts on the ground but flourished as a psychological myth that provided a political context for those facts. The Westernizers and Slavophiles absorbed ideas from the West and turned them inside out. Through some alchemy of moral longing, the Russian intelligentsia was able to transform the shame they felt before Europe into a point of pride.

"We are one of those nations which does not seem to form an integral part of humanity," Chaadaev wrote, "but which exists only to provide some great lesson for the world."[15] Russians, then, were of the same ilk as their American contemporaries, who saw themselves as heirs to a revolution that had ushered something new and uniquely precious into the world, something morally superior to the decadent European regimes.

Given the context of Chaadaev's letters, particularly his religious and quasi-mystical orientation, it seems odd that the fruition of his thought comes about in Marxism-Leninism. But it is precisely Chaadaev's grand unifying idea—the special destiny of Russia leading the world toward a higher state of universal moral seriousness—that is found in Lenin's bold appropriation of proletarian revolution for an agrarian society. It is unlikely that Chaadaev's writings had any direct influence on Lenin. (At a minimum, he would have been dismissive of their religious content.) Russian revolutionaries devised a new, site-specific theory of historical development that in the end defied the logic of all existing models. A determined faction of the Social Democratic Labor Party led by Vladimir Lenin (1870–1924) took Marxist theory, performed radical surgery on it to remove the required proletariat class leadership, and replaced it with a bourgeois intellectual party vanguard. They, the bourgeois intellectuals of the Bolshevik faction, would execute the will of the proletariat. That they succeeded was a marvel to the world—for some, an inspiration; for others, a caution.

Lenin's hybrid of Western positivism and Russia's historical messianism created the Frankenstein idea that Marxism would triumph in a country that was not industrialized and had few proletarians. Lenin's revolution contravened all the essential requirements Marx and Engels placed on the realization of communism. This didn't matter. Chaadaev prophetically wrote that "this past is no longer within our powers, but the future belongs to us. . . . In order to achieve definite results, we need only a powerful will," like that of Peter the Great.[16]

That is exactly what Lenin brought to the revolution. So, too, did the foremost revolutionary of aesthetics, Kazimir Malevich (1878–1935), the man who invented nonobjective art. Malevich claimed ownership of the future and launched an uncompromising frontal assault on European art in 1913. By 1915, he had broken through the line, defeated the enemy, and finally "escaped from the circle of things."[17]

MALEVICH AND THE ECLIPSE OF THE PAST

By the time Russia entered the war in August 1914, the hope for an evolution from an autocracy to a constitutional democracy was long gone. Time and again, the moral longings of the Russian reformers met insuperable obstacles to moral action. In its place was escalating frustration, despair, and extremism.

When the war began, Lenin was abroad, where he had been for seven years and where he stayed until months after Nicholas II abdicated in February 1917. Russian artists, meanwhile, breached the barrier of passivity and alienation to create an art that threw off all reference to the past and staked their claim on the future. By force of will and imagination, Kazimir Malevich led the revolutionary brigade of artists. His art distilled an unbounded ambition to annihilate all barriers to human strivings, equal in scope and scale to any Marxist vision of humanity's transformation.

Envisioning the future was a widely shared passion among European artists at the time. For inspiration they looked to "primitive" and pre-Christian cultures in search of an authenticity of form and affect that had been buried under the macadam of modern life. Picasso and Brancusi found their inspiration in cultural objects from sub-Saharan colonies that entered the art markets of Paris, Rome, and Berlin. They were seeking aesthetic perspectives uncorrupted by the materialism of the bourgeoisie and their fixation on creature comforts.

By contrast, Russian artists didn't need to look abroad if they wanted to move beyond the worn-out mimetic arts. For them, the primitive and pre-industrial was nearby in the countryside. In creating *The Rite of Spring*, Igor Stravinsky, Vaslav Nijinsky, and Sergei Diaghilev needed only travel a short distance outside St. Petersburg or Moscow to find a world untouched by Western influences, beyond the occasional incongruity of a gentry manor house styled as a Greek temple or French chateau. *The Rite of Spring* premiered in May 1913 and has gone down in history as the most notoriously daring of the artistic scandals that year. But that is because it took place in Paris. Considerably more radical was "the first Futurist opera," *Victory over the Sun*, staged in St. Petersburg for four performances, alternating with the self-styled tragedy, *Vladimir Mayakovsky* by Vladimir Mayakovsky. The opera had a libretto by Aleksandr Kruchenykh, score by Mikhail Matyushin, and set, costume, and lighting design by Kazimir Malevich. The poet Velimir Khlebnikov wrote a prologue in verse that included scores of invented words. Russian futurists had almost nothing in common with their more renowned Italian brethren of the same name, other than their embrace of movement. In contrast to Marinetti and company, the Russians were anti-machismo, anti-war pacifists.[18]

In every way imaginable, *Victory over the Sun* was a far more substantive departure from bourgeois banalities than *The Rite of Spring*. The plot, such as it was, was simple. In the first act, the Sun, nature's greatest power and the source of light, life, and energy—and metaphorically of logic and reason—is taken captive and incarcerated by Futurist Strongmen. In the second act, the audience is transported to the future, to a land remade into a zone of fantastical freedom from the tyrannies of nature, time, and history—of cause and effect, of logical language, and of gravity's bondage (figure 4.1). So marvelous is this world that its inhabitants hardly know what to do with their ease and "extreme lightness": "how extraordinary life is without a past / With risk but without remorse and memories."[19]

Victory achieves complete integration of sound, light, voice, costumes, set designs, and gestures. It slams the "antiquated movement of thought based on laws of causality." The poets Khlebnikov and Kruchenykh improvised a new language that transcended logic, which they called "transrational" or "beyond reason" language (*zaumnyi iazyk*). Futurism sought to "destroy the antiquated movement of thought which follows the law of causality, toothless common sense, 'symmetrical logic' wandering about in the blue shadows of Symbolism, and to give the creative pre-vision of the real world of the new people. . . . The noise of exploders and the carnage of scarecrows will shake up the redhead by the art that is coming!"[20] If this sounds obscure today, it was in 1913 as well. (After the war broke out, it began to make more sense.) Half of the small audience present for the first performances decried the opera's outrageous defiance of theatrical convention. The other half may not have made much more sense of it, but they took great pleasure in its jubilant defiance of sense-making. To this day, the opera's willful obscurities make rich feasting for scholars eager to decipher its artistic codes. Its references to war, though, are unmistakable, and its maximalist exaltation of an imminent transformation of the human condition prophetic.

As Malevich worked on the opera that summer, two things preoccupied him: war and time. In June, Balkan hostilities broke out again. The First Balkan War had barely reached a negotiated peace when it failed. Now the Second Balkan War convulsed the region, pitting Serbia against Bulgaria. It may have been little noticed in the West outside diplomatic circles, but the

Figure 4.1

In the opera *Victory over the Sun*, Futurist Strongmen overpower the "antiquated movement of thought based on laws of causality." Malevich's backdrop design has objects of war painted over with black quadrilaterals, precursors to his *Black Square*. Kazimir Malevich, Stage design for *Victory over the Sun*, 1913.

Russians followed the war closely because they feared being drawn into it. The following summer, when a Serb anarchist assassinated the heir to the throne of the Austro-Hungarian Empire, this event was not taken to be a serious threat to peace in Western capitals. Nonetheless, a few weeks later, it served Austria as the pretext for a series of retributions that soon escalated into total war.

What did Malevich make of the Balkan conflict? He wrote to his collaborator Matyushin that "we should use the war for the preparation for a final disintegration of academism."[21] *Victory over the Sun* was Malevich's opening salvo in his battle to reset the clocks of natural and historical time. In contrast to *Rite of Spring*, *Victory* turned its back defiantly on the past. It dwelt on a future when humans do not submit to the power of nature, as they do in the *Rite*. Instead, it is nature that submits to the power of humans. Humanity was emancipated from time, decay, entropy, contingency itself—in other words, history.

In 1915, in the midst of the First World War, Malevich made his great breakthrough in a single painting through which he finally "escaped from the circle of things." The breakthrough was a canvas measuring 79.5 by 79.5 centimeters on which a black square was painted against a white ground. It was called *Black Square* (figure 4.2). The painting was exhibited along with other Suprematist paintings, placed ostentatiously in a corner under the ceiling, exactly the spot where icons were placed in Russian homes. The artist described his creation as a eureka moment because he saw that with black, the zero of color, he could paint a quadrilateral, the zero of form. The year before, Russia had experienced a full solar eclipse, with the moon passing in front of the sun and darkness covering the face of the earth. This was taken by the futurists as an omen. When he painted his *Black Square*, Malevich's intention was explicitly to eclipse the entire history of Western art. The *Black Square* was, in fact, an eclipse of the past and more. Forensic examination of the painting reveals that the artist used a canvas which had a painting about war on it, thereby blotting it out (see figure 4.3).[22] Just as Khlebnikov wrote poems beyond rational language, Malevich made art that was beyond painting. To be clear, the *Black Square* is not an abstract painting, nor is it a painting of black. It is not a painting at all. It is the end point of a spiritual quest for the supremacy of feeling above reason.

In 1913, Malevich was done with depicting and dissecting material reality. By 1915, he banished objects altogether from his paintings. The

Figure 4.2
The *Black Square* was intended to eclipse all past art, like the earth eclipsing the sun. By uniting the zero of color (black) with the zero of form (the square), Malevich escaped "the circle of things" and created a painting that "does not belong solely to the earth." Kazimir Malevich, *Black Square*, 1915.

paintings are truly objectless or *bespredmednyi*, usually translated as "nonobjective." The translation can be misleading. In English, the term "objective" connotes the opposite of subjective. Malevich believed his art was completely objective and scientific, untainted by one scintilla of the mystical or symbolic. For the futurists, subjectivity was the essence of symbolism, and symbolism was everything that was wrong with art. As Malevich understood it, for symbolist writers and artists nothing existed in and of itself; all

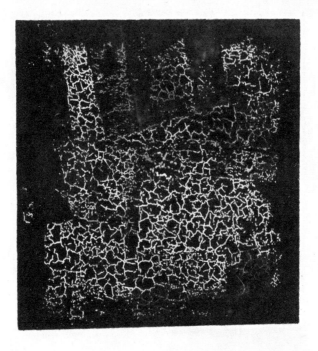

Figure 4.3

Malevich claimed he discovered the Black Square in 1913 (see figure 4.2), but only grasped its significance in 1915, when he painted over a canvas about war, seen here in x-ray. How often does war prompt people to blot out all memories of it? Kazimir Malevich, *Black Square*, 1915, x-ray.

that appeared to our senses was simply a symbol or point of reference for something beyond human reach. For Malevich, this idea was anathema. The entire notion of immateriality and the pull of nostalgia trapped creators in a dream world that does not exist.

Suprematism and, specifically, the *Black Square* were products of the war that was destroying the world before people's eyes. Malevich welcomed the destruction of the old to make room for the new. In 1915 the war in all its terrifying destruction called forth the *Black Square* as a negation—of the war and of painting itself. "The keys of Suprematism," Malevich wrote to Matyushin, "are leading me to discover things still outside cognition. My new painting does not belong solely to the earth. The earth has been abandoned like a house, it has been decimated. Indeed, man feels a great yearning for space, a gravitation to 'break free from the globe of the earth.'"[23] He discovered a "new painterly realism" and, from this time forward, dedicated himself exclusively to Suprematism. He used the word variously to mean "the dominance of the object by color," and the supremacy of pure feeling over reason, contingency, space, and time. All symbols, referents, and associations were banished from the canvas. People, landscapes, objects, movement—all the subjects of his previous paintings—disappeared. He used primary colors—reds, blues, occasionally yellows. And always there was black, the zero of color. In 1916, he worked his way to the final apotheosis of Suprematism—a white quadrangle on a white canvas. This was the end of the known world and there was no going back.

How did Malevich come to such millenarian ambitions? In tracing his artistic evolution, Malevich recalled that as a child he was surrounded by religious artifacts, including icons, though his parents were not religious. He claimed that icons had no effect on him at the time because they were not objects of the natural world; they did not represent people and there was no attempt to make them look like things in the real world. He was fascinated by nature itself—primarily inanimate nature such as clouds, rivers, thunderstorms, and the play of light and shadow on the surface of objects. By his own account, when he began painting, he was singularly interested in transferring onto his canvas a perfect likeness of what he saw, an absolutely faithful replica of nature.

This is the art he came to reject. "If likeness was still maintained," he wrote, "then it was only because the painter hadn't yet found that form which would portray painting 'as such,' without evoking associations with nature and objects, without being an illustration or a story, but as a completely new artistic fact, a new reality, a new truth."[24] This is what he achieved when he renounced naturalism and the naturalization of humankind that underwrote it. Malevich's break from natural representation was a declaration of freedom from nature itself. *Victory over the Sun* told the story of how humanity emancipated itself. The *Black Square* was the act of emancipation.

Icons instructed Malevich in the authority of color and frankness of form to create emotional truth. Icon painters, he came to see, "had achieved a great mastery of technique, convey[ing] meaning outside of spatial and linear perspective. They employed color and form on the basis of a purely emotional interpretation of theme."[25] The icon's primary value was its physicality, its very physical presence, because through the object—as object, not as symbol or representation—the spheres of the sacred and profane, the visible and invisible, the mortal and immortal exist equally in the same space at the same time and are accessible to us. Unlike the religious paintings of the West, which vividly depict the suffering of Christ or saints to prompt the faithful to contemplate their own mortality, Russian icons were not intended to prompt contemplation or introspection per se. They were simply present as a tangible artifact of the transmundane world. Malevich wanted nothing to do with the limitations forced on him by the human condition. If nature itself was the ultimate limitation, then nature must be transcended.

In the space of sixteen years, he had quickly traversed the styles of impressionism, pointillism, symbolism, fauvism, cubism, and neo-primitivism, then fevralism (briefly) and futurism, as if on a forced march to conquer European influences and leave them behind.[26] In 1915, he found the holy grail of Suprematism. By 1919, Malevich had exhausted the possibilities of the canvas and abandoned painting altogether. He followed the logic of aesthetic modernism that was flourishing in several European cities, but he followed it to its logical end and beyond—to its translogical end. He was the very model of the extravagant Russian artistic imagination that he shared with Natalia Goncharova, Vladimir Tatlin, Vladimir Mayakovsky, Mikhail Larionov, Dziga Vertov, Sergei Eisenstein, and especially Velimir Khlebnikov. If he went further and faster than they did, it was because he was spurred by his competition with Tatlin and Larionov to establish the priority of Suprematism over Tatlin's constructivism and Larionov's rayonism, of form and color over material. The battle for priority among artists was as fierce then as it is today among scientists for discoveries and patents.

Malevich took up a teaching post in Vitebsk at the school where Marc Chagall was teaching. (Chagall left eventually when it became obvious that Malevich attracted more students and they enthusiastically embraced Suprematism.) The school secured for Malevich and his family housing and food, absolutely critical in those starving times of the civil war. He attracted so many students—they were acolytes, really—because he invited them not merely to imagine but to create the world they wanted to live in.

Malevich was big-boned, compact of build, with a big square head. He spoke and wrote in the declarative mode. In 1919, he was forty-one years old, teaching students who were too young to have experienced the world before the war and revolution. All they knew of it were the shards that lay strewn about on every street. They were ready to be led in the job of building the new world upon the ruins of the old, and Malevich was eager to lead them. In thorough-going revolutionary mode, everything about daily life was in the midst of transformation. Malevich and his students formed an art collective, the Champions of the New Art (*Utverditeli novogo isskustva*), or UNOVIS. Malevich wrote: "If we want to attain perfection, the self must be annihilated—just as religious fanatics annihilate themselves in the face of the divine, so the modern saint must annihilate himself in the face of the 'collective,' in the face of that 'image' which perfects itself in the name of unity, in the name of coming-together."[27]

His students worked in all media and together they created a Suprematist environment. They made books, pamphlets, broadsides, posters, crockery, furniture, speakers' platforms, and panels to be displayed on the sides of buildings, buses, and propaganda trains. In 1920, the filmmaker Sergei Eisenstein came through Vitebsk on a propaganda train and recalled years later that "like many of the border towns of Western Russia, it's built of red brick. Sooty and cheerless. Here the red brick streets are covered with white paint, and green circles are scattered across this white background. There are only squares. Blue rectangles, this is Vitebsk in 1920. Its brick walls have met the brush of Kazimir Malevich. And from these walls you can hear: 'The streets are our palette!'"[28]

Malevich devoted his creative energies, somewhat frenetically, to producing a veritable Niagara of theoretical tracts, manifestoes, instruction manuals, and all manner of didactic materials. All this testifies to what was widely reported at the time, a sense of excitement about infinite horizons, the opportunity, even the need, to completely change the relationship between the individual and society, to make it more equitable, less atomized. Through their collective art-making, Malevich and his students embodied the spirit of the new society.

Over the course of the 1920s, Malevich produced fewer and fewer images and more and more words, analyzing the history of art, forms, media, and the basic elements of art-making. Like his contemporary Marcel Duchamp, Malevich was a master at surrounding his works with dense word-fogs of theory, now in lieu of producing art. (These two artists working on the far distant edges of innovation were apparently unaware of each other.) Malevich had a strong end-time orientation to art, and in this, his Suprematism was distinct from all other avant-garde art movements of the time. Cubists, Dadaists, and surrealists never envisioned an end-time; they never abandoned representation, but instead dissected it, mocked it, or excavated the unconscious to reveal a deeper and more irrational reality. Above all, they were art movements, aesthetic first and last.

These were not the ends pursued by Malevich. He sought the total transformation not merely of art, or of the world, but of humanity itself. Malevich's eschatological vision of humans transcending the constraints of gravity, reason, nature, and entropy had affinities with Karl Marx's own vision of humanity transcending nature to achieve freedom. The origins of this vision run deep in Russia. They found resonance in Marx's theory of history, where they finally found the path to a political agenda that just might turn their dreams into reality. The alignment of the Marxist political vision and Suprematist artistic ambitions came together in the most incongruous of circumstances to raze the old and build the new moral order. Then, they believed, humanity will be free from nature's dominion. History will end.

5 THE TYRANNY OF HISTORY

RUSSIAN MESSIANISM MEETS MARXISM

Every culture has essential ideas about where ultimate power lies—in the heavens, on the earth, or in the hearts of women and men. For Eastern Europeans, the source of their historical thinking has been Christianity, the offspring of an awkward marriage between the story of the Jewish Messiah, come to deliver his people from political tyranny, and a strain of Greek philosophy that endowed human reason with particular virtue. History became more than the tales of great men, great battles, and great empires—nor was it the myth of the lost Golden Age. It was the theater of humanity's salvation, a dynamic of consequential actions unfolding in mortal time. Adam and Eve chose knowledge over obedience, thereby cursing their progeny with pain, suffering, and death. In his infinite mercy, God gave them a way out by sending his son into the world to assume the burden of their guilt. What followed from there was a steady progression toward the consummation of God's plan—the end of the world and the day of judgment. History will end, and with it, all conflict. Humanity will no longer be subjugated to nature. There will be no pain, no labor, no death. Time itself will cease to exist, and with it, the past, present, and future. There is only eternity.

The spiritual and intellectual ambitions of the malcontent Russian intelligentsia were seldom satisfied by Russian Orthodoxy. Its rituals of worship and calendar of saints might be fine for the pious, illiterate peasant, but the educated gravitated instead to socialism and many ultimately to the communism of Karl Marx and Friedrich Engels. The Marxist theory of history is also a tale of salvation that works its way from the paradise of humans owning their own labor to the hell of capitalism in which all labor has been expropriated by capitalists, then back to freedom through class struggle and revolution.

Those urging reform grew increasingly impatient after the end of serfdom. Some saw revolution as the only way forward and found Marxism a surprisingly good fit. It was a respectably rational belief system that nonetheless commanded the heart as well as the mind. It prophesied a society of complete freedom and equality—freedom, because humanity would overcome the existential alienation of humans from their true nature as creative beings; equality, because there would be no exploiting class. There would be no class system at all, therefore no conflict and therefore no state. In the end, Vladimir Lenin and the Bolsheviks made communism the modern Russian Orthodoxy. Lenin was, if you will, its founder and spiritual leader. His corpse is preserved by a dedicated team of chemists who replenish the fluids (a secret formula) and perform ministrations to the body to keep it from evidencing corruption. His incorruptible body is displayed as a holy relic in a sepulcher built into the wall of the Kremlin. For close to a century, people from all over the world have made a pilgrimage to his tomb to be granted a glimpse of his body. Russian Orthodoxy has a particular cult of mortal remains, believing that those who are truly blessed do not show corruption after death. There is a splendid depiction of this cult in Dostoevsky's novel *The Brothers Karamazov*, where the particularly holy monk Zosima lies in state after death. When people begin to detect a smell in the room, doubt is cast on his true saintliness. Scandal ensues.

According to Marx, creativity—that is, labor—is the essence of humanity. Through labor we create ourselves and we create the world. History is thus the theater of humanity's self-realization through labor. It moves through distinct stages, propelled by change in modes of production. In the beginning was the Garden-of-Eden stage, before the division of labor separated ("alienated") people from their creativity. What they made was theirs. People were spontaneous because they were unrestrained by anything except their own will. Then tradition came to dominate in tribal societies. Hierarchies were established and cultural beliefs ("superstructure") inculcated the acceptance of this state of affairs as the natural order of the world. With each change in the mode of production, expropriation of labor grew in scale, so that property removed more and more of labor's fruits from the laborers to private control. This theft eventually generated opposition, which in turn led to the overthrow of the old order and established new overlords.

Marx took great pains to make the dialectical mechanism of change "scientific" and "objective." Through the law of dialectical change, the ruling class generates resistance. From the conflict between the rulers and the ruled, a new stage of historical development comes into existence. According to the *Communist Manifesto*, written in 1848 and translated into Russian in 1869, "the bourgeoisie forged the weapons that bring death to itself; it has also called into existence the men who are to wield these weapons—the modern working class—the proletarians."[1] The next stage of the historical dialectic requires the active will of the proletariat to rebel against the bourgeoisie. The revolution would not be a spectator sport.

The law-like logic of the stages of history and the Marxist spirit of positivism filled the sails of revolutionaries with a mighty wind. Feelings of powerlessness that had so long plagued Russian reformers and revolutionaries alike vanished when they allied themselves with a theory of history that was inexorable yet not, strictly speaking, deterministic. The manifesto states that in bourgeois society, "the past dominates the present; *in Communist society, the present dominates the past*."[2] Russian Communists interpreted this liberally to mean that they could take certain liberties with history to bring it into alignment with Marxist theory.

Followed through to the very end, the class struggle will lead to a new paradise. All conflict will cease because all want will be gone. There will be no need to compete for the resources that sustain life. History itself will carry humanity beyond the tyrannies of contingency, chance, and nature. Life will never again be a zero-sum game. A taxi driver, a housewife, a kindergarten teacher, a neurosurgeon—all are equally qualified to govern themselves and to share in governance of the commons. (It is a libertarian's dream come true.) Humans will no longer experience alienation. Peace will at last prevail.

This view of human potential will strike many in the twenty-first century as naive at best, dangerous at worst. Marxism posits a one-dimensional nature for all human beings, so that perfect freedom for one is perfect freedom for all. Marx and Engels are explicit that the values of any given society are created by the consciousness of the ruling class, and thus, the values of society at, say, the feudal stage of development differ in characteristics from those of the bourgeois stage. Values, in other words, mirror the modes of production; they change as technology advances. Since the rise of anthropological studies of cultures, contemporary scholars have seen values not as absolute across time and space, but as intrinsic to specific cultures as embodied by their mores and customs. Marx appears to say something similar but is actually saying the opposite. For Marx, values are not the product of cultures as they develop organically; they are the products of the modes of production. Therefore, when communism truly reigns, there will be no plurality of values. Culture understood anthropologically is itself a mirage, a bourgeois idea. Proletarian values will be good for all because all will be proletarian. Individualism is a bourgeois value. As long as it persists, true communism has not been achieved. Those valuing individualism and individual freedom were consistently labeled enemies of the Communist parties of the USSR, China, and Cambodia. It's impossible to know what Marx would say about these regimes, but he did hold that violence and the dictatorship of the proletariat were necessary to create communism. They were not necessary to maintain communism.

Freedom, then, is not freedom to exercise one's will. Nor is it the freedom to choose between different values or decide for oneself what is right or wrong. Rather, it is freedom from the oppression of nature. Marx, like Malevich, believed that oppression comes from the material conditions that nature imposes on human potential. Humans can be free only when they dominate nature completely. Leszek Kołakowski notes the remarkable fact that "Marx did not believe in the essential finitude and limitation of man, or the obstacles to his creativity. Evil and suffering, in his eyes, had no meaning except as instruments of liberation; they were purely social facts, not an essential part of the human condition."[3]

Marxism offered the most comprehensive, the most *meta* of metanarratives. It created an ontological unity of cosmology, history, and art, the first such unity since the dissolution of Christendom. Perhaps for this reason, Marxism is often seen as the secular successor to religion. For the Russians who felt bereft of a religion that offered intellectual or spiritual gravitas, communism acted as a special balm to their troubled souls. In the Marxist ontology, sin is the alienation of a person's creativity through property. This idea resonated in a nation that had little tradition of property rights to begin with. All land, all labor, all service, even all speech were held not outright, but by sufferance of the tsar, God's chosen leader. Much the same would obtain under communism—without the tsar, of course, but with the Party.

In the end what distinguishes Marxism from religion is its lack of a sense of mystery. It does not recognize the limits of human capacities to plumb the depths of creation. No matter how complicated life is, how inscrutable the ways of humans, how perplexing the arbitrary catastrophes that shape individuals' lives, and how unfathomable the nature of evil, Marxist materialism explains it all. Pain and suffering have no redemptive value but are nonetheless necessary because they are generated by the friction between classes.

The mesmerizing appeal of Marxism to the revolutionaries in Eastern Europe is most eloquently and accurately described by those who fell under its sway. The poet Aleksander Wat (1900–1967) grew up in Poland, part of the Russian Empire until 1917. He describes being oppressed by a sense of nihilism and negativity before he embraced communism: "There was only one alternative, only one global answer to negation. The entire illness [i.e., communism] stemmed from that need, that hunger for something all-embracing. In fact, communism arose to satisfy certain hungers. . . . One of those hungers was the hunger for catechism, a simple catechism. That sort of hunger burns in refined intellectuals much more than it does in the man on the street. The man on the street always had a catechism; he replaced one catechism with another."[4]

Leszek Kołakowski (1927–2009) was another Pole who fell under the spell of communism. He traced it to living in Warsaw during the Second World War. The Red Army liberated Warsaw and saved his country from the Nazis. The Russians were the white knights, the ones with the purest ideology, who embraced the fellowship of all people. Kołakowski was a committed Communist until 1950, when he went to Moscow for the first time. There he saw the logical conclusion of the philosophy he admired for its spiritual strivings. Marxism resulted in Stalinism, which brought not liberation to Russian laborers, but a new type of serfdom. Bodies and souls were held captive to the collective goal of building an ideal society. Kołakowski saw desolation and depression in the wholesale destruction of one civilization to make way for another that, he realized in a flash, would never, could never, be built. He became a committed, though nonideological, anti-Communist. (He rejected ideologies as such and urged caution about all demands made by maximalists.) He went on to write *Main Currents of Marxism*, widely viewed as the definitive work on Marxism in its philosophical context (as opposed to economic or political). As a historian, philosopher, Polish patriot, and (former) Communist, Kołakowski does full justice to the power of the ideas he once held to be true but then renounced:

> [It appeared that] Communism alone makes possible the proper use of human abilities: thanks to the variety of technical progress it ensures that specifically human activity is freed from the constraints of physical need and the pressure of hunger and is thus truly creative. It is the realization of freedom, not only from exploitation and political power but from immediate bodily needs. It is the solution to the problem of history and is also the end of history as we have known it, in which individual and collective life are subject to contingency. Henceforth man can determine his own development and freedom, instead of being enslaved by material forces which he has created but can no longer control. *Man, under communism, is not a prey to chance* but is the captain of his fate, the conscious molder of his own destiny.[5]

Dialectical change is supposed to happen under its own power. But it also requires that people take action to effect it, and that is its sweet spot. It is going to happen, and at the same time it requires people to make it happen. It puts a premium on action over contemplation. Its ethical imperatives went straight to the aching heart of the reformers and revolutionaries who felt complicit in the system they were trying to change. Aleksander Wat said that he "went over to communism" because "the motivations that inclined us to socialism were markedly social: questions of worldview, ideology, conscience, the cause of social justice. There were few political motivations, little politics in the strict sense of the world—little manipulation of reality. We lacked political passion. That was one of the features of the pre-Stalin Communist guard, especially the Polish one: the unmistakable predominance of ideological, philosophical, and social motives over the political."[6]

The creation of the moral society would not rely on supernatural forces or strokes of blind luck. It would not be mediated by church prelates or elected representatives. And while it doesn't paint the world as black-and-white, it does say that feudal lords and bourgeois capitalists couldn't be other than they were. Without troubling about any theological niceties, such as the doctrine of original sin, the need for divine intervention, and the prospect of eternal damnation spent in the fiery pits of hell, there was instead the simple catechism of the right side of history versus the wrong side of history. Everyone knew who the enemy was—they were the enemy of history. Evil as such does not exist as an absolute; it is the result of the historical process of expropriation. It will cease, in the end, when the expropriators are defeated by the proletariat. The process of history generates its own evil and then abolishes it. There was not and could not be radical evil.

And it goes without saying that the end will justify the means.

Communism promised to erase the distinction between my needs and your needs because, in the end, it abolishes the distinction between you and me. The claims of the self that are so often in conflict with the claims of the collective are artifacts of the bourgeois individualism that has created private wealth at the expense of the commons. Marx flattens the individual into only those dimensions shared by all. This insistence on the universal nature of humanity is evidence that he was an inheritor of the Enlightenment's emphasis on reason and rationality per se. It is probably this feature that makes Marxism seem dated and even irrelevant today—it is psychologically obtuse. Marx pays no heed to individual diversity as part of the human condition. He makes no mention of biological distinctions between people: those born healthy and whole or unhealthy and impaired, male or female, white or black. Does he think that these biological distinctions are just part of the structures of alienation that will eventually wither away with the state? He has such a totalizing view of humans that pain isn't even considered in its biological sense. Nor is death. We are not to concern ourselves with these things. Today it is inconceivable to think of the good society as one that disregards the particulars of humans—health, ethnicity, gender—and that discounts the effect of pain and suffering on individuals. But it is a common feature of ideologies to indulge in essentialism that slots humans into categories of being, some of greater value than others. To a significant degree, the identity politics of today makes essentialism respectable again, even obligatory, as those politics ironically codify identity into an ideology.[7]

The voluntaristic action demanded of Marxists gave intellectuals in particular a salutary feeling of strength and self-worth. They were fighting for the good and it made them feel good. George Orwell, in Spain to fight with the Republicans in 1936, wrote about the extraordinary atmosphere of the committed Communists he lived among:

> Many of the normal motives of civilized life—snobbishness, money-grubbing, fear of the boss, etc.—had simply ceased to exist. The ordinary class-division of society had disappeared to an extent that is almost unthinkable in the money-tainted air of England; there was no one there except for the peasants and ourselves, and no one owned anyone else as his master. . . . One realized afterwards that one had been in contact with something strange and valuable. One had been in a community where hope was more normal than apathy or cynicism, that the word "comrade" stood for comradeship and not, as in most countries, for humbug. One had breathed the air of equality.[8]

During the Cold War, the West turned Marx into an economic theorist. The conflict, we were told, was between two competing political economies, one benignly promoting free enterprise and the other cynically impoverishing their people for the benefit of the Party oligarchy. Political wars were waged through the proxy of competing economic models, with nuclear weapons. But at the beginning of the last century, avant-garde artists and revolutionary politicians were not arguing about economic models as much as embracing the power of ideas to change the moral order of the universe. The identification of so many Russian avant-garde artists with the Bolshevik revolution testifies to the way their millenarian vision coincided with Marx's prophecy of a harmonious time when everyone has what they need and *wants no more*. It was a glorious vision of the future in which, through Marxism, the Russians found a way to jump to the head of the line. They would no longer be, as Chaadaev lamented, "outside of the times" but instead be at the very center of them. Russian messianism could at long last board the express train to the future.

MARXISM MEETS LENIN

In 1913, while Malevich and fellow futurists were performing the funerary rites for the dead world and its dead art, another Russian was in Zurich plotting world revolution. Vladimir Lenin spent years of foreign exile (1900–1905, 1907–1917) forging his theory of revolution and creating his Bolshevik party with monomaniacal focus. Like Malevich, Lenin was short, compact of build, with a large head. Like Malevich, he was a man who skulled through every aspect of a problem by writing. (His collected works, collated and edited as reverently as scripture, comprise fifty-four volumes, each about 650 pages.) Lenin spent increasingly isolated years in exile writing his way into harmonizing Marx and Engels with the shifting political winds. He concentrated on creating an orthodoxy, born of his conviction that there was only one true Marxism. He was its avatar. (My use of the term "Bolshevik" rather than "Communist" is meant to clarify that there were several versions of Marxism developed in Russia.) Lenin's orthodoxy was distinguished by virulent partisanship and maximalist demands. These were the DNA of Marxism-Leninism until its shriveling into something empty and theatrical under Brezhnev.

Lenin paddled furiously against the tide of fellow socialists who were eager to argue and debate. He was interested in power and had contempt for those who merely signaled their revolutionary virtue. His language, which today would be called hate speech, was a tireless onslaught of exhortation and vituperation. He brooked no difference of opinion or interpretation. There was orthodoxy—his brand of Marxism—and there was heresy—everything else. "Deviationism" became a favorite invective, a curse he unloosed with abandon on his political rivals. His keen single-mindedness, together with his zeal for purity and demand for complete control, was the key to the unlikely triumph of Bolshevism over all rivals. Lenin was not alone in his revolutionary cruelty, but he set the ruthless tone for his party's leadership. His instrumental use of power to rush the revolution was not born of personal vanity; it was not wielded against personal enemies for vengeance's sake, as Stalin's was. Instead, it was all in service to the revolution, guarded by Lenin with the instinctual ferocity of a she-bear protecting her cub. Kołakowski commented, "If political calculation so required, he could pelt a man with mud one day and shake hands with him the next."[9] Lenin canceled comrades left and right. If they admitted their error, he just as freely uncanceled them.

During most of the war years, Lenin was living in the mountain fastness of Zurich. The city was alive with radicals and artists seeking a neutral port during the storm of the war. From there, world revolution looked increasingly remote. Rather improbably, Lenin frequented the Cabaret Voltaire, the infamous birthplace of Dada. In conversation with the Romanian Dadaist Marcu, Lenin is reputed to have said that "one must always try to be as radical as reality itself."[10] Yet, for one of the most successful politicians in modern history, he had a feeble sense of that reality. In 1913, Lenin wrote to his friend and fellow socialist Maxim Gorky, lamenting that "war between Austria and Russia would be a very useful thing for the revolution (in the whole of eastern Europe), but it's scarcely likely that [Emperor] Franz-Joseph and Nikolasha [Nicholas II] would grant us this pleasure."[11] Yet within the year, this is exactly what they did. In addition to his flawed sense of the times in which he lived, Lenin had little feeling for the proletariat. He mistrusted the peasants and felt contempt for "sentimental little intellectuals."[12]

Unlike Marx, Lenin was no philosopher. What he added to Marx and Engels's theory of communism was a bristling instinct for power and a readiness to exercise it without self-doubt or moral scruples of the bourgeois kind, totally alien to revolutionary consciousness. He was able to achieve what Marx himself thought illogical—proletarian revolution in an agrarian society—by sacrificing philosophical consistency for radical political action.

Karl Marx was asked by the Russian Populist revolutionary Vera Zasulich if it was possible to move from the feudal stage of production—serf and landowner—directly to socialism, and thence to communism, eliding the capitalist stage. What about Russia transitioning directly from peasant communal organization to communism? This would violate Marx's philosophy that history moves through specific and necessary stages, with one stage producing the preconditions for the next. The penultimate stage had to be capitalism because it created the proletariat that would destroy the bourgeoisie after they created the technological and industrial preconditions for communism. The question Zasulich posed amounted to asking if there could be a Communist revolution first and the building of capitalism second.

Marx lived long enough to have outgrown his earlier dogmatism. He was open to considering various ways non-European political economies could become Communist. In particular, he was impressed by the earnestness of the Russian revolutionary movement and eager to encourage its leaders. In his reply to Zasulich in 1877, he conceded that it may be possible to skip the capitalist stage, but only if, after the manumission of serfs in 1861, the commune became the basis for socialism. That moment had passed. Russia was already into the stage of capitalist production, and the proletarian revolution in Europe (the Paris Commune of 1871) had failed. Proletarian revolution in Europe would be needed to bring Russia along. A solo journey into the final phase of history was not possible.

This obstacle was extremely inconvenient for Lenin, who was working on a much tighter timetable than industrialization would allow. He had to create the dictatorship of the proletariat first, then develop capitalist means of production.[13] True, there was a growing proletariat, but the bulk of the population was still illiterate peasants. Renaming them as agrarian workers didn't change their consciousness.[14] Even the Russian proletariat—scarcely 3 percent of the population—didn't have the right consciousness. Instead, as Lenin said scornfully, theirs was trade-unionism at best. The revolutionary vanguard, made of bourgeois intellectuals like Lenin, would have to lead the revolution on their behalf. Still, one problem remained: the revolution could not succeed in one country, especially one as backward as Russia; it had to be a worldwide revolution to succeed.

When the opportunity presented itself in October 1917, the Bolsheviks did not hesitate to seize the day and start what they knew was a premature stage of the worldwide revolution. Lenin, the Bolsheviks, other socialist parties, the workers' councils (*soviets*), and the millions of others who joined the revolution "from below" felt they were living through a moment of transformation that could not be wasted. At this point, Lenin and the Bolsheviks were certain that their seizure of power was the spark that would ignite proletarian revolution in Europe. This would save the revolution. Bolshevik success in seizing power and keeping it was high risk and high reward. In late 1918, the European war ended and the collapse of empires fast followed. Bolshevik expectations were met when Communist uprisings broke out in Hungary, Estonia, and Bavaria, yet they were quickly put down. Bolshevik Russia, to her very great peril, stood alone, isolated, besieged by hostile armies on multiple fronts. The revolution was in danger as soon as it began. The Bolsheviks were faced with the task of jury-rigging their revolution in an agrarian nation, a difficult task akin to fitting a square peg in a round hole: it would require a great deal of force.

Lenin created a series of economic policies intended to hurry along the transition to proletarian supremacy, but he was forced to retreat. He created a set of instruments to enforce policy by silencing, isolating, or judicially murdering any and all opponents. In December 1917, he established the secret police, called the Cheka or the Extraordinary Commission for Combating Speculation and Counterrevolution. In 1918, Leon Trotsky, head of the Red Army, opened a concentration camp to incarcerate enemies captured during the civil war. More camps opened to accommodate an increasing number of political enemies. Everything that is today synonymous with Stalinism got its start under Lenin—draconian economic plans, the secret police, the Gulag, grain requisitioning, massive famines resulting from deliberate policy decisions, the stamping out of phantom conspiracies everywhere, all accompanied by the liberal application of terror. During de-Stalinization in the 1950s, many of the policies that were exposed and excoriated were attributed to Stalin, even though they had been set in motion by Lenin. Lenin's reputation as the father of the revolution had to be kept pristine. Otherwise, the revolution itself would be seen as the ultimate culprit behind all the sins committed in the name of the Communist Party. At that juncture, it was expedient to let Stalin take the blame. Their tactic was not to argue against the truth of the facts that were public at this time. Instead, the party created a context in which they could use those facts to substantiate a completely different history of Soviet criminality. This sleight of hand with facts and theory was itself part of Lenin's legacy.

Once Lenin decided to foreshorten the future by "deviating" from Marx's philosophy of history, he made violence and the threat of violence necessary and intrinsic to Russian Marxism. In *The State and Revolution*, Lenin explained that "the replacement of the bourgeois state by the proletarian state is impossible without a violent revolution. The eradication of the proletarian state, i.e. the eradication of the state as such, is impossible except through the process of 'withering away.'"[15] Violence was always part of the proletariat destruction of the bourgeoisie. But it was to be directed at the enemy, the bourgeoisie. Because Russia (after 1922, the USSR) didn't have a robust capitalist economy with a healthy class of capitalist exploiters, it was necessary to find enemies that could unite an exhausted and hungry population in a shared bloodlust for retribution. To accommodate this need, Lenin created categories of enemies that had not existed before. For example, he called the peasants who resisted the Bolsheviks *kulaks*, a term that before 1917 connoted a wealthy peasant ("wealthy" being a highly relative term). Resistance to the regime came from many types of peasants because the government was requisitioning food, sometimes even seed grain itself, to feed the starving cities. During the civil war (1918–1922), the rural population suffered terror under the revolutionary Reds, counterrevolutionary Whites, peasant Greens, Ukrainian Blacks, and an assortment of foreign armies, from Czechs and Poles to Americans and British. Yet there is something particularly chilling about the premeditation of Lenin's approach to resistance. In August 1918, only ten months after the Bolsheviks took power, Lenin set the standard for treatment of so-called state enemies. To comrades in Penza, a district to the west of Moscow, Lenin wrote:

> Comrades! The revolt of five kulak *volosts* [districts] must be suppressed without mercy. The interest of the *entire* revolution demands this, because *we have* now before us our final decisive battle "with the kulaks." We need to set an example. "The last decisive battle" with the kulaks is now underway *everywhere*. An example must be demonstrated.
>
> 1. You need to hang (hang without fail, so that the *public sees*) at least 100 notorious kulaks, the rich and the bloodsuckers.
> 2. Publish their names.

3. Take away *all* of their grain.
4. Execute the hostages—in accordance with yesterday's telegram.

This needs to be accomplished in such a way that people for hundreds of miles around will see, tremble, know and scream out; *let's choke* and strangle those blood-sucking kulaks.

Telegraph us acknowledging receipt and *execution* of this.

Yours, Lenin.

P. S. Use your *toughest* people for this.[16]

By cheating history, Lenin changed the fundamental moral order that Marx defined as the communist end-state. Instead, Lenin found a way to achieve what Chaadaev only dreamt of—Russia leapfrogging Europe's essential phases of development. He took Marxist political theory and turned it into a strategy for the seizure of power and the moral justification for embracing any means necessary to achieve the end he desired. It was not an end that he alone desired. Millions joined the revolution "from below," including the thousands of artists, of whom Malevich was perhaps the most original, who were eager to destroy the old world and build anew.

History cannot be cheated, though, not when you have made it into an ontological entity and a jealous god. The past can be erased, but without it, humans lose their bearings. Contrary to what the futurists predicted in *Victory over the Sun*, the "extreme lightness" of the present without a past brought no ease. The past was gone, and the future for which generations of Soviets were sacrificed never arrived. People were marooned in an eternal present with faltering hope for their future.

Lenin was true to Marx when he wrote:

We are not utopians, and do not in the least deny the possibility and inevitability of excesses on the part of *individual persons* or equally the need to suppress *such* excesses. But in the first place, no special machine, no special apparatus of suppression is needed for this; this will be done by the armed people itself with the ease and simplicity shown by any crowd of civilized people, even in modern society, stepping in to put a stop to a brawl or to prevent a woman from being assaulted. And, secondly, we know that the fundamental social cause of excesses which consist in the violation of the rules of social intercourse is the exploitation of the masses, their want and their poverty. With the removal of this chief cause, excesses will inevitably begin to "*wither away*." We do not know with what speed and calibration; but we do know that they will wither away. With their withering away the state will also *wither away*.[17]

Lenin makes the Party vanguard (of which he was the undisputed leader) out to be an instrument of the people's will without respecting, let alone trusting, the people. The state never withered away. It had to grow stronger and stronger simply to get through each winter with fuel shortages and each summer with inadequate harvests.

This state was a world away from the utopian expectations that animate so many of Chekhov's characters. They, too, dream of a better, nobler way of being human. In the final moments of *Uncle Vanya*, when Vanya gives way one more time to his gloom and unhappiness, his niece Sonya—who has her own reasons for despair—rallies to console him:

> You and I, Uncle Vanya, we have to go on living. The days will be slow, and the nights will be long, but we'll take whatever fate sends us. We'll spend the rest of our lives doing other people's work for them, we won't know a minute's rest, and then, when our time comes, we'll die. And when we're dead, we'll say that our lives were full of pain, that we wept and suffered, and God will have pity on us, and then, Uncle, dear Uncle Vanya, we'll see a brand-new life, all shiny and beautiful, we'll be happy, and we'll look back on the pain we feel right now and will smile . . . And then we'll rest. . . . We'll hear the angels singing, we'll see the diamonds of heaven, and all our earthly woes will vanish in a flood of compassion that overwhelms the world! And then everything will be calm, quiet, gentle as a loving hand.[18]

The revolutionaries refused to take whatever fate sent them. Yet, for all that, they ended up in the same eschatological cul-de-sac, talking of the time in the future when they would be happy, when the cares of work and labor for other people, never for themselves, would at long last end. The Communist Party leaders were forced to explain why the time of arrival kept receding over the horizon. There was an endless spontaneous generation of enemies, saboteurs, wreckers, cosmopolitan parasites, blood-suckers, deviationists, and other malign forces that required stamping out first. The search for enemies became moot on June 22, 1941, when Hitler launched Operation Barbarossa and history released the Soviet people from the purgatory of Marxism-Leninism. They had a real enemy to fight now. Its name was not capitalism. Its name was fascism.

When Russian messianism met Marxism, the two joined forces to promote Russia's mission to usher in a new moral order. When Marxism met Leninism, it set aside its commitments to philosophical consistency and embraced the reality of power. Marxism-Leninism replaced bourgeois individualism, with its sense of identity, freedom, and responsibility, with a class identity that fixed people into essential categories, analogous to the racial and ethnic categorizations prevalent today. History became an ontological entity unto itself, akin to the Prime Mover whom Christian theologians identified as God. As such, history acted as judge, jury, and executioner. People could be on the right side of history or on the wrong side of history, but wherever they stood, they were oriented to the bright, shining future. The historian Lesley Chamberlain notes that Marx's idea was to rescue labor from capitalist exploitation and restore to humans their full dignity. Instead, the Communist Party of the USSR ended up creating a system that debased work itself.[19] Soviet citizens liked to jest that "they pretend to pay us and we pretend to work."

The greatest crime committed by the regime in the name of the Future Perfect was to fake a past in order to manipulate people's sense of identity. Kołakowski goes so far as to say that there really is no difference between *them* and *us* because "in its perfect form, totalitarianism is an extraordinary form of slavery: slavery without masters. It converts all people into slaves; because of this it bears certain marks of egalitarianism."[20] Freedom, too, was debased because the difference between freedom and necessity disappeared. After twelve hundred pages analyzing the origins and fate of Marxism, Kołakowski concludes *Main Currents of Marxism* with the observation that any society which intends to create perfect equality must use coercion because it must first eliminate freedom: "In real life more equality means more government, and absolute equality means absolute government."[21] When the USSR finally died in 1991, people of the former Soviet Union and the satellite nations of the Warsaw Pact then faced their greatest fear—that more freedom means more anarchy, and absolute freedom means absolute anarchy. The countries that had living memories of democracy, such as Poland and the Baltic nations, knew better. But the Russians had no such memories of effective self-rule. Their fears of anarchy, then, were justified, and when they came true in the 1990s, Russians were not surprised. For this fear, Vladimir Putin offered a reassuringly familiar answer—to make Russia great again under the protection of a strongman.

It is ironic that Putin blames so much of what went wrong in Russia over the past three decades on the father of the revolution, Lenin. It's ironic because Putin's style of leadership has so much in common with Lenin's—for example, his ostentatious ruthlessness to enemies and liberal use of scatological language to cast doubt on the humanity of others. It was Lenin, after all, who created the Cheka, precursor to the KGB. Putin was a longtime mid-level officer in the KGB and early on resorted to KGB tactics such as disinformation to consolidate his power. In 2016, *The Guardian* reported that in an address to pro-Kremlin activists in Stavropol,

> Vladimir Putin has denounced Lenin and his Bolshevik government for their brutal repressions and accused him of having placed a "time bomb" under the state. . . . Putin was particularly critical of Lenin's concept of a federative state with its entities having the right to secede, saying it has heavily contributed to the 1991 breakup of the Soviet Union. He added that Lenin was wrong in a dispute with Joseph Stalin, who advocated a unitary state model. Putin has in the past denounced Stalin for the purges that killed millions, but noted his role in defeating the Nazis in the Second World War.[22]

Some observers claim that since the war in Ukraine began, Putin has gone one step further and is shaping his internal security apparatus to resemble the notorious NKVD, the Cheka's successor, which Stalin forged into the critical instrument of terror.[23] The claims of national security have already been used preemptively to arrest people who voice dissent, effectively intimidating the public into keeping their opinions to themselves.

The fears of Russians *in extremis* present a mirror image of Americans' fears. In the twenty-first century, many Americans who fear any encroachment on their liberties believe the country is headed in the wrong direction. They don't fear an excess of freedom devolving into anarchy. On the contrary, because "this is America and I'll do what I want," there can hardly be enough liberty *for them*. Equality of such liberty for *all* citizens is a different matter. Segments of the civilian population are heavily armed and the habits of vigilantism still very much alive. There are Americans ready to take up arms to protect their exclusive claims to liberty. They are afraid of the excesses of equality, believing that absolute equality means absolute government. The language of absolutes is seductive in times of social upheaval and an array of socioeconomic changes that are beyond understanding. Lenin was a master of the rhetoric of absolutes. He demonstrated that when it is combined with the rhetoric of good versus evil, the language of history as destiny is a license to kill.

6 FINAL THINGS ARE FOR CHILDREN

THE PROBLEM WITH PERFECTION

European empires saw the Great War as the armed conflict that might end conflict itself. Perhaps this view was merely a way to justify the uncontrollable carnage they could not find a way out of. That said, the quixotic ambition to wage war on war had the power of self-hypnosis. It was effective in blinding millions to the reckless carnage unfolding before their very eyes. Historians Stephane Audoin-Rouzeau and Annette Becker conclude that "the central paradox of the Great War is that from the beginning, and probably even most strongly during the bleak period when the belligerents were discouraged, . . . each side believed they were waging war because it would bring a new and radiant world in the future, a purified world rid of its central flaw: war. . . . *There was a genuine eschatology of peace, of the triumph at long last of redeemed humanity over the forces of evil.*"[1] In hindsight, it's obvious that this is not what the armistice brought. Instead of suturing wounds that long festered among the imperial powers, the war ripped open old wounds and inflicted new ones. The death toll was stupefying. Yet, being real, it had the power to strip reality of its veil of coherence. The dead called upon the living to be "as radical as reality itself."

The Russian Empire was only one of the combatant nations that struggled to rationalize the irrationalities of trench warfare, poison gas, and mechanized murder. The pursuit of a more perfect world took a different shape in the United States. In 1917, the US entered the fray in the role of *deus ex machina*, volunteering to bring the curtain down on the conflict and secure a permanent peace. President Woodrow Wilson believed that "we are at the beginning of an age in which it will be insisted that the same standards of conduct and of responsibility for wrong shall be observed among nations . . . that are observed among the individual citizens of civilized states."[2] Wilson's eschatology of peace developed into the liberal internationalism that pursued the mission of spreading democracy across the world. American intervention proved profoundly consequential. It contravened the unilateralist instincts and policies, held by Americans since George Washington's presidency, that had kept the nation out of foreign entanglements and obligations.[3] The long-term consequences of Wilson's vision was far from evident to Americans at the time, but it put an end to the delusion that a nation of such economic might and technical expertise could choose freely when, where, and how it could engage beyond its borders.

Drawing an analogy between the present and events from a century ago doesn't permit predictions about how the current moment will turn out for either post-Communist Russia or post-neoliberal America. For one thing, the consequences of the Great War continue to unfold to this day in the combatant nations and their former dominions in the Middle East, the Balkans, Australia, Manchuria, Vietnam—the list goes on. The war was only the beginning of the end of empires. The unwinding of imperial power carries on today, economically, militarily, politically, and culturally. In each of these spheres, the ghost of empires continues to broadcast the seeds of new conflicts and novel imperial ambitions.

History doesn't repeat itself, but habits of mind and patterns of human behavior do. Now, thirty years after the Soviet Union's demise, it is clear that Russia's pre-Revolutionary autocratic political culture has emerged intact and continuous with its Soviet instantiation. Within a decade of the USSR's dissolution, Russia defaulted to authoritarian rule after failed attempts at devolving power to the Duma and the states. The Putin regime's ambition to restore Russia's starring role on the world stage with status equal to the West drives his domestic as well as foreign policies. Tragically, Putin insists the invasion of Ukraine is a domestic matter, not foreign. He bitterly resents what he sees as NATO's encroachment on the territorial integrity of Russia.

Once again, the West both attracts and repels Russians concerned about their place in the larger global order. In particular, they envy the United States while simultaneously accusing it of rank egoism, materialism, and soullessness. The heavy doses of Western economic theory applied by Western economists in Eastern Europe and Russia in the 1990s left many Russians with a bitter taste in their mouth. Daniel T. Rodgers remarks that "notions of monoeconomics and monopolitics, good for all times and places, transportable through the conduits of internationally mobile experts and pressure groups, were at their height" when the Iron Curtain lifted in Berlin.[4] Western ideas of the universal and progressive development of *homo economicus* were planted in Russian soil only to find the ground barren, or worse—toxic.

The case of the Russian Empire transforming itself into the USSR reveals how existential crises can induce national communities to fall into a dream of deliverance from chaos and evil in the hope that when they wake up, the dream has become reality. What happens when they awake to confront the truth and are forced to reckon with the consequences? How are they to understand the extent to which their identity and self-image has been supported by a distorted and at times wholly fictional past? Their government told them, in the words of Simone Weil, that "by walking straight ahead [they] would rise into the air," and the people believed them, or wanted to, or pretended to because they had no choice. What happens when they fall back down to earth? As a nation, they can get rid of the government that lied to them and put a different one in place. But how do they account for their own role in the duplicitous past?

The Soviet Union is often characterized as a totalitarian regime that ruled through coercion and terror. It is just as true to say that the regime controlled its population by manipulating their sense of reality, past, present, and future. The presence of terror was the regime's key instrument in rendering the population psychologically vulnerable to their manipulation. The moment the Bolsheviks seized power, they imposed strict control over the organs of information, from media and publishing to libraries and archives. Lenin did not hesitate to use terror to hold on to power, but it was not intended to be the sole source of legitimacy. Terror was educational, in Lenin's view—the terrible swift sword of revolutionary justice used with equanimity against class enemies and corrupt comrades.[5]

The Party's promise was that in the end, freedom would come as freedom from want, and equality would come as the end of class distinctions. This was a powerful projection of desire onto the future. It wasn't Marxism alone that inflated the utopian imagination of Russians in the decade after the October Revolution. A new and distinctive sense of reality transfixed the population in the 1920s. Utopian projects proliferated across the multiple time zones of the former empire before they were suppressed by the government. Kazimir Malevich's Suprematism stands out among many of these projects because of its continued influence on art today. Yet he and his cohort launched but one experiment into a sea of a thousand experiments. It was indeed as if they were all ascending higher and higher into another realm of existence. In 1923, Trotsky waxed lyrical about humanity's immanent transformation:

> It is difficult to predict the extent of self-government that the man of the future may reach or the heights to which he may carry his technique. Social construction and psychophysical self-education will become two aspects of one and the same process. All the arts—literature, drama, painting, music, and architecture will lend this process beautiful form. . . . Man will become immeasurably stronger, wiser, and subtler; his body will become more harmonized, his movements more rhythmic, his voice more musical. The forms of life will become dynamically dramatic. The average human type will rise to the heights of an Aristotle, a Goethe, or a Marx. And above this ridge new peaks will rise.[6]

A more convincing picture of the future was recorded by Yevgeny Zamyatin (1884–1937) in his novel *We*. It depicts a utopia, the One State (*Edinoe Gosudarstvo*), with all the promised virtues of a Communist world, except one: there was no withering away of the state. This is the novel's most prophetic and, for the Bolshevik dictatorship of the proletariat, most dangerous insight. There is no end-state. Nothing is ever final. As the protagonist, D-503, says, "The ideal (clearly) is a state where nothing actually happens anymore." The people of the One State are told by the authorities that they reached that state long ago. Yet there is trouble in paradise—"something unforeseen, something that couldn't be calculated in advance, has occurred."[7] Zamyatin's novel is a profound meditation on disillusionment. Through the eyes of D-503, the reader experiences the enchantment of the perfect state. The reader sees how the government apparatus hypnotizes the population into believing they have achieved the harmonious state, while also signaling to them that this harmonious state is under constant threat and they must be vigilant. At the same time, the reader senses D-503's temptation to wake up, to open his eyes, to gain knowledge of the real world at the expense of being cast out from the safety of the One State.

The novel is written as a journal kept by D-503. Its style is almost impenetrably avant-garde—with fractured syntax, occluded imagery, and stochastic narrative—and mirrors the jumbled and chaotic consciousness of the future. (The novel was written in 1920 but was set at least twelve hundred years in the future.) D-503 is the chief engineer of the spaceship *Integral*, being built to explore the possibility of creating settlements on new planets. He is a privileged denizen of the One State, a city state surrounded by the Green Wall. It's shielded from the sun by a dome erected a thousand years ago at the end of the Two Hundred Years' War to keep the outside world out—and invisible. Within the confines of the Green Wall, the One State is virtually transparent, made mostly of glass buildings that ease the tutelary job of the secret police (known as the Bureau of Guardians). Everything is hyper-rationalized and regulated by the Table of Hours according to the efficiency rules of F. W. Taylor, "the most brilliant of the Ancients . . . with the ability to see ten centuries ahead."[8] (Taylor was greatly admired by many Russians in this period, most notably Vladimir Lenin.)

Individuals are units, names are numbers, clothing is uniform, sex partners are assigned, and all are spared the burden of choice. After all, choice relies on imagination, the ability to project different paths and outcomes into the future. But imagination is a mental illness. Choice only creates vertigo. In the One State there is one way to thrive and be happy. For all units, it is the same. The unity of desire is true equality and with equality comes order: "Oh, the great, divinely bounding wisdom of walls and barriers! They may just be the greatest of all inventions. Mankind ceased to be wild beast [*sic*] when it built its first wall. Mankind ceased to be savage when we built the Green Wall, when we isolated our perfect, machined world, by means of the Wall, from the irrational, chaotic world of the trees, birds, animals."[9] On the annual Day of the One Vote, people come together to elect the Benefactor with the joy, D-503 says, that must be like that of the Ancients' Easter: "The mighty chalice of unanimity, the reverentially raised hands. Tomorrow, once again, we will offer the Benefactor the keys to the unshakable stronghold of our happiness." The Ancients voted with secret ballots as if, like thieves, they were hiding something. The day of the One Vote "does not resemble the disordered, disorganized elections of the Ancients, when—it seems funny to say—the result of the election was not known before-hand. Building a government on totally unaccounted-for happenstance, blindly—what could be more senseless? And yet still, it turns out, it took centuries to understand this. It is hardly necessary to say it but in this, as in everything else, there is no place for chance and unexpected events are not possible."[10] Like a great spider, the Benefactor "wisely binds us by our hands and feet with His bene-factorly [*sic*] threads of happiness."[11] The One State is superior in all ways.

Trouble in paradise begins when D-503 is possessed by an ungovernable attraction to I-330, a woman who tempts him to drink, smoke, and visit forbidden parts of the city. From the Ancient House, where relics of life before the Two Hundred Years' War are stored, they travel through tunnels that thread their way into the world outside. There, beyond the Wall, live people who, like their accursed ancestors Adam and Eve, inexplicably chose freedom over happiness. How could they make such a choice? With non-freedom, there is no crime, "no more confusion between good and evil: everything is very simple, heavenly, childishly simple. The Benefactor, the Machine, the Gas Bell Jar, the Guardians—all these are good, all these are majestic, wonderful, noble, sublime, crystal-clean. Because they guard our non-freedom—that is, our happiness. Those Ancients would be discussing it, deliberating and racking their brains: is it ethical, is it unethical . . . et cetera."[12]

D-503 breaks down under the seductive powers of I-330. First she reveals to him that she is a member of the revolutionary underground, the Mephi. Then he discovers within himself a second self, one with a soul and an imagination, and comes to know the agony of self-doubt. Who is he? How could he be more than one person? Which one is real? Yes, the imagination must be an illness. For D-503, Builder of the *Integral*, a critical job fit only for the most trustworthy, it is dangerous, even life-threatening, to discover his capacity for fantasy and desire for things the Benefactor has proscribed. Fortunately, there is a cure for this dread disease; scientists have isolated the location of the imagination in the brain and devised a procedure—the Great Operation—that disables it through three doses of x-rays. D-503 knows all this, yet he does not wish to be cured.

How could something new happen, something he feels within himself, when the revolution has reached its end-state and nothing can change? I-330 turns his engineering expertise on him to prove that there is no such thing as a final revolution. She reminds him that the number of numbers is infinite. So, she adds, it is the same for revolutions: "There isn't a final one. Revolutions are infinite. Final things are for children because infinity scares children and it is important that children sleep peacefully at night . . ."[13] In the end, D-503 submits to the operation that zaps his imagination and returns him to non-freedom. Yet the Green Wall has been breached, and the sun, for centuries hidden behind the giant dome covering the One State, comes pouring through. Once more birds appear in the skies high above.

Zamyatin wrote *We* at the height of the Civil War. It was impossible to publish the book in Russia, and so its first printing appeared in English translation in 1924.[14] (It likely influenced Aldous Huxley's *Brave New World* and certainly George Orwell's *1984*.) Thus, the novel followed in the hallowed Russian tradition of dissident literature banned by the tsarist (now Soviet) regime, only to circulate freely in the West and make its clandestine way back into the hands of Russian (now Soviet) readers. Its first publication in Russia was in 1988, during the period of glasnost.

Zamyatin's prophetic vision of Marxism-Leninism was so acute because he himself had been a true believer. Since university days he had been a member in good standing of the Bolshevik Party. His political activities in the 1905 Revolution landed him in jail, then exile in Siberia. Within a year of the Bolshevik seizure of power, he grew troubled by their ostensibly tactical pursuit of violence and terror. He realized that terror would be the watchword of the regime.

Zamyatin understood from the start that the new relationship between the individual and society promised by the Leninist regime would result in the opposite of what was imagined. Rather than the individual being fully and freely integrated into the collective, becoming a productive, unalienated member of society whose labor was not expropriated, and therein finding freedom, the collective would absorb and zero out the individual. The use of terror began in October 1917 and the threat of it never disappeared. The population was atomized by fear. In the end there was no community, no society as such. The effects of exposure to intense and repeated fear, the syndrome now known as post-traumatic stress, create distorted perceptions of reality. People are disposed to see mortal threats where there are none. They are unable to trust other people and, eventually, come to distrust themselves.

This is exactly how Zamyatin depicts the inhabitants of the One State. There are individuals who are confident in themselves and their ability to make choices, but they are the dangerous and endangered exception. Zamyatin's was an artist's vision of freedom, that is, the freedom of the imagination. The freedom to dream, to frame alternative realities, and pursue those to their logical end allows individuals to make informed choices about their actions. They can imagine the possible outcomes that might develop and choose to take the action that promises their desired result. This is not the freedom of speech, assembly, or religious affiliation that Americans see as their birthright. It is freedom of an entirely different kind, freedom from fear that is so deeply internalized that the most private of human experience—the free play of the mind—becomes a source of anxiety that people must actively repress simply to feel safe.

Zamyatin was hardly alone in his knowledge that the moral aims and political strategy of the revolution were at odds. Censorship was reimposed on all publications after the October Revolution, and this was an unmistakable omen of things to come. (The only time there was no government censorship was the brief period between the February and October revolutions.) A steady stream of artists, writers, philosophers, and painters started exiting for safer harbors abroad.[15] In 1935, the infamous directive that art must conform to the official artistic policy of Socialist Realism was decreed from on high. More than a decade before the policy was official, the government had controlled what was published and exhibited because it was the sole patron for all the arts. There were no private entities to commission art. What was forbidden at home could be published abroad, but that was a dangerous move. The appearance of *We* in translation led to Zamyatin's arrest. He was silenced and fellow members of the Writer's Union drowned his voice with choruses of condemnation—the equivalent of today's tweet storms that cancel dissenting voices.

Zamyatin tried more than once to emigrate without success. Finally, in 1931, he wrote to Stalin that "to me as a writer, being deprived of the opportunity to write is nothing less than a death sentence. Yet the situation that has come about is such that I cannot continue my work, because no creative activity is possible in an atmosphere of systemic persecution that increases in intensity from year to year."[16] As Zamyatin's alter ego, D-503, dutifully notes in his journal, the One State "tamed and saddled the once-wild natural force of poetry. Now poetry is no longer a brazen nightingale call. Poetry is a state service; poetry is purpose."[17] The writer's case was headed to a fatal outcome until Maxim Gorky intervened on his behalf with Stalin and he was finally allowed to emigrate.

Zamyatin and his wife moved to Paris. There he knew the full measure of freedom and ate the bitter bread of exile. He lived in poverty, isolated from other émigrés. (Zamyatin was ever loyal to the Revolution.) In 1937, his heart gave out and he died. He was fifty-three.

ART AS STATE SERVICE

It is in the nature of orthodoxy to generate heresies. The Soviet aesthetic orthodoxy was summed up by Maxim Gorky as art that has "the ability to see the present in terms of the future." The grave heresy of Zamyatin was that he had a different future in mind, one he thought more true to Marxism than what the Bolsheviks created. This was Kazimir Malevich's heresy as well. To an even greater degree than Zamyatin's vision, Malevich's view of the Suprematist future was more radical than the Bolsheviks could contemplate. Malevich proclaimed, loudly and often, that art-as-creation was an end in itself. This was anathema to Marxism. Culture has no intrinsic value; it is merely an instantiation of the ruling class's consciousness. Neither Malevich nor Zamyatin were dissidents who were against communism. On the contrary, they were both true believers. This only made matters worse for them.

The artistic and intellectual classes who refused obedience to the new order either found their way abroad or stayed and accepted silence. If not silent, they were exterminated. In the dark times of the 1920s, some died of disease or starvation. The futurist and transrational poet Khlebnikov died in 1922 at the age of thirty-six, suffering from gangrene and probably toxemia. Khlebnikov was laboring on his uniquely prescient vision of the future in which all human knowledge would be broadcast throughout the world—a Universal Library Radio Network that bore uncanny similarities to the internet. At the same time, the poet-philosopher was in the midst of parsing time into quasi-musical intervals according to Pythagorean theory. These he called *Tables of Destiny*.

Malevich worked in Leningrad as director of the State Institute of Artistic Culture (GINKhUK). There he labored sedulously to expand the reach of Suprematism across all arts and crafts media. He created a wealth of pedagogical materials that classified the entire history of European art, its forms and genres, into theoretical categories. He also created a prodigious number of *arkhitektons*, theoretical models of architectural space. In 1926, the institute mounted an exhibition of his work that drew condemnation from zealous critics acting as shills for the state. The institute was vilified as "a 'monastery' run by a couple of 'holy fools' engaged in counterrevolutionary sermonizing while the state footed the bill."[18] The institute was closed. In 1930, Malevich was jailed for several months, accused of "artistic formalism." He was released without being charged. The message was received.

Malevich had "destroyed the ring of the horizon and escaped from the circle of things" for only a decade before he fell back down to earth, where human affairs were ruled by the inexorable law of causality he so despised. He returned to his easel and circled back to the figurative paintings of peasant laborers that had preceded his Suprematist moment. He escaped the worst of consequences that killed thousands in the paroxysm of purges in the 1930s. He died in his bed in 1935—an enviable fate for a nonconforming artist in the USSR.

Malevich's late figurative paintings are too easily dismissed as retrograde after the maximalist nonobjective formalism of Suprematism. These late works are infused with Suprematist aesthetics but are now freighted with humanitarian significance that had never appeared in his art before. The canvases are still paeans to the supremacy of color and form. His peasants, invariably rendered as hieratic figures, are given all the dignity and pathos of the Suprematist colors and forms of his pre-revolutionary period. But they are haunted creatures, stripped of any individuality. Their featureless faces, torsos, and missing limbs are composed as ciphers, precise visual analogs to the characters from *We* (figure 6.1).

Aleksander Wat testified that avant-garde artists "learned that the road to the party absolutely did not lead through a revolution in art; on the contrary, only traditional art, the most retrograde art, not innovation, could be the instrument of the party."[19] The totalitarian regime that consolidated its grip on the USSR sanctioned the one kind of art that in the twentieth century was deemed to be wholly void of true content—Socialist Realism. In 1916, Malevich had, he thought, secured a completely different future for art: "Things have disappeared like smoke; to gain the new artistic culture, art approached creation as an end in itself and domination over the forms of Nature."[20] Unfortunately for Malevich, in the USSR creation could never be an end in itself.

By the mid-1920s, if not before, Malevich realized that his ends and those of the state were in conflict. He was invited to give an exhibition of his work in Berlin in 1927. When he accompanied the work abroad, he stopped in Warsaw, where he applied for residency (that is, asylum) on the basis that he was Polish by birth. His application was rejected, and that seemed to put an end to any plans he might have hatched to go into exile. (When he was diagnosed with cancer in 1933, he applied to go abroad for treatment, but his request was denied.) In 1930, he was arrested a second time, this time on suspicion of engaging in espionage while in Germany. The case never came to trial, but he was dismissed from his job.

Figure 6.1

His utopian dreams betrayed, Malevich produced a series of paintings during the brutal collectivization of the late 1920s that depict peasants as hieratic figures, adorned in Suprematist colors, but lacking identity. It's as if labor is glorified at the expense of the laborer. Kazimir Malevich, *Woman with a Rake*, 1928.

For a decade Malevich had wielded influence as a visionary. He was free to pursue the logic of his aesthetic creed to extremes. Until the first Five-Year Plan was promulgated in 1929 and the state began to exercise greater and greater control over all aspects of cultural life, utopian groups—some political, some religious, some artistic—flourished throughout the Soviet Union.[21] Many paths to a moral life were hacked out of the ruins left by the First World War, the two revolutions of 1917, the influenza pandemic of 1918–1920, the civil war of 1918–1922, and the great famine of 1920–1921. By 1929, those few that remained were finally repressed.

Malevich never abandoned his commitment to an art focused completely on remaking the future into the world of non-objectivity. He would not let death stop his efforts to change the world. When diagnosed with cancer, he created detailed instructions for his funeral. In accordance with his directives, a funeral procession took to the streets of Leningrad filled with Suprematist art and rites.

It is only because he left his paintings behind in Berlin when he returned to Moscow that knowledge of Malevich's work continued abroad. From time to time his paintings were on display in Russia as well, but after 1935, abstract art was deemed illegitimate bourgeois "art for art's sake." His paintings were consigned to the basement storerooms of Russian museums, only to be taken out of storage during glasnost, when they were recruited as an ambassador of Russia's unique contributions to worldwide culture. A flurry of Malevich exhibitions were co-curated by Western and Russian specialists. In 1990 his work was showcased during a disarmament summit between the US and the USSR. An exhibition opened at the National Gallery of Art in Washington, DC, traveled to the Armand Hammer Museum of Art and Cultural Center in Los Angeles, and thence to the Metropolitan Museum of Art in New York. The catalog opened with letters from President George H. W. Bush, President Mikhail Gorbachev, and Raisa Gorbachev. Bush wrote, "It is significant that this exhibition is the result of multinational cooperation, coming as it does during a time of renewed hope for world peace." Subtly conceding that "the creative forms of Kazimir Malevich may be complex," he adds: "It is my sincere hope that all those who view this exhibition will gain a deeper understanding of the dreams—and the timeless truths—that form a common bond among members of the human family." President Gorbachev in turn wrote, "Malevich's artistic quest was an attempt to comprehend the warning of approaching world tragedy. Today it is incumbent upon all of us, and especially our two great nations, to rid this world of its mortal dangers and together explore an avenue that will lead to a new era in the history of mankind. To this end, it would be indeed enlightening to penetrate the artist's conceptions and premonitions."[22]

The victory of the Bolsheviks over all rivals was a matter of historical contingency and therefore so was their imposition of one true vision of the moral relationship between individual and community. There could have been other outcomes. Analysis of how and why the Bolsheviks prevailed over their opponents continues as new information comes out from the archives; new explanations are proffered, critiqued, modified, and absorbed into the general narrative of the revolution happening from above and from below. The Bolsheviks' one undeniable advantage stands out: their conviction that the end justifies the means. They were unconstrained by what they contemptuously called bourgeois morality and instead embraced a revolutionary morality, one that was truly Jacobin. As Robespierre said, "Pity is treason." The deaths of millions in civil war, extrajudicial murders, and starvation were seen simply as necessary costs, a down payment for the future. They did not monopolize the tools of terror. The White Army and other combatants in the civil war were infamous for perpetrating pogroms and sadistic attacks on civilian populations. But the Red Army was steeled by fierce commitment to the future. The White Army sought to restore a world already gone forever.

Over a century after Malevich painted the *Black Square*, it's routine to condemn the politicians and their collaborators who conscientiously dismantled the pre-revolutionary Russian culture. They are roundly censured for snuffing out the talents of visionary artists such as Malevich, while the visionary artists are looked on with admiration and as inspiring contemporary artists. But not everyone agrees that Malevich was, in the end, on the right side of history. The contemporary Russian writer Tatyana Tolstaya doesn't see Malevich as an undisputed hero of the avant-garde artistic movements in Russia. On the contrary, she accuses him of participating fully in the nihilistic destruction of a humanistic culture. In 2015, to mark the one-hundredth anniversary of the *Black Square*'s creation, she wrote a commentary calling it a "sinister canvas" and an assault on the very premise of art. The painting was a negation as soul-destroying as communism. If anything, it was more pernicious because it was art, not politics, that was undermining culture itself. Art is the ultimate, the only bearer of truth. Malevich practiced and proselytized an aesthetic that fit wholly with the tenor of the times. It was maximalist, uncompromising, and pitiless: "Malevich became the author of the most famous, most enigmatic, and most frightening painting known to man: 'The Black Square.' With an easy flick of the wrist, he once and for all drew an uncrossable line that demarcated the chasm between old art and new art, between a man and a shadow, between the rose and a casket, between life and death, between God and the Devil. In his own words, he reduced everything to the 'zero of form.' Zero, for some reason, turned out to be a square, and this simple discovery is one of the most frightening events in art in all of its history of existence."[23]

WHAT REALLY HAPPENED

Zamyatin resigned from the All-Russian Writers Union in 1929. In his letter of resignation, he protested their resolution against him for publishing his novel in the original Russian in a Prague journal. He wrote: "But facts are stubborn, they are more stubborn than resolutions. Every fact can be confirmed by documents or people."[24] Civil society and civility itself begins and ends with the shared acknowledgement of the truth. What are the facts? This question is never easy to answer definitively. Facts are slippery. They are human things, representations of reality based on our observations, which in turn come to us filtered through the mind's perceptual frameworks. A scientific fact is one that holds true across cultures. A political fact is embedded in a culture that in theory may share ideals, laws, and principles, but in reality vigorously contest them. In polarized societies, this makes answering the question of what really happened a kind of Rorschach test. The same facts can be put into different frames of reference and come out with different meanings. For a long time in the United States, views on police brutality were one thing in the Black community, and another in white communities. When video evidence of George Floyd pleading for his life under the knee of a white police officer, surrounded by other police officers, went viral, the views of white and Black communities aligned quickly. But it didn't take long for some people to declare the video evidence doctored, faked, or simply not what it looked like. These accusations could gain traction because the environment was full of faked videos. It didn't take much computer power or software expertise to create authentic-looking but entirely fabricated videos. Everyone looking at the video saw the very same images. But if the audio was manipulated or if chyrons ran under the images declaring them faked, interpretations of Floyd's death inevitably varied greatly.

In closed narratives, as literary critic Frank Kermode points out, the way things end must have origins that harmonize with that end. As Soviets liked to joke, the future is certain; it is the past that keeps changing. The state controlled all information and the official documentary record was kept up-to-date with current orthodoxy. In this inversion of ordinary time, the past is always more dynamic, more *uncertain*, than the future. The past was shaped to serve neatly as prologue to the future, but it took some serious carpentry to fit the history of Muscovy and imperial Russia into the procrustean bed of the historical dialectic. All the actors were cast into a mere handful of available roles. There were feudal rulers (though Muscovy never experienced feudalism), who were superseded by the bourgeoisie (though industrialization was in early stages). The nation was populated chiefly by peasants. If they had any property—a barn, livestock, a house, a plow—they were cast in the role of the "petty bourgeoisie," despite the meagerness of their property holdings. Thus, the primary problem of inconvenient facts that didn't map to the Marxist theory of history was glossed over with the careful use of well-chosen words. The historical past was replaced with a false, highly schematized history. People were given new identities—the petty bourgeoisie, the agrarian proletariat (landless peasant), the kulak (rich peasant), and so forth. The Russian language itself gave way to a vocabulary and syntax imported from Europe. The alphabet was modernized. Time was reset from the Julian calendar to the Gregorian of the modern world. The day after January 31, 1918, the Russians awoke to February 14. Thirteen days disappeared as the nation lurched into the modern era.

Authentic history endures, unacknowledged yet carefully preserved in archives, the equivalent of the Ancient House. This scrupulous record-keeping by twentieth-century totalitarian regimes, even of criminal behavior, is a well-known if seemingly counterintuitive feature of both the Soviet and Nazi bureaucracies. When Soviet-era archives were opened briefly after 1991, records of the Red Terror of 1918, the Gulag's beginnings in 1921, the forced grain requisitions that caused famines, and reprisals against so-called counterrevolutionaries were all there, intact and carefully filed. (The letter Lenin sent to comrades in Penza ordering the hanging of a hundred kulaks was among the records made available at that time.) These were not, in Communist Party terms, crimes; they were necessary means. The logic of the ends justifying the means was ready to hand when Putin started his invasion of Ukraine in 2022. All he had to do was declare the people under assault to be enemies—Nazis, fascists, puppets of the West—and the brutality of the assault was justified by the urgency of the task to annihilate them. The goal of the 2022 invasion is the recovery of territory wrested away from the bosom of Mother Russia. Many Westerners were shocked by the brazen violation of Geneva Convention rules of war. Many were baffled by the illogic of seizing territory by razing it to the ground and rendering it useless upon possession. But they overlook the power of shock and awe in war time. Ironically, Putin, on the other hand, overlooked the fact that the Ukrainians are well acquainted with what would happen if they fell to the Russians. They had been in that position several times in the last century alone. Russian commanders did not anticipate Ukrainian ferocity in self-defense and their determination to hold the ground unto death.

In contrast to authentic facts kept in the deep freeze of the Soviet archives, authentic identities—authentic selves, as it were—were destroyed. How do people recover from learning that millions of people perished because of false promises? Some may cling to their belief that their expectations have not failed, believing they had merely misunderstood how and when the final outcome would unfold. This was the case of the first Christians who expected the return of Christ within their lifetime. In such circumstances, many of the disillusioned—possibly the majority—give up their willing suspension of disbelief, accept the evidence, and struggle to understand what happened. They look back anxiously to trace the steps they took to arrive at a place they had not planned for. Had they wandered from the path they were certain fate was taking them? Or were they sleepwalking the whole time? Did they mistake the symbolic for the literal? Whatever the answer, they experience a kind of whiplash that induces pain and disorientation that may last the rest of their lives.

In *We*, the twist of the knife comes from the reader's understanding that the world Zamyatin depicts is a precise fulfillment of the Bolshevik promise, but turned upside down. There is equality, but it is achieved by eliminating individuality and identity. There is no conflict, but that is because there is no freedom. There is unanimity of purpose, but that is because there is an enforced ignorance about the world beyond the Green Wall. The cruelest reversal of expectation in *We* is that there is no withering away of the state, despite the fact that there are no classes and thus no class warfare, and all the "units" in the One State are of one mind. It has even achieved a victory over the sun, though not by locking it up, as the futurists imagined. It is the human-built world that is immured under the Glass Dome, locked up, walled off from nature.

We've noted that a hazard that arises when looking retrospectively for the causes of a phenomenon is to believe the mirage that things have turned out the way they have because it is the only way they could have happened. Individuals, groups, and nations committed to goal-directed beliefs find it unimaginable that anything of significance happens purely by chance. They think humanity, in distinction from all other creatures, moves through time in fulfillment of a specific end, some kind of spiritual transfiguration such as salvation or a world of permanent peace and freedom from want. In the case of Russia, the goal could be the creation of a morally just society based on true equality among all the peoples of the world. This goal affirms the belief that Russia is to play a special salvific role in world history. In the case of the United States, the goal could be exporting democracy to the peoples of the earth, which in turn affirms the special salvific role America is to play in world history.

The expectation of imminent change lends an intensity of meaning to the everyday lives of American evangelicals, as it did to the ardent supporters of the Bolshevik regime. A goal-directed orientation that lends a sense of purpose is also a component of technocratic societies that believe they are pursuing progress on behalf of the whole human race. This claim is easily challenged—who gives them the right to decide what is good for the whole human race?—but nonetheless pervasive. Without that psychologically reassuring sense of an ending, people can perceive themselves as "prey to chance," their individual existence always subject to the whims of an indifferent and ultimately cruel universe, "these bloody insults, these jeers coming from nowhere." As Kołakowski pointed out, in communism, history's logic culminates in the fulfillment of human destiny. People are no longer prey to chance, but captains of their fate, conscious molders of their own destiny. If we substitute the word "democracy" for "communism," he could be describing the political philosophy held by many in the United States. Clarity of purpose and a welcome release from self-doubt are the magnetic forces that pull so many people into the orbits of political ideologies. Deliverance from doubt is the lodestone of all ideologies.

There are powerful reasons why, time and again, individuals and nations avoid accounting for the consequences of acting in ways incompatible with the ultimate goals of equality or freedom. Without grappling with the truth and consequences of beliefs and the actions they prompt, people are likely to repeat the cycle of belief, action, reversal of expectation, only to begin again. Given the need for accountability to avoid further bad consequences, why do we fail to deal with the truth, as citizens and as a nation? One answer is that we don't like what we find when we start digging, so we stop. But there is more than that. Both the Russians and the Americans have been weaned on stories of their nation being destined to play world-historical roles as bearers of the highest values. Yet, past action does not match present aspirations. If there is not enough confidence in their ability to change things in the present, for whatever reason—economic depression or political stalemate, for instance—people find it nearly impossible to sit for long with feelings of powerlessness. That is when revisiting the past can serve as a springboard to the future.

HISTORY AS A RESCUE MISSION

The belief that Russia has a special destiny was carried in the bloodstream of the body politic for centuries before Chaadaev articulated it. During the Middle Ages, it was an explicitly religious idea: that Moscow, the seat of Russian Orthodoxy, was the Third Rome. First, there was the founding of the church in Rome. Then in 1054, Western and Eastern Christendom split over theological controversy, and the true center of Christianity moved to Constantinople, the Second Rome. Finally, in the century after the fall of Constantinople to the Ottomans in 1453, Moscow declared itself the Third Rome, the true successor to the Roman Empire. Somewhat ironically, what was first a theological justification of Russia's messianic role was carried forward most ardently and successfully by the Communist leaders. The Bolsheviks had passionate faith that their seizure of control in Russia would be the spark for a global revolution. Faced with the failure of revolution abroad, they dedicated themselves to "socialism in one country." Average Soviets, who suffered through famines, wars, measureless deprivations, and back-breaking work as they built a modern industrial economy, came to feel pride in their endurance, fortitude, and dedication to the work of communism. Russia would offer a lesson for the rest of the world, Chaadaev had predicted. What was that lesson?

In 1991, an American scholar in Moscow talked with an old man of peasant background whose family members were murdered during the first decade of Bolshevik rule. They were accused of being rich peasants. Only one or two generations before he was born, the man's family had been serfs, just as Chekhov's family had been. Perhaps they had been accused of being *kulaks* by covetous villagers. Perhaps they resisted expropriation of their land, buildings, grain, and livestock during collectivization. Perhaps they were simply disliked. Whatever it was, they were cursed and so was all their seed. This old man helped defend Moscow against the invading Nazi army as a soldier in the Great Patriotic War (World War II). Yet the man was unable to find work later. "After a long recount of his incredibly painful and rich life experiences," the scholar wrote, "he looked at me and said: the worst thing is that we have nothing to give to the young, and to future generations. What is the benefit from all this? We worked all our lives, and we can give nothing. Perhaps what we can give is a lesson: that this was all senseless, and that these socialist ideas go nowhere. Otherwise unable to see how this worthless past could provide a bridge to the future, he looked upon the country's prospects with trepidation."[1] His past was robbed of value and, as an old man, he had no future to look forward to. Worse, he could no longer look back at his life as a tale of worthy sacrifice—unjust, perhaps, but necessary to benefit future generations. The younger generation of his family were sick and tired of hearing about the sacrifices made by his generation for the socialist future. It had all turned to dust and death. How could an entire nation be duped? What had millions died for? Nothing. The chain Chekhov conjures up in "The Student" connecting generations across time was broken beyond repair.

Chekhov's advice to writers works well for anyone facing such disillusionment: "It's about time that everyone who writes—especially genuine literary artists—admitted that in this world you can't figure anything out ... If a writer declare[s] that he understands nothing of what he sees—that alone will constitute a major gain in the realm of thought and a major step forward."[2] It's important to know the truth but just as important to know what to do with the truth, so that those who are wronged can act to set things right. But truth has more than instrumental value. A truthful historical narrative has the power to recover meaning from the past, no matter how blighted. If nothing else, it carries in it the significance of experience. Sometimes that is all that can be recovered. It's especially powerful when confronting a loss or failure for which people paid dearly. If we lose hold of the truth, the narrative can be twisted to any purpose at all. It can constitute the narrative arc that Wolf-gang Schivelbusch describes as the culture of defeat, a way of writing history that embeds defeat and humiliation into an exculpatory narrative.[3] This is the power of the American South's narrative of the Lost Cause. Why else would the vanquished cling so tenaciously to the history of their defeat? It's so powerful a legend that it is now the byword adopted by some Americans who have no connection with the South, let alone the Confederacy. It stands in for the loss of a way of life that the nation has rejected and cast scorn upon. Perhaps it's especially in the case of ignominious defeat that a person feels the deepest need for community. If a community shares recognition of and honors what once existed—or might have existed—and now is gone, there is the consolation of fellow feeling. The shared memory of loss can motivate deeply antisocial behavior, as it has with alt-right groups in America, ethnic groups in the Balkans and the Caucasus, and Sunnis and Shias in Iraq. That hardly lessens its power to create solidarity. It is precisely this kind of narrative that we must be wary of in times of uncertainty, when the world order as we understand it isn't turning out well for us, doesn't make sense to us, or bodes ill for the future. It takes a master storyteller to draw our attention to this narrative and to convince us that if only we believe it, things will be better. The storyteller may be a popular media figure, like Tucker Carlson. It could be head of state like Viktor Orbán or Vladimir Putin. It could be a popular media figure who becomes head of state, as Donald Trump did.

This desire for a shared understanding of the past is a psychological need, but it is more than that: it's a necessary grounding in the present and a critical component of personal and collective identity. What the Red Army veteran faced in 1991 was the prospect that all he could give to the next generation is the lesson that there is no meaning to the sacrifices made by three generations of Russians. He knows this meager lesson is of no value to the next generation. They're already deeply cynical about the government as an instrument of social amelioration. They're tired of hearing about the past, as it appears to have no relevance to their future. At most they're interested to learn more about the pre-Revolutionary culture that was destroyed, silenced, or exiled. This is now the past that needs to be rescued. This is past that, in the minds of the young, this old man helped to destroy.

A truthful accounting that follows failed expectations begins by establishing the facts of the case. Like the demands made by the ethnic studies students at Harvard, this work rests on the claim that people are entitled to an authentic history. This is a political claim, for it is about power. (Knowledge is power.) It's an existential claim, for it's about grounding identity in an identifiable beginning. It's a moral claim, because an authentic history is a precondition for people to flourish as individuals and as members of society. It does not require a narrative with beginning, middle, and end. In her memoirs, Nadezhda Mandelstam argues that, in fact, trying to create a logical narrative from a blighted past creates a moral trap.

Nadezhda Mandelstam (1899–1980) wrote two volumes of memoirs after the death of her husband, the poet Osip Mandelstam (1891–1938). He's judged today as one of the great poets of the twentieth century. The fact that we have his poetry to judge at all is because Nadezhda committed his poetry to memory and survived long enough to see it published. Memory saved his poems, but memory also saved her: "If the verse I have preserved is of some use to people, then my life has not been wasted and I have done what I had to do both for the man who was my other self and for all those people whose humane, that is, human instincts are roused by poetry. If this is so, it means that I probably had a preordained task to fulfill and that I have correctly understood it."[4]

Osip Mandelstam was deeply knowledgeable about European and Russian literature. He felt himself a direct heir of the long line of poets from the Greeks and Romans, through Dante and Goethe, to Pushkin. He welcomed the end of the old regime but was far from a supporter of the Bolsheviks. Their view that art was merely instrumental to politics as superstructure was anathema to him. In 1934, he was arrested and exiled for having written a bitingly satirical poem about Stalin. The poem, "We Live," is more often called the "Stalin Epigram." It refers to the Soviet leader as "the Kremlin gremlin," describing his mustache as "a hairy cockroach" and his hands as "a grubworm clutch, all oil and vile," and likens him to "a pig farmer who's plucked a blackberry from the vine, / Savors the sweet spurt, before he turns back to his swine."[5] The poem was never published, but Osip Mandelstam read it aloud to a group of like-minded friends, one of whom informed

PLATES

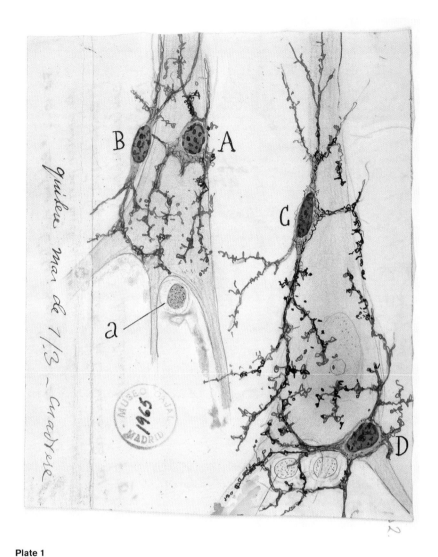

Plate 1

Santiago Ramón y Cajal drew neurons from the hippocampus, the seat of memory and "the oldest center of association in the brain" (quoted in *Beautiful Brain*, ed. Newman, Araque, and Dubinsky, 140). They receive signals at one end and transmit them at the other, thus creating and changing associations and memories. Ramón y Cajal, *Glial Cells Surrounding Pyramidal Neurons in the Human Hippocampus*.

Plate 2

Photographs both create and edit collective memory. At the height of the purges (*top*), the head of the NKVD Yezhov (right) strolls with Stalin. After Yezhov was purged, he became a nonperson, so evidence of their relationship was erased (*bottom*). Anonymous artist, *Stalin, Ezhov, Molotov, and Voroshilov at the Moscow–Volga Canal Embankment, 1937.*

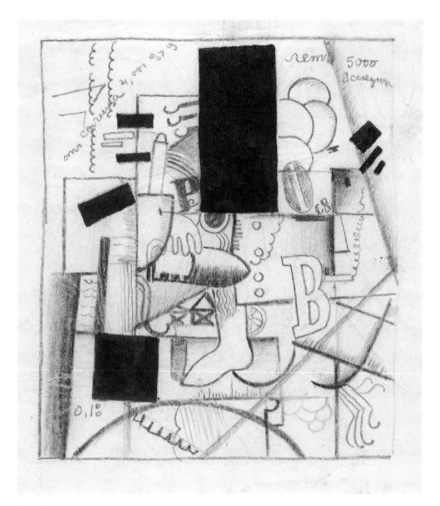

Plate 3

In the opera *Victory over the Sun*, Futurist Strongmen overpower the "antiquated movement of thought based on laws of causality." Malevich's backdrop design has objects of war painted over with black quadrilaterals, precursors to his *Black Square*. Kazimir Malevich, Stage design for *Victory over the Sun*, 1913.

Plate 4

The *Black Square* was intended to eclipse all past art, like the earth eclipsing the sun. By uniting the zero of color (black) with the zero of form (the square), Malevich escaped "the circle of things" and created a painting that "does not belong solely to the earth." Kazimir Malevich, *Black Square*, 1915.

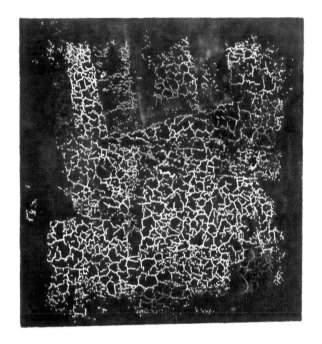

Plate 5

Malevich claimed he discovered the Black Square in 1913 (see plate 4), but only grasped its significance in 1915, when he painted over a canvas about war, seen here in x-ray. How often does war prompt people to blot out all memories of it? Kazimir Malevich, *Black Square*, 1915, x-ray.

Plate 6

His utopian dreams betrayed, Malevich produced a series of paintings during the brutal collectivization of the late 1920s that depict peasants as hieratic figures, adorned in Suprematist colors, but lacking identity. It's as if labor is glorified at the expense of the laborer. Kazimir Malevich, *Woman with a Rake*, 1928.

Plate 7

Duchamp's notorious cubofuturist nude, mocked as an explosion in a shingles factory, protests retinal art that appeals only to the eye. Instead, Duchamp aims for "visual indifference." Marcel Duchamp, *Nude Descending a Staircase, No. 2*, 1912.

Plate 8

"What can art do?" Gerhard Richter asked. His encounter with contemporary Western art after he left East Germany led him to study Duchamp's work. Here he thinks through Duchamp's *Nude* by painting a nude that is not "visually indifferent" yet also engages the mind. Gerhard Richter, *Ema (Nude on a Staircase)*, 1966.

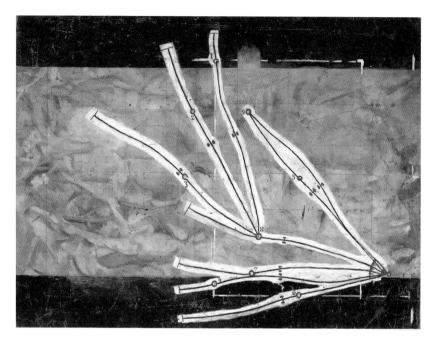

Plate 9

"Can one make works that are not works of 'art'?" Duchamp wondered. Following the creation of nonretinal art in the *Nude*, Duchamp experimented with chance. This became "the first gesture liberating me from the past" because it bore no reference to any previous work of art and demoted the role of artistic subjectivity. Marcel Duchamp, *Network of Stoppages*, 1914.

Plate 10

Duchamp then went on to invent the readymade, inspired by a bicycle wheel he set up in his studio. He'd give it a spin from time to time to amuse himself. By declaring this to be art, he reiterated his conviction that art is an act of perception, not craft, happening in the mind, not the eye. Marcel Duchamp, *Bicycle Wheel*, 1951 (after lost original of 1913).

Plate 11

Richter explores whether art is a depiction of the world or a mirror. Obliquely referring to the solipsistic mystifications of Duchamp's *Large Glass*, Richter answers this question by installing clear glass panes that both reveal reality (viewers see the world) and serve as a mirror (viewers see reflections of themselves in the world). Gerhard Richter, *4 Panes of Glass*, 1967.

Plate 12

Over his lifetime, Richter has amassed a large archive of images and photos from which he draws inspiration. Here he is in his studio working on the *October 18, 1977* series. The fifteen paintings were based on newspaper and police photographs. Behind him are two paintings of Red Army Faction leader Gudrun Ensslin, who hanged herself in her cell. Timm Rautert, *Gerhard Richter*, Köln, 1988.

Plate 13

The *October* series depicts idealism and utopianism gone to murderous extremes. Richter said the paintings "provoke contradictions through their hopelessness and desolation; their lack of partisanship" (*Writings*, 204). Ulrike Meinhof was a pacifist when young, a journalist and mother of two, before starting the RAF. Richter takes pains to show her humanity, which caused considerable controversy. Gerhard Richter, *Youth Portrait*, 1988.

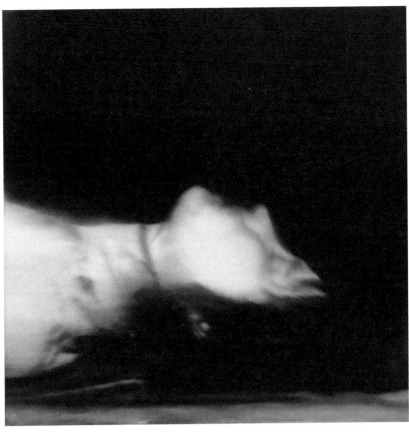

Plate 14

Growing disillusioned and impatient, Meinhof turned to terrorism to accelerate the destruction of corrupt capitalism. She was arrested in 1973 and hanged herself in prison three years later. This death portrait memorializes her transformation from idealist to terrorist. Richter's image engages the viewer in seeing what they are not prepared to see. Its objectivity makes her neither martyr nor devil. Gerhard Richter, *Dead*, 1988.

on him. (Who did so and under what circumstances is not known, and Nadezhda does not share her speculation about who it was.) From that time until his second arrest and eventual death in the Gulag, Osip and Nadezhda Mandelstam lived as nomads, eking out a living translating and teaching.[6] The poet took sly pride in the regime's "boundless, almost superstitious respect for poetry." He told Nadezhda that one shouldn't complain, because "Poetry is respected only in this country—people are killed for it. There's no place where more people are killed for it."[7]

Nadezhda Mandelstam's first volume, translated as *Hope against Hope*— *nadezhda* is Russian for "hope"—is about her life with the poet, beginning in 1919. The second volume, *Hope Abandoned*, is a longer and more trenchant account of her life and times as the poet's wife and widow. In the first volume, it is clear that she is making the case for her husband's legacy as a willing martyr for poetry. Memorizing his poetry and writing this book was a moral commitment that anchored her to something sane in a world gone mad. Year after year she silently recited the poems, fixing the words firmly in her memory, hearing her dead husband's voice in her head, and giving her a reason to endure what would otherwise be unendurable. Hers was a heroic vision of art as the incorruptible repository of human dignity. Perhaps such a vision of verse is also possible in an open and free society, yet it seems strange, even alien, to the practical Yankee mind of Americans, for whom poetry hardly registers in their education and everyday life. What *is* comparable to the power of poetry as both witness and salvation is the music of African-Americans that carried them from slavery and Jim Crow to Black Lives Matter, while producing the blues, jazz, and hip-hop, the most original and recognizably American art forms.

Nadezhda Mandelstam makes no claims to have perfect recall. Nor does she claim that what she does remember is reliable. She knows she will be met with disbelief in the West, and denial in the Soviet Union. She suffered like everyone from the distortions that trauma forces on perceptions and the ability to remember. Nonetheless, she had several advantages as a witness. First, she was a woman. Women were not taken seriously as political actors in the USSR.[8] The men in their lives were taken as serious political threats, and the women were punished for the men's supposed crimes through exile, deprivation of work, and so forth. But their punishment was usually little more than leverage over the men themselves. The second advantage was simply that she survived: "I was saved by chance. Our lives were ruled by chance, but it more commonly led to death than to survival."[9] The third was that the regime's bureaucrats, secret police, and collaborators among the general population did not bother to hide their crimes. They did not believe that their victims would ever survive to testify against them:

> All the murderers, provocateurs and informers had one feature in common: it never occurred to them that their victims might one day rise up again and speak. They also imagined that time had stopped—this, indeed, was the chief symptom of the sickness. We had, you see, been led to believe that in our country nothing whatever will change again, and that it was now up to the rest of the world to follow our example and enter the "New Era," after which all change would cease everywhere. And the people who accepted this doctrine worked sincerely for the greater glory of the new morality which followed from historical determinism taken to its extreme conclusion. . . . It never entered their heads that these ghosts [of those sent to camps] might rise up and call the grave-diggers to account.[10]

People were hypnotized into thinking that they had entered a new era. What they were experiencing was historically determined. All that was required of them was to submit to historical necessity. There was simply no reason to resist or fight back, because nothing would change. Even after Stalin's death, the sense of this new reality persisted like an after-image burned onto the retina.

Khrushchev's campaign to change course and bring the Soviet Union back down to earthly time began with selective revelations of Stalin's most egregious crimes. Many prisoners of the Gulag were released and allowed to settle elsewhere. Mandelstam began to breathe more easily. Her task of committing to paper the poems held in memory was possible now. It was safe to begin writing about all she had seen and heard. She was able to remember what life was like in the Before Times, before the world went mad. Her narrative toggles back and forth in time just as memories do, working not chronologically but through associations of sense perception and emotional valence. She knows how valuable each detail is, and makes little effort at concision. The reader can feel her moments of exhaustion and elation in the rhythm of her prose. She autopsies the process of memory itself, writing:

> The capacity of memory, both collective and individual, to gloss over, improve on, or distort the facts is particularly evident at periods when the foundations of a society are collapsing. Those disorders to which memory is prey—the tendency to embellish or suppress "awkward" detail, the need to vindicate oneself—show how dangerous it is to rely on one's own conviction of being right; since this is all too often based on a false criterion, our main task is to find a true one. There is also the problem that, while distorting our recollections and thus hindering a proper appreciation of individual or historical experience, memory is yet the one feature that distinguishes us as human beings.[11]

She spares the readers little, and spares herself absolutely nothing: "Small as my part has been, I must nevertheless bear full responsibility for it—to a larger extent, perhaps, than those who aided the work of destruction unconsciously and therefore at least never tried to find ways of justifying themselves."[12] To know is to accept responsibility.

Among the general population, memory of life before the Revolution was gone, replaced entirely by their experience of the new Soviet reality, the one that comes with its own bespoke history textbook. Being all that people knew, this was for them as real as reality gets. It was a reality greater than common sense, greater than logic, greater than all evidence to the contrary. Once, when Mandelstam was traveling by train to Moscow, she fell into conversation with a stranger about Solzhenitsyn. This was in the 1960s, after Solzhenitsyn's novella *One Day in the Life of Ivan Denisovich*, a lightly veiled description of the author's life in the Gulag, had been published. The fellow passenger had not read the novella but felt free to protest its publication. Why tell stories about the Gulag, he griped, when it was a historical necessity?

> "Why necessity?" I objected, "We're now being told it was all a historical accident due to Stalin's bad character."
> . . . "You must've forgotten what [Marx] says about accidents—they also happen by necessity, but people aren't aware of it."[13]

That's how it is: If it hadn't been Stalin, it would have been somebody else. It had all been necessary.

The sole instrument of power truly critical for the success of a totalitarian regime is control of people's sense of reality, of what is possible and what is not. That is the coin of the realm, and on the obverse side of the coin is the injunction to be arbitrary in implementing its own rules. The regime must periodically violate its own rules of conduct, or suddenly reverse them; that way no one can ever predict what is going to happen. Surprise is the key. (Think of how Trump created a state of distraction as people waited for his next tweet storm.) People are kept on tenterhooks day in, day out. Soviet citizens lived in a world turned upside down. Nights terrors are good, too, to keep people off balance. Everybody knew that when the secret police came, they came at night. People went to bed, a just-in-case bag packed, not knowing what the night could bring. Even if their conscience was clear—especially if their conscience was clear—they knew they could still be arrested because they knew people who were surely innocent, but still had been arrested and never heard from again. They disappeared into the night and no one ever spoke of them again. If there was no knock in the night, you could live another day. But it was another day without a decent night's sleep. (Sleep deprivation was an easy, cheap torture technique for people in prison.) This torture was inflicted on the innocent as well as the guilty, and even if you were never arrested, all the nights a person kept an ear out for the knock on the door added up to a population suffering from sleep deprivation. Emotions were hard to regulate. Memory and cognition were impaired. People internalized a dread that weakened their will and made a mockery of their powers of reason.

People were fed lies about their collective past and future, and *their memories codified the lies as reality*. There were some—it is hard to know how many—who could see exactly when and how the Big Lie machine was in operation. Varia Shklovsky, Nadezhda Mandelstam's friend, could make sly jokes about the need to edit pages of her textbooks whenever Party members were cast into the darkness of oblivion, but joking hardly helped. These edits, too, were "necessary." The sole act of volition available to her was to be aware she was lied to. But she was required to collude in the lie simply to be safe from harm to herself or her family. Where was the joy in laughter?

Throughout the two volumes of her memoirs, Mandelstam says over and over that people gave up their will because it was a danger to them. They all believed things could end only one way. There would be an end to it all eventually. All evil things exhaust themselves, she came to believe, but "in destroying itself, evil may destroy all life on earth as well."[14] According to Frank Kermode, when people are in the thrall of apocalyptic thinking, they "make considerable imaginative investments in coherent patterns which, by the provision of an end, make possible a satisfying consonance with the origins and with the middle. That is why the image of the end can never be *permanently* falsified. But they also, when awake and sane, feel the need to show a marked respect for things as they are; so that there is a recurring need for adjustments in the interests of reality as well as of control."[15]

Kermode was talking about literary forms, not the Stalinist regime. That said, historical narratives are a literary form—fact-based, but a genre none-theless. When historical accounts of the past are composed with beginnings, middles, and ends, they convey a sense of completeness and purpose. Mandelstam's mode of narration matches precisely the experience of having lived in and survived a collective madness, moving in and out of this apocalyptic frame of mind. What makes her memoirs so striking and self-evidently reliable is that she does not tell the story chronologically, nor in any particular thematic order. There is a jumping back and forth not only of time, but of moods and states of mind. At times she is grimly pessimistic and at times wildly optimistic. She was damaged by her experience, like everybody else. She makes no effort to hide it. On the contrary, it is the ultimate truth of her testimony.

The critique that Zamyatin made of the One State was personified in an individual—the unit I-330—who refused to be absorbed totally into the sum of the One. True, she had to forgo happiness in this world, but she was free. Mandelstam's memoirs show us the real-world result of making the choice for freedom and living with the consequences. She carefully depicts individuals whom she knew and the actions they took and did not take. She remembers who said what to whom, who sat with them in times of trouble, and who stayed away. To survive and remember was sometimes all it took to be moral in the world. It sustained the continuity and dignity of human experience. Mandelstam stands in contrast to the veteran who was unable to see his own life justified in the continuity of humanity because he felt he had nothing to pass forward. He had a truth to tell, but he knew it fell on deaf ears.

Memory works by association, categorization, and patternmaking, which make things that by themselves seem random easy to remember. Chance cannot sort for value. But while aleatory art may better reflect the reality of modernity as we experience it, it defeats memory. Memorizing aleatory music and text is far harder than remembering patterned things. Osip Mandelstam's poetry was classical, tightly structured, and thus easier to remember than, say, the aleatory poetry of Khlebnikov, which was full of neologisms and nonsense patter. Nadezhda Mandelstam's memoir follows the inspiration of her husband's poetry, but in prose. It is long, episodic, and spares no details. For Chekhov, memory is a filter that leaves only the most significant memories. Mandelstam's memory has a different function, which is not to distill but to bear witness. She confesses she can hardly distinguish what is important from what is not, and errs on the side of including everything. She battles with amnesia to prove to herself that she is an optimist, despite all. She believes that "all we have been through will have served to turn people against the idea, so tempting at first sight, that the end justifies the means and 'everything is permitted.'" She tells herself that in the end, suffering will always be redeemed:

> Alas, my faith and optimism are shared by almost nobody: people who know the difference between good and evil are more inclined to expect new misfortunes and new crimes. I realize the possibility of a return to the past, but I still think the general outlook is bright. We have seen the triumph of evil after the values of humanism have been vilified and trampled on. The reason these values succumbed was probably that they were based on nothing except boundless confidence in the human intellect. I think we may now find a better foundation for them, if only because of the lessons we have drawn from our experience. We can see the mistakes and crimes of the past, and the seductive delusions of former times have lost their glamour. Russia once saved the Christian culture of Europe from the Tatars, and in the past fifty years, by taking the brunt on herself, she has saved Europe again—this time from

rationalism and all the will to evil that goes with it. The sacrifice of human life was enormous. How can I believe it was all in vain?[16]

After all her suffering, she defaults to the messianism of Chaadaev, of the Slavophiles, and of the Russian revolutionary movement. This Russia saved the world from Marxism, just as it saved Europe from the Nazis. This Russia took upon itself the pain and suffering of the world in order to extinguish evil. But in the end, the question remains—was all this death necessary for progress, which is the secular word for salvation? Only if Chaadaev was right and Russia was "called upon to resolve most of the problems in the social order [and] to accomplish most of the ideas which arose in the old societies [i.e., Europe], to make a pronouncement about those very grave questions which preoccupy humanity," then the enormous sacrifice of human life was not in vain.[17] This was the final judgment.

FACTS ARE STUBBORN

The curious thing about historical evidence is that it endures even when buried alive. It will resurface to trip you up when you least expect it, like the roots of old trees breaching the ground of a newly dug-in trail. The bones of the many thousands who were victims of summary executions in the forests of the borderlands of Eastern Europe, or the rude graves of those who died on their way to the camps, are exposed more and more often to the light of day. The warming planet is uncovering physical evidence of the unacknowledged murders of the twentieth century. As permafrost thaws in Siberia, human remains are lifted to the surface. Lidar is now used to pinpoint evidence about the scale of murders committed in Poland by retreating Nazi troops. In one case among many, lidar detected the location of burial pits covered over by grass and trees. DNA analysis of the four hundred or so victims is being matched by archival and family records. Proper names are being restored to the relics. Advanced technologies provide ways to decipher material evidence, but it still takes words to do justice to what was lost here.[18]

The climate of public opinion is changing, as well. In parallel to this interest in recovering the past is the careful and reverent excavation of Southern plantations and Northern construction sites whose foundations reveal the graves of the enslaved. There is an abundance of written documentation that complements the material evidence. Whether it is the bureaucratic records of those arrested and sent to labor camps in the Gulag, or the business records of the auctioneers who bought and sold human beings treated as property, there is a body of evidence which is far from complete but nonetheless richly informative. The most immediately affecting of these records include individual remembrances of those who suffered and bear witness, such as Nadezhda Mandelstam and Frederick Douglass. Equally rich are the stories passed from one generation to another through the cultural artifacts, cuisines, religious practices, and songs that encode shared experiences. Increasingly, historians are turning to non-textual sources to broaden the scope of people who are now recognized as historical actors. The historian Tiya Miles reconstructed the life of an illiterate enslaved girl, sold away from her mother, through the scant but deeply meaningful material evidence she possessed and her heirs preserved—a sack.[19] Working with such materials requires a new set of disciplinary skills in a profession that's long relied on textual sources. To use an artifact such as a sack as primary evidence is novel at the moment. But with time, it will be understood to be as rich a source of information about the past as a photograph, a sound recording, or a book.

With increased access to trustworthy evidence comes the opportunity to see how facts were understood and framed at the time. Separating fact from fiction is a tricky business, especially when looking through the rearview mirror of historical retrospection. The most convincing fictions always build on facts. Cherry-picking evidence can legitimate narratives that ignore the facts' logical inferences. Instead, facts are sprinkled like fairy dust over a fanciful tale to give it a patina of legitimacy. A few well-chosen facts placed into a narrative will fundamentally change the context and the meaning of the facts. This is the pattern we see routinely in conspiracy theories. Such narratives always suggest a deeper significance than the insignificant facts warrant because they draw connections between otherwise random events. The everyday world becomes pregnant with meaning. Every believer experiences the thrill of detection, like Sherlock Holmes, able to find clues to crimes in the seemingly insignificant.

Looking at the use of such facts (or pseudo-facts) reveals distinct patterns of deception, and the patterns of deception are the same as the patterns of self-deception. There are people who weave selected facts into a narrative, and there are people eager to hear them and believe them. The symbiosis between narrator and audience is the nexus of narrative power. It creates the strong magnetic field that from time to time seems to defy gravity and allow people "to rise into the air." It takes a community that colludes in the deception to bring others along, for fear of missing out. A changed perception of reality then changes the reality itself. Mandelstam put it this way: "The fundamental rule of the times was to ignore the facts of life. Holders of high office were supposed to see only the positive side of things and, once ensconced in their ivory towers . . . , to look down indulgently at the writhing human masses below. A man who knew that you cannot build the present out of the bricks of the future was bound to resign himself beforehand to his inevitable doom and the prospect of the firing squad. What else could he do? We were all prepared for the same end."[20]

She was most acutely distressed by the indifference of those around her who witnessed the humiliations inflicted on them as exiles. They were almost ostentatiously indifferent. For whom were they performing their callousness? At the same time, she knew that everyone, everywhere, felt they were being watched: "They could do anything to a prisoner—shoot him down, kill him, torture him—and nobody would interfere. Bystanders would just turn their heads, not to be upset by the sight."[21] The Mandelstams were helpless, but still, she concludes, "if nothing else is left, one must scream. Silence is the real crime against humanity."[22] Perhaps this is the only way to understand why Osip incautiously wrote a satirical poem about Stalin and even more incautiously read it to friends. Poetry was his scream. Once he screamed, it was only a matter of time before he was cancelled and the state "stepped on the throat of poetry."[23]

Identifying the source of attraction between narrator and audience is the crucial task for a society to reckon with the truth. It is not enough to identify the people who have created the big lies to understand their power to seduce, to comfort, and to persuade. They have no power without members of society being eager to hear and willing to believe them, even when they suspect they are being lied to. The source of deception's power is usually simple—it focuses the gaze outward. No introspection is necessary. How pleasant it is to imagine that all the ills you suffer are perpetrated by an identifiable enemy. And who is the enemy? Whoever they name.

Ultimately, the only way to disenthrall ourselves from these magic narratives is for people to acknowledge they were deceived and refuse to be deceived further. This is the last and most daunting step in reckoning, because it requires looking inward. People must accept responsibility for what they have done and failed to do, and all the consequences that flow from this. They can point to others who behaved the same way, trusting this will provide them some cover. But this is self-defeating. They must put themselves firmly in the role of free historical agents, ultimately accountable for individual actions and those taken as part of a community. That is why the movement toward reckoning needs a community and leadership; it cannot be done alone. Terror is very good at atomizing society, creating a sense of distrust and alienation from others, a desire to be delivered of doubt by a strong leader who can create a sense of community. Authoritarian leaders excel at uniting a community. They do so not by building a model of the good society from within, but by identifying enemies and allowing scapegoating and punishment of the enemy to be thought of as a moral act in itself. Building up a sense of community among those who feel alienated happens not by connecting people with one another, but by connecting them with a single leader or party.

Dismantling the façade of Soviet legitimacy was the work of generations of dissenters. In the post-Stalin era, there were many of them—Elena Bonner, Andrei Sakharov, Larissa Bogoraz, Lyudmila Alexeyeva, Vladimir Bukovsky, and others—who were aligned in their commitment to truth. Each individually put themselves, their families, and their friends at risk because of their actions. As for the hard work of exposing lies, no one worked more steadfastly and achieved greater visibility than Alexander Solzhenitsyn. He made it his life's work to establish the factual base of Soviet history, knowledge that he committed to the page, especially in *The Gulag Archipelago*. What he revealed over the course of his life was shocking to many—for some it was the shock of facts unknown, to others the shock of recognition, and yet others incredulity that they lived to see these facts come to light. Contra Mandelstam, the most painful and morally courageous part of his mission was his refusal to believe that the death and suffering of millions had any meaning at all. There was not and could not be any meaning in the atrocities inflicted by humans on other humans. To say that there was meaning or purpose in any of it would be only to justify it. Solzhenitsyn was determined to reveal the truth and to force the Soviet people and the world to reckon with it, not to explain it away or endow it with the dignity of meaning. He refused to claim that there was any meaning to the loss of life but understood that the need to assert meaning was an act of desperation. The search for meaning in the reckless mass casualties preoccupied the survivors of the First World War as well. In the end, none could be found.

A significant difference between Solzhenitsyn, born in 1917, and Mandelstam, born in 1899, was that the former had no direct exposure to European culture, only that which passed through the filter of Marxism-Leninism. Unlike Mandelstam's generation, Solzhenitsyn never believed there was unique value in the civilization of Europe and the West. On the contrary, he condemned what he took to be its crass materialism and shameful spiritual poverty. In the USSR, portrayals of the West were uniformly negative. The material prosperity of the average French or American citizen was concealed behind a thick wall of silence or caricature. Solzhenitsyn was grateful that the United States took him in when he was expelled from Russia. But he was a deeply conservative Slavophile. When he was able to, he moved back to Russia, where he continued his lifelong project of documenting the crimes of Soviet communism. As Clive James astutely pointed out in his 1974 review of *The Gulag Archipelago*, Solzhenitsyn's dedication to writing revisionist histories was forced upon him as a novelist. He had to write history in order to write fiction. James argued: "The most pressing reason he writes history is to make the truth public. But a subsidiary reason, and one that will perhaps become increasingly important, is *to make his own fiction intelligible.* He writes history in order that his historical novel might be understood."[24]

Solzhenitsyn was in the unenviable position of being an artist writing truthfully about his own society, aware that his society does not know the truth about itself. His prose has an inevitable didactic tone because if he wrote too allusively, as artists are supposed to, nobody would understand what he was alluding to. Fortunately, his prose was suited to this task. When his novels are read abroad, they are valued less for their aesthetic than their educational qualities. James cautions against the mistake of going to his novels looking for the twentieth-century Tolstoy: "Tolstoy's novels are about the planet Earth and Solzhenitsyn's are about Pluto. Tolstoy is writing about a society and Solzhenitsyn is writing about the lack of one. . . . [Solzhenitsyn's novels] are not really concerned with society. They are concerned with what happens after society has been destroyed."[25]

It took only one generation to break the bonds of memory. Nadezhda Mandelstam notes that sometime in the 1920s people began to avoid one another. This was a symptom of a world already atomized by the eschatological fervor of the state. People avoided one another not out of fear of betrayal to authorities so much as due to the general numbness that set in as people turned away from the reality of the street to the other, newer reality. People couldn't forge connections in a society bombarded by lies about the past and the future. The past that people knew from their own experience disappeared from public view and was replaced by the expedient fictions dictated by ideology. The deep past that binds people and communities simply ceased to exist. What once held them together as a society was papered over by the lies that they could either accept or reject at their own peril.

All peoples and nations have a history and identity, but not all have a sense of destiny. Belief in a fate that is ordained and necessary endows a nation's actions with moral responsibilities other countries do not claim. In the best of times, this sense of a shared destiny can unite a people in the pursuit of a common moral purpose. In the worst of times, it becomes a license to act without regard to those who stand in the way of a nation's pursuit of its preordained greatness. The twentieth century was a protracted "worst of times." The destruction of the European imperial order created a vacuum filled by three nations with messianic visions. The Third Reich believed it had a destiny to save the Aryan race from communism, Zionism, and "racial pollution." The Soviet Union had a destiny to lead the global Communist revolution to accelerate "the eradication of the state as such."[26] President Woodrow Wilson claimed that America had a God-given destiny "to show the way to the nations of the world how they shall walk in the paths of liberty."[27] The US proved its mettle by saving civilization from the barbarism of Nazis, Communists, and latter-day terrorists.[28]

The twentieth century also spawned reactions to messianic goal-directed politics. (Existentialism is the best-known philosophical articulation of this rejection of historical determinism and its attendant moral crusades.) In the long run, the most influential counterpoint to end-state narratives was the development of evolutionary biology. It inaugurated a slow but sustained revolution in how humans understand their own nature and place in the world. Advances in physics and astronomy kept expanding the dimensions of time and space, pushing the human imagination far beyond the finite scale native to humanity. At the same time, various versions of Freudian theory opened new vistas onto the hidden dynamics of human nature. In *Civilization and Its Discontents*, Freud concluded that the conflicts within individuals and within civilization writ large are ultimately irresolvable. Equality, justice, and individual liberty can never be achieved. At core, they are antagonistic to the demands of society and rub against the grain of the human psyche. They are literally unnatural. Believing they can be natural is "an untenable illusion. . . . Nature, by endowing individuals with extremely unequal physical attributes and mental capacities, has introduced injustices against which there is no remedy."[29] Unlike Marx, Freud saw human history as inescapably tragic.

Seen in the context of evolution through natural selection, human history has no intrinsic aim, let alone predestined moral trajectory. Life is an open-ended system. It is poised to take advantage of any chance event that advances the fortunes of one species or culls others who don't adapt. Culture is implicated in all aspects of human evolution because it's the singular critical feature of human adaptability. Culture works to share practices and knowledge across generations, along with the tools and technologies that support adaptation to a given environment. Belief systems—ideologies, religions, worldviews such as empiricism or animism—are among humanity's most robust adaptive strategies. It's hardly surprising that when the natural and human-made environments change as rapidly as they do today, coherent belief systems struggle to cope with those changes. They begin to unravel or morph into something baroque and illogical. Faced with radical uncertainty, people will gravitate to a belief that offers radical certainty. The center is always grounded in the reality of indeterminacy and the need to consider conflicting perspectives. Certainty lies at the extremes of human beliefs. When people run to extremes in pursuit of certainty, the give-and-take between differences needed to find common cause is perceived as a threat. Compromise becomes a token of bad faith, and clinging to a sense of reality makes one a pariah. In the First World War, the center did not hold. So much of the Old Order was destroyed in the midst of combat that when peace was finally negotiated, there was little of it to restore. The survivors faced an unknown landscape. It couldn't even be called a New Order because there was no order. To regain footing in this landscape meant reckoning with human nature that is irrational and human affairs that are prey to chance.

8 PREY TO CHANCE

THE FIRST TASK

Nadezhda Mandelstam was born in the Old World and lived to see it utterly destroyed. The New World was a work perpetually in progress. People were treated as mere handmaidens of the future. Mandelstam reports that those who survived the first decade of Soviet rule were unable to accept as real what was evident before their eyes. They seemed not to know what was at stake and so failed to defend themselves. Most who did know didn't acknowledge it. They saw the price others paid for acting on their sense of reality—exile, prison, murder, or suicide. The most they could do was protect themselves from the worst. But no one escaped. Anyone who was not as radical as reality itself found themselves unfit for the reality of the twentieth century.

After experiencing the atomization of society under pressure by the regime, Mandelstam feared people were no longer capable of doing what is necessary to avoid such a fate in the future: "I shall not live to see the future, but I am haunted by the fear that it may be only a slightly modified version of the past. . . . We have to get over our loss of memory. This is the first task. We have to settle the accounts presented by the past—otherwise there will be no way ahead."[1]

What does settling "the accounts presented by the past" look like in action? It means establishing the facts of the case through well-provenanced evidence. It means acknowledging through private and public acts what trustworthy evidence reveals. Public acknowledgment actively engages society in all spheres, from the classroom to the boardroom, to legislative bodies and courts, to what makes it into talk shows, newsfeeds, and social media. The more unsettling the evidence, the greater the need for public leadership to acknowledge and make sense of what comes to light. The crucial last step is to reframe this evidence in a way that makes the past visible as a source of regeneration, not of recrimination. Reframing doesn't demand the past be made coherent, with a beginning, a middle, and an end. On the contrary, the incoherence, irreconcilable differences, chance events, and inscrutable motives of various actors should be seen as such, as real as they are in the present. If the future is open for humans to act, the past must also have been indeterminate. *Acknowledgment of life's indeterminacy is precisely what we have to defend.* That is why overcoming the brutal and cynical editing of memory becomes a moral imperative.

Many emerged from the 1910s with a contempt for the past equal to that of Lenin and Malevich. In contrast to them, though, these people didn't rely on the future to resolve the conflicts and divisions among the peoples of the earth. On the contrary, in their minds, dreams of perfectibility were vain, even delusional. There is no end to time, just as there is no end to war. Peace and harmony among nations never reigns for long. Millenarian expectations of deliverance are the ultimate failure of hope; they appeal to people who lack faith and must be assured they will not be prey to chance. This ground truth—the failure of sense and the rule of chance—is the quintessence of modernism.

Is the refusal to believe in any historical narrative promising radical change *for the better* the only appropriate response to failed expectations? If so, history unravels into a series of *things just happening*, one thing after another. This is most famously described by Macbeth when he finally grasps the grotesque irony of the Weird Sisters' prophesies about his reign and death. Life appears to him as "a tale / Told by an idiot, full of sound and fury / Signifying nothing." That recognition acknowledges the end of certainty but not the end of human dignity. Macbeth is a tragic hero, after all. He is brought low by his ambition, but in the end is ennobled by his pity for others and lack of pity for himself. Anton Chekhov created beautiful stories out of weak humans scratching meaning out of bleak nature. Their suffering is real. Acknowledging that suffering and the ultimate failure to make sense of life gives them a nobility greater than those who turn a blind eye to it. Simone Weil, whose life is a study of suffering, believed that "theories about progress and the 'genius which always pierces through,' arise from the fact that it is intolerable to suppose that what is most precious in the world should be given over to chance. It is because it is intolerable that it ought to be contemplated."[2]

In the decades following World War I, scientists elaborating theories of evolution developed an appreciation for the role of chance and contingency in natural selection. Recognition of evolution as a change in species over time dates back to the pre-Socratic Greeks, but Charles Darwin's and Alfred Russel Wallace's proposals of natural selection as the mechanism for change proved revolutionary. The theory of natural selection stands in fundamental opposition to goal-directed narratives of change because it recognizes random changes in genetic codes and equally random changes in the environment as effecting change over time. It could be argued that there is a goal—survival. But that is merely redundant. The specific mechanisms, scales, and dynamics of natural selection continue to be debated and refined. Do they operate at the individual level, at the group level, or some combination of the two? Given the observation of altruistic behaviors among flora and fauna, the notion of competition to the death and survival only of the fittest rings hollow today. Understanding organisms that exist as colonies, such as corals and ants or the microbiome inhabiting the guts of animals, raises profound questions of identity involving the permeable boundaries between an individual, a group, and the environment. Ants live exclusively as communal, eusocial beings. Trees are now said to communicate with one another through the soil and establish symbiotic environments that allow wounded trees to borrow the energy and nutrients stored in healthier trees.[3] At times, the descriptions of these phenomena betray a somewhat romantic, even anthropomorphized, view of the natural world, no doubt prompted by our fear that we are killing it. That said, such language signals a necessary rapprochement between humanity and nature. It doesn't so much impute human qualities and intelligence to other living things as it recognizes that human intelligence is merely one kind of intelligence that animates the natural world.

For humans, the boundary between the individual and the collective is always shifting. Individuals who are unable to recognize and adapt to changes in that relationship do so at their own peril. Dostoevsky, for example, was an individual thrust into the hostile environment of forced labor in Siberia. He had to find his place in an alien, hostile collective or shrivel into nonbeing. Several of his alleged co-conspirators were not able to adapt and did not survive their ordeal intact. Their mental and physical health was destroyed and their lives wasted. Some committed suicide, others went mad. Dostoevsky does not seem to have known about or at least been influenced by Darwin's *Origin of Species*. (It was published in 1859 and appeared in Russian in 1864.) He arrived at his rejection of utopian narratives, together with the morality of rational egoism, through a different route—the overwhelming evidence he saw in Siberia of humanity's desire for self-assertion, even unto death.

"Group-level adaptations" usually refer to biological modifications and/or cultural practices that enable survival in hostile environments. Classic examples cited are pastoral societies' retaining an enzyme for digesting lactose long after being weaned from breast milk. Genetic instructions to produce the enzyme are usually silenced. This exception makes dependence on cattle for nutrition possible.[4] Another example of group-level adaptation is the physical adaptations to Arctic weather by carrying more insulating body fat in a more compact build seen among Indigenous populations. These physiological modifications were as important as cultural practices to the Inuit, Sami, and other populations living in subzero weather, who devised technologies to build durable dwellings out of snow and ice. People sustain a network of mutual obligations within a group that allow its members to rely on one another for survival.

A further rethink of how history is made and unmade was catalyzed by the new discipline of human culture itself, anthropology. Franz Boas (1858–1942) was a German émigré to the United States who immersed himself in the study of the Inuit and Pacific Coast Indians. At the end of the nineteenth century, he settled in New York and taught for decades at Columbia University. He was a staunch opponent of the science-based race theory which held that the differences between the peoples of the earth were biologically determined. He rejected the idea that there is one ideal type of culture which achieves its greatest fruition in the civilization of Western Europe. Boas argued instead that each culture emerges from the relationship between the natural environment and the people who live there. Given the diversity of different environments, culture will reflect that diversity.

A culture can be deemed successful if it creates and maintains a nurturing relationship between humanity, nature, and the technologies humans create as they adapt to their environment. In Boas's view, the Indigenous people of the Pacific Northwest had deep, coherent cultures that allowed for full realization of human potentials, equal to that of any other culture. He went against the prevailing view that these cultures were primitive forms of the ideal type and would—or should—over time develop into the advanced form of Western civilization. Boas insisted that they were not immature or lesser versions of a higher culture. Their values, family structures, marriage and mating practices, belief systems, and political economies were well adapted to their reality. Boas influenced a large number of his students who carried on his work, including Zora Neale Hurston, Margaret Mead, A. L. Kroeber, and Ruth Benedict. These anthropologists didn't study cultures with a view to finding evidence of either progress toward Western-style civilization or regress from a lost Golden Age. This is not to say Boas and his students were the ideal type of disinterested investigator. Margaret Mead, for one, was happy to have her work on sexual relations among the adolescent females of Samoa stand in contrast to that of Americans and serve as an example. What's distinctive is not the partiality of her work but the novel idea that the West had something to learn from so-called primitive societies, not the other way around.[5]

The work of Boas and his students as well as the work of other anthropologists mount a significant argument against the idea of a universal culture as the goal of historical development. Cultures across the globe are not to be understood by measuring linear progress to an ideal state that elevates freedom and equality as the greatest among all possible values. In that view, traditional societies should outgrow values such as loyalty, piety, and moral purity because they are barriers to equality among genders, ethnicities, and abilities. The spirit of Woodrow Wilson's mission to bring democratic ideals of freedom and equality to countries with traditional but not necessarily democratic values still inspires American foreign policy. The irony in that mission is that the freedom to choose one's values is intrinsic to democracy. Further, a healthy pluralism of values is advantageous to cultural adaptability in a changing world. Monocultures, whether agricultural, economic, political, or ideological, will prove too fragile in the twenty-first century to survive.

THE FUTURE COMES FIRST

If chance influences events as much as or more than human decisions, actions, and interventions, what is the use of the past to us today? After all, history is not a catechism valuable for the lessons it teaches. Aleksander Wat warned against feeding the human hunger for certainty by turning, as he had done, to a doctrine that answered questions about the past, present, and future. In his case, it had been a turn to communism. But he cautioned against any ideology or creed that attempted to smother doubt. Nor does history repeat itself if it is ignored. History is made by context-specific forces acting on the sum of all that has gone before. It is *temporally dynamic*, taking place over time and neither reversible nor repeatable. The actions taken today will determine the range of options available to future generations. This feature of history is the stuff of counterfactual exercises and thought experiments in time travel. What if Fanny Kaplan's assassination attempt against Lenin in 1918 had been successful? What if Hitler had never been born? Ideologies that lay down a specific end-state may leave plenty of room for individuals or groups maneuvering within those parameters. But the sum of those actions in no way affects their ultimate destiny. Worldwide communism and the withering away of the state may happen quickly or slowly, in Asia and then South America, or in South America and then Asia. The speed of revolutionary transformation and its geography may be affected by individuals and groups. The triumph of the proletariat over the bourgeoisie will happen this way or that, but it will happen. By the same token, people can be too quick to interpret the precipitous collapse of Soviet communism as the necessary precursor to the stage of democratic development. In this view of history, knowledge of the past has little use except to reassure the living that things are happening the way they are meant to, because history tells us things always happen as they have to.

Our expanding knowledge of how totalitarian states have used history as a tool of persuasion and coercion hasn't stopped the practice of turning the past into an instrument of mind control. This is why Kołakowski concluded that "we learn history not in order to know how to behave or how to succeed, but to know who we are." The past reveals patterns of human responses to natural and human-caused pressures. People born into a world where the past is obscured, censored, distorted, or cast entirely as a prologue to the future spend their lives caught in the maze of a world detached from reality.

The work of creating a different, fact-based past from the shards of the Soviet Union has not gone the way Solzhenitsyn expected or hoped. It is not a more open society, nor is it one that values the dignity of humans as individuals. Nonetheless, it is on the basis of a shared past that Vladimir Putin is trying to build a vision of a shared future. He aims to project power on the world stage and at home by harkening back to centuries of traditional authoritarianism and Russian Orthodoxy. He is capturing (framed as "reuniting") territories such as the Crimea and the Caucasus to reassemble a Great Russian empire. One of Putin's narrative innovations is to redefine the USSR not as a failed Communist state, but as the great power that defeated fascism. Never mind that Stalin began the war by allying with the Third Reich in order to carve up Poland, part of Russia's lost imperial territories. This alliance turned disastrous when the Nazis began their "surprise" invasion of Russia. (There is plenty of evidence that the Russian military knew of the plan to invade and informed Stalin, but he for some reason did not act to counter the threat.)[6] In the new, improved version of the Great Patriotic War, communism has become anti-fascism, and the USSR is rebranded as the great nation that saved the world from Nazism.[7] Because Stalin was the leader of the Soviet Union during the Great Patriotic War, he has been rehabilitated as one of the greatest leaders in all of Russian history, with Lenin now playing second fiddle. Since 2014, it has been a criminal act to cast aspersions on the Soviet conduct of the war. Anniversaries of the Russian Revolution are slighted, while celebrations of victory over the Nazis are the key national holidays. Even the centenary of the October Revolution came and went with little fanfare. Once again, the Russians' fear of being prey to chance has been mobilized to justify limiting certain economic and civic freedoms. The recent experience of chaos and economic stress during the 1990s is not allowed to be forgotten.

Perhaps the case of the Soviet Union and the crimes committed over decades in the name of an ideology is so extreme as to appear to be an outlier. Yet it can hardly be seen as an outlier, given that in the twentieth century alone, regimes in Germany, Hungary, Cambodia, China, and other countries followed suit. Perhaps communism, like fascism, seems like a horrid relic of the twentieth century. Things have changed. That was then and this is now. We have learned our lesson and it is inconceivable today, with the all-seeing eye of the internet and the multiple town-hall-style commentaries of social media, that these practices could possibly continue. But they do.

Ideological crimes of such scale are far from outliers. The forced feeding of Communist ideology is taking place in China at "re-education camps" for Uighurs, even though many Chinese have living memory of the Great Leap Forward and the Cultural Revolution. In December 2019, a *Washington Post* reporter filed a story about Chinese library officials burning their books because they were deemed not to conform to the party line. One library "declared it had removed 'illegal publications, religious publications and deviant papers and books, picture books and photographs' in an effort to 'fully exert the library's role in broadcasting mainstream ideology.'"[8] A recent addition to the Chinese criminal code bans citizens from mocking or slandering a Chinese hero: "Since it went into effect in March [2021], the statute has been enforced with a revolutionary zeal, part of an intensified campaign under China's leader, Xi Jinping, to sanctify the Communist Party's version of history—and his vision for the country's future." The law sanctions prison time for anyone found guilty of such slander. It has encouraged mobs of vigilantes to gather on social media to attack those thus accused, whether the accusation has any merit or not: "Officials have defended the law as a necessary tool to fight what one director with the Cyberspace Administration of China, Wen Youhua, called 'historical nihilism,' [a term] which officials often use to describe deviant views."[9] Through social media, the nature and especially the scale of embracing "people's justice" means a tiny wave of dissent can create a tsunami of media attacks, all with virtually no cost to the instigators.

Unlike the use of force, the fabrication of a false past can be achieved without people noticing. There was a flurry of attention paid to the new official history textbook approved by the Central Committee of the Chinese Communist Party in 2020, but it has faded. It rewrites the role of the current president, Xi Jinping, as the equal of Mao Zedong and Deng Xiaoping. "This is about creating a new timescape for China around the Communist Party and Xi in which he is riding the wave of the past towards the future," said Geremie R. Barmé, a historian of China based in New Zealand. "It is not really a resolution about past history, but a resolution about future leadership."[10] There will be a rigorous propaganda campaign accompanied by uncompromising enforcement that will create memorable examples of the punishments meted out to dissenters.

The personal psychologies of those in the vanguard of artistic and political utopian thinking, be they Malevich and his fellow futurists, or Lenin and his fellow Bolsheviks, no doubt influenced the historical roles they played. They were shaped by their times, and they in turn shaped their times. Their personalities may have disposed them to lead millenarian movements into the future, but they say nothing about the susceptibility of the people whom they led. Important and fascinating as the leaders are, they are of circumscribed relevance to the task of accounting. That is still up to the present generation.

In the second volume of her memoirs, Mandelstam describes her abiding fear that like everyone else, she'd lost her grounding and sense of self. She experienced "an inner pain greater than anything caused by the worst of heart attacks. If you lost your self, the sense of life vanished with it."[11] The regime hid the past from view so effectively that by the time Solzhenitsyn came along in the period of the Thaw, when there was widespread desire to rebuild society post-Stalin, there was no empirical foundation to build on. There was no continuity with pre-revolutionary Russia. The most tragic consequence of historical amnesia was that people were "uncertain of what we had to defend." Solzhenitsyn, together with tens of thousands of Soviet and post-Soviet citizens working to recover the facts of the Communist era, has staked a claim for a future based on a transparent, if difficult, past.

What do they have to defend? For Solzhenitsyn, a latter-day Slavophile, it was the restoration of a pious, Orthodox, unmaterialistic nation. For Putin, it is that same collective identity plus the projection of world power. Before his invasion of Ukraine, Putin was busy writing a lengthy historical essay arguing that Ukraine is, has, and always shall be at the core of Russian national identity, where Christianity was first embraced and the Russian Orthodox culture flourished.[12] He will not recognize Ukraine as a separate and sovereign nation with the right of self-determination, but only sees it as a criminally separated territory. Textbooks are revised to codify this false history, and the schoolchildren of today are taught this story. Yet without an authentic and evidence-based past, Russians will not find solid ground to build on, no matter how much territory they conquer.

There is a significant difference between the way Eastern European countries have addressed the past, and Russia's way. Mandelstam's countrypeople have dealt with the past in a pattern familiar in Russian history. Periods of a cautious but open public discussion of the worst parts of Russian history—in particular, the "excesses" of the Soviet period—alternate with closing down discussion. Then the regime shapes various historical accounts that deftly avoid implicating the present generation in the moral pollution of the previous generation. On the one hand, certain charismatic poets and artists who suffered repression are carefully exhumed for public display. In St. Petersburg, the one-and-a-half-room apartment the poet Joseph Brodsky shared with his parents before emigration to the United States has been opened as a house museum with the support of individuals and a private foundation.[13] Here people are allowed to come and contemplate the riches of Russia's unique poetic culture. On the other hand, thousands of people who suffer in obscurity have found little relief from the legacy of repression that still affects them.

There is a generation of children whose long-dead parents served time in the Gulag. The parents received amnesty after Stalin's death but were not allowed to return to the city they came from. Their children are now in their seventies and eighties. They live in expectation of receiving the compensation they are legally entitled to, the most important of which is an accommodation in the city from which their parents were exiled. A seventy-two-year-old woman who is entitled to move back to Moscow has been living with her two daughters in a village five hours from the capital in a single room that measures 430 square feet. Her case has been taken up by an activist lawyer, and over 80,000 signatures have been collected in a petition to the government on behalf of her case: "Supporters say it is the least the country can do for the remaining victims of Stalinist terror—a period of history that Russian authorities often ignore, highlighting instead moments like the Soviet Union's victory over Nazi Germany."[14] As of 2022, the women have not moved.

What happens to a post-utopian society? Is there a proper way to acknowledge its death, perform appropriate funeral rites, and learn how to live in the present, for the present? In 1988, the émigré philosopher and historian Isaiah Berlin, born in the Russian Empire and eyewitness to a mob murdering a policeman during the 1917 Revolution, gave a speech summing up why Marxism and all other goal-directed philosophies of history will die:

> Marxists tell us that once the fight is won and true history has begun, the new problems that may arise will generate their own solutions, which can be peacefully realized by the united powers of harmonious, classless society. This seems to me a piece of metaphysical optimism for which there is no evidence in historical experience. In a society in which the same goals are universally accepted, problems can be only of means, all soluble by technological methods. That is a society in which the inner life of man, the moral and spiritual and aesthetic imagination, no longer speaks at all. Is it for this that men and women should be destroyed or societies enslaved? Utopias have their value—nothing so wonderfully expands the imaginative horizons of human potentialities—but as guides to conduct they can prove literally fatal.[15]

Marxism-Leninism had all the coherence of a satisfying historical narrative. It clearly articulated the mechanism by which humanity's destiny is realized through time. It specified the role humans play in this historical narrative: individuals are the means, a just society the ends. The moral order was crystal clear. Pain, suffering, and evil itself come from exploitation of the laboring class and the alienation of the creative powers of all humans. The striving of the working class to reclaim their labor and human dignity will triumph. That end-state will be worth whatever price must be paid today.

The opposite of utopia is not dystopia. They are identical landscapes seen through different lenses, one rose-colored, the other darkest gray. In *We*, Zamyatin depicts the world imagined as a utopia. But it is a dystopia because the One State fails in the execution. The fact that some people will always choose freedom over happiness means utopias require coercion. Attempts to realize utopian dreams at a national scale reveal the staggering price paid for believing this world to be a battleground between good and evil. People invariably become the enemy they despise when they hold the conviction that fire must be fought with fire. They rationalize the evil that people do to one another in the name of some higher destiny. A regime based on such a vision requires control over people's imagination. Imagination doesn't duplicate memory, but it is generated from memory. Think of the young woman from Vladivostok who simply couldn't imagine a place where butter was stocked in every food store but could imagine that a visiting scholar from America would lie about it. These images arose in her mind from the collective narrative she was raised on. The regime shamelessly exploited the capacity of humans to make sense of the world. To be fair, everyone in Russia, including the leaders, were born in the USSR and were all raised in the same bizarre faith that "by walking straight ahead one would rise into the air." Their sense of time was as surreal as their sense of gravity. In a magical reversal of natural law, the future is predicate and the past all speculation. Unlike the leaders of the regime, though, the woman from Vladivostok had no ready defenses at hand when the regime changed course during glasnost and the curtain shrouding Russians from the outside world was lifted. People are reluctant to acknowledge that they've been duped for many reasons, but wounded pride is the least of these. It is the greater existential threat that they find hard to grapple with—that they were lied to all their lives. What was real and what was fake? How could they know who they really were if they didn't even trust in the truth of their own stories?

It's a fundamental error to believe that a shared past is needed for shared future. For better or for worse, a shared past is easy to make up. A persuasive narrative can be stitched together by carefully editing a handful of recognizable truths. What people need after a shattering reversal of expectations is a way to envision a path forward that inspires hope but makes no false promises of peace and prosperity, or the triumph of their values over the world, or a glorious future that will vindicate the moral pollution inherited from the past. What is needed is a shared sense of reality based on the real, not a counterfeit confection.

9 RADICAL REALITY

PEOPLE INTO PATIENTS

Eastern European artists who came of age after World War II attended art schools that taught Socialist Realism as the sole legitimate form of art-making. They grew up in the midst of war and the dreary aftermath of occupying armies, bombed-out cities, displaced persons camps, and chronic food shortages. In the wake of fascism's failure and Communism's triumph, they struggled to find a point of leverage on traumas still fresh in their minds. They knew there was no vindication possible for the moral pollution of fascist racial ideology or Communist class warfare. Maybe it would be enough to acknowledge the past for what it was. But what was that past? The facts were elusive. There was the hard reality of staying fed and housed. That took all the energy survivors had for over a decade. It was premature to autopsy the ideologies that took hold of people and turned them first against the world and then against themselves.

In contrast to their counterparts in other Eastern Bloc countries, Russian artists and writers were forbidden from reckoning with the past. The facts of Soviet crimes were self-evident, there for all to see. But so was the price everyone paid to survive the Nazi onslaught—somewhere between 20 and 27 million casualties, and at least one in every family.[1] Reckoning was impossible as long as Stalin was alive. There were efforts to allow glimpses into the archives after his death, first under Khrushchev and to a greater extent under Gorbachev. These were calculated political moves by the regime to strengthen their own positions in advance of the reforms they were putting into practice. To see what happens when a population wakes up to a new reality, we must look further west. Among Eastern Bloc artists who saw their way to a radical reality, none has taken a harder look than Gerhard Richter.

Richter was born in 1932 in Dresden, then part of the Weimar Republic. He hadn't reached his first birthday before Hitler came to power and Richter's home town was absorbed into the fascist Reich. All through the 1920s, Germany had struggled to overcome its defeat in the Great War and the humiliation imposed as a condition of peace. Wolfgang Schivelbusch notes that, mired in the agony of defeat, "like all other losing nations, Germany began to search for the origins of the false path that led it to the abyss."[2] They were vulnerable to, if not actively seeking, the messianic deliverance promised by Adolf Hitler and the National Socialist Party. By 1945, Dresden lay in utter ruins, carpet-bombed by the Allies in a deliberate attempt to crush the hope out of the civilian population by exacting a punitive revenge. Richter and his family lived on the outskirts and witnessed the destruction. The city was then occupied by the victorious, vengeful Red Army before it was incorporated into a Soviet client state, the German Democratic Republic (GDR). East Germany was stripped of its assets by the Soviets and rendered poorer than before and dependent upon a country still burning with rage for what the Nazis had done to Mother Russia.

Richter's was a world of sudden, bewildering reversals. One day Germans living in the eastern half of the defeated nation were fascist pariahs, the next day they were Communist comrades, overseen with zealous efficiency by the Stasi. Anna Funder, an Australian living in Berlin in 2002, reported that "almost overnight the Germans in the eastern states were made, or made themselves, innocent of Nazism. It seemed as if they actually believed that Nazis had come from and returned to the western parts of Germany, and were somehow separate from them—which was in no way true. History was so quickly remade, and so successfully, that it can truly be said that the easterners did not feel then, and do not feel now, that they were the same Germans as those responsible for Hitler's regime. This sleight-of-history must rank as one of the most extraordinary innocence manoeuvres of the century."[3]

Shortly after the Germans tore down the Berlin Wall, Richter wrote in his notebook that "all theory is absolutely circumscribed, almost unusable, but always dangerous."[4] He taught himself to see through theory to the reality that was hidden behind utopian sloganeering and tales of innocents victimized—first of the Germans being victimized by Jews and Bolsheviks, then the Germans being victimized by materialistic capitalists. His attention to the outside objective world, rather than to his own subjectivity or identity, has enabled him to acknowledge the past and strip history of its tyrannical power. His work from 1961, when he moved to West Germany, through 1988, when he painted the series *October 18, 1977* about the deaths of Baader-Meinhof terrorist revolutionaries in a high-security prison, documents his struggles with Eastern Europe's postwar loss of memory. He had to come to terms with the legacy of the ancestral sin he was born into as a German. Nazis had done a comprehensive job of implicating all Germans in the commission of their racial policies. Though the Nazis' actions were shrouded in obfuscations and stubborn silences, it now appears implausible that any German didn't know, directly or indirectly, what those racial policies were and the measures taken to enforce them.[5]

"What can art do?" It is the pointed question artists asked themselves after the invention of photography. The question arose again, for different reasons, in 1945. Many postwar Europeans doubted whether it was even possible to do art in the wake of revelations about the Holocaust. What can art possibly add to the world in light of humanity's capacity for radical evil? Can humans create beauty, let alone cherish it? For artists in the GDR, though, "What can art do?" was a meaningless question. Art, like history, science, philosophy, and literature, self-evidently served the construction of the socialist state. Its function was already determined. Artists did not ask themselves what to do, but how to do it. That was also determined. The only proper aesthetic form was Socialist Realism.

Richter wanted something else out of art, though: "My concern is never art, but always what art can be used for."[6] He wanted to know what reality is and how to represent it. In contrast to Malevich, Richter does not erase history but makes it newly visible. He neither propagandizes nor philosophizes. In his approach, he resembles Anton Chekhov, who believed that writers must be like chemists—renouncing subjectivity, setting aside any squeamishness, and committed to reporting the truth, "no matter how terrible something seems." Richter presents the past as an indeterminate, elusive power animating the present and manifesting humanity's capacity for both good and evil.

For twenty-nine years he lived under two regimes that inculcated a historical determinism which denied individuals the possibility of choosing freely between good and evil. Richter lived under fascism for his first thirteen years and under communism for the next sixteen. He saw little difference between the mentalities of the fascist and communist regimes, despite their professed ideological antagonisms. Shortly after the fall of the Berlin Wall, Richter entered the following obituary for the Reich and GDR in his notebook:

> From 1933 to 1989, that makes it 56 years of uninterrupted dictatorship for the East Germans. Included within that, as the necessary concomitants of dictatorship, were the catastrophes, the crimes and the constant deprivations, offset by a vast effort of lies, slander, distortion and self-deception, an effort that could have been made only under the strictest control, in extreme duress—in a dictatorship, in fact. There is a very simple and familiar logic to all this: from time to time, our capacity for hope and faith (which are the same thing in this case) has generated a delusion, or ideology, which initially energizes people to achieve some real successes, and which from the very outset makes them selectively blind: blind to all that fails to fit, blind to anomalies and crimes. Psychological repression takes place; and, when the privations and sufferings and catastrophes come along, the delusion becomes a dogma, which prevails, prohibits, controls and punishes for so long that people are transformed into patients. The GDR.[7]

Both fascist and communist regimes wielded a potent instrument of control: the calculated obliteration of the boundary between *me* and *us*. The individual was fully absorbed into the community. Only in the collective could a person find a grounding reality. The *Volk* and the working class were essential, inelastic categories of the human. Anyone who found themselves outside that boundary was a pariah and clearly marked out as such. In the Reich, Jews wore yellow stars. In the USSR, dissenters were labeled class enemies. Whether they were non-Aryan or part of the bourgeoisie, their fate was isolation, exile, prison, or extermination. For everyone inside that collective identity, any question they posed about their own past was inextricably intertwined with investigations into Nazism and communism. Both histories were, strictly speaking, verboten. The weight of ancestral sin burdened both personal and collective consciousness. Everyone was implicated in the atrocities perpetrated by the Third Reich. The Nazis' blurring of the distinction between private and public, personal and collective identities, was replaced by the GDR's very same blurring of *me* and *us*. The GDR offered survivors of fascism "atonement" through becoming good Communists who reported bad Germans to the Stasi. Everyone became complicit all over again. After 1989, the same Germans confronted their complicity in the crimes committed by the GDR on top of those of the Reich. Richter confronted this grotesque legacy early in his career. He rejected the ideology of determinism, and was attracted to artists for whom chance and contingency played significant roles in art-making.

In 1961, Richter surreptitiously moved to Düsseldorf in West Germany and pursued his education. "I did not come here to get away from 'materialism': here its dominance is far more total and mindless," he wrote the following year. "I came to get away from the criminal 'idealism' of the Socialists."[8] Here he was exposed to contemporary artists, such as Joseph Beuys (who taught at the art academy), Jackson Pollock, Barnett Newman, Fluxus, and Pop artists, including Andy Warhol and Roy Lichtenstein. He began painting simple domestic objects—a table, a chair, a roll of toilet paper—in shades of black, white, and gray. These were the first paintings he included in his catalogue raisonné, thereby exiling all the work he did in the GDR to the attic. He began again.

His ideas about what art can do were honed by his early engagement with the art of Marcel Duchamp (1887–1968). Though Duchamp was taken by many to be anti-art, Richter understood him quite differently. A look at Duchamp's work and its influence on Richter can illustrate the knowledge necessary for someone behind the Iron Curtain to catch up with the West. As an East German, Richter was doubly disadvantaged. He would never have seen art deemed either decadent (according to Hitler) or bourgeois capitalist (according to the Party). He first became interested by Duchamp in 1965, when he saw an exhibition of his work in Krefeld. It reminded him of Joseph Beuys.[9] At that stage, Richter was troubled by the failure of traditional oil painting and its tradition of *peinture* to represent reality rather than foreground painting as such. Richter wanted to know if it was possible for oil painting—his preferred medium—to represent reality rather than itself. He believed that "everything made since Duchamp has been a readymade, even when hand-painted."[10] This is because "the artist's productive act . . . has nothing to do with the talent of 'making by hand,' only with the capacity to see and to decide *what* is to be made visible. *How* that then gets fabricated has nothing to do with art or with artistic abilities."[11]

Over the years, he made a series of experiments using Duchamp as a touchstone because of what he discovered in that art. Primary were Duchamp's ideas that art happens in the mind, not the eye; it does not serve an ideology but is the ultimate act of human freedom; and history is not directed by grand teleological laws, nor even by humans, but purely by chance. Richter did not agree with all these ideas in the end, but they were his first deep encounters with a serious art that was the polar opposite of Socialist Realism. With Duchamp, Richter was grappling with an artist who in many ways is also the polar opposite of Kazimir Malevich. Where Malevich gave Richter too much theory, Duchamp gave him a lot of reality, all of it declared to be art by the artist. Where Malevich saw all human activities straining to transcend the brutal power of nature over humans, Duchamp saw no grand plan, no transcendence, and certainly thought of strain itself anathema. That said, Duchamp and Malevich had much in common.

Duchamp and Malevich were roughly contemporaries (Duchamp was nine years younger than Malevich). They did not know each other. Nonetheless, they are closely linked in the history of art as godfathers to contemporary art—Duchamp to conceptual art, Malevich to abstract art. Different as they were, they were men of the same generation, shaped by many of the same experiences and sharing the radical's instinct to push everything to its extreme. Duchamp was every inch and brainwave as uncompromising and maximalist in his approach to art and life, as ambitious and demanding of himself and others, as Malevich. Both men stopped painting mid-career when they had exhausted the potential of the easel. Both wrote extensively about their art, and their work is impossible to grasp fully without reference to their notebooks, annotations, and letters. They elevated art to the highest value in life, and while assiduously pursuing recognition, they never pursued commercial success. Both longed for a kind of unconditioned existence, not limited by space, time, politics, or physical constraints. Duchamp believed "that art is the only form of activity in which man shows himself to be a true individual. Only in art is he capable of going beyond the animal state, his art is an *outlook towards regions which are not ruled by space and time.*"[12] Their artistic temperaments, then, were very similar and their subsequent influence on art history equal and yet complementary, as their art was antithetical.

The artists' fundamental dissimilarity as creators was their point of departure, derived from their theory of history and temporality in general. Malevich started from his vision of the end, and kept the image of transcendence and transformation always in mind. Duchamp, by contrast, focused on the beginning of things and stayed always with the present, so that his art was about the process of creation itself. Many of his works were never finished, but live on as works-in-progress. (This makes him the precursor to both digital and conceptual art.) The means and the ends were the same. Duchamp had no expectation of an existential transformation of the human condition; he preferred to take life on its own terms. What makes his art so radical is the nature of that bargain: not only does history as such have no end-state or object in mind, but it has no existential value. Duchamp's attention was devoted to the logic of the moment, in which chance and contingency stand strong against all other forces. It is in chance that freedom lies. The past cannot rule over the present, let alone the future. In his view, "the dead should not be permitted to be so much stronger than the living. We must learn to forget the past, *to live our own lives in our own time.*"[13]

Duchamp was fascinated by what results when humans give themselves over to chance. His art and writings put on display multiple dimensions of indeterminacy. He made art, played chess, and recorded reams of notes on his thought experiments. He made no attempt to synthesize his artistic practices into a *summa aesthetica* that would guide contemporaries and future artists.

Figure 9.1
Duchamp's notorious cubofuturist nude, mocked as an explosion in a shingles factory, protests retinal art that appeals only to the eye. Instead, Duchamp aims for "visual indifference." Marcel Duchamp, *Nude Descending a Staircase, No. 2*, 1912.

He never taught, he had no students, and he formed no school. That would be work, and as he said, he preferred breathing to work.

Duchamp was dissatisfied with the turn that Western art took in the nineteenth century with Gustave Courbet. This art gave priority to the visual over the intellectual. He referred to this errant art dismissively as "retinal," meaning appealing to the eye alone. According to Duchamp, art happened in the mind, not the eye. True art was intellectual, not retinal. Certainly Duchamp's works are among the most intellectually engaged and visually indifferent created in the last century. *Visual indifference*—his phrase—was absolutely critical to the success of his work. Duchamp's extensive writings about his art, together with the complicated, almost opaque presentation of the art itself, demanded the mind experience it. The eye was incidental. In retrospect, this makes him the putative father of conceptual art.

The priority of the mind over the eye was prominently on display to all who visited the New York Armory Show in 1913. There Duchamp created a *succes de scandale* with a painting noted more for its title than its excellence as a work of art. Hung alongside contemporary European paintings by Matisse, Vlaminck, Cezanne, Rouault, Picasso, and Braque, the canvas depicts a moving body, or so the title indicates—*Nude Descending a Staircase* (figure 9.1). The painting combines the angular delineation of volume seen from multiple perspectives characteristic of cubism with the dynamic simultaneity of motion typical of Italian futurism, all painted in the drab brown palette he had come to favor. Because the painting is so familiar to us today as the emblem of modernism (an irony Duchamp surely would have enjoyed), it is hard to understand the frisson of shock it produced in New Yorkers. This shock had to do with the uncanny way that Duchamp upended the expectations of art critics, connoisseurs, and the general public. He flaunted the tradition of depicting the naked female figure with a mixture of reverence and self-indulgent eroticism.

The year before, Duchamp's two older brothers, the artists Jacques Villiers and Raymond Villiers-Duchamp, invited him to exhibit at the Salon des Indépendants in Paris, organized by a group of cubist painters. Duchamp was twenty-six and in a great hurry to become an artist. By 1912, he arrived at his cubist phase and offered to hang his recently completed *Nude*. The cubist organizers asked Duchamp's brothers to ask Duchamp to change the title. Different versions of the story are told about what offended whom.[14] Yet, all versions report that the painting was viewed as a violation of the canonical treatment of the nude in European art and simultaneously a violation of the newly minted canons of cubism. The nude was a traditional subject that emphasized stillness, passivity, and varying degrees of eroticism. Duchamp's nude was not passive but engaged in action. Nor was she remotely erotic. In fact, there is nothing decisively female about this body. In the meantime, the cubists organizing the show insisted there was entirely too much motion in the picture, given their disdain for Italian futurism. Duchamp had offended both the past and the future, it seems, by not toeing any party line.

Duchamp refused to change the title.[15] He later recollected that "I didn't discuss it with anyone, but it was really a turn in my life. I saw that I would never be very much interested in groups after that."[16] He was against the idea of ideologies and -isms in art and life. He wanted no part of any collective identity. His biographer Calvin Tomkins cites his "attitude of complete freedom: freedom from tradition, freedom from dogmas of any kind. . . . He spoke about how he doubted everything and, in doubting everything, found ways to come up with something new."[17]

The *Nude* is hardly a great painting, but it has a great title. Though it offended the cubists, the canvas was shown elsewhere in Paris and again in Barcelona. In neither case did it draw special attention.[18] The reception at the Armory Show was quite different. The painting was widely covered in the press and became a must-see because it was guaranteed to shock. Its notoriety sprang to a large degree from the Americans' desire to get over their self-conscious provincialism by proudly showcasing contemporary European art. Among the culturally ambitious and status-conscious, it was necessary to see the *Nude* in order to say that they had seen it. People hardly knew what to make of it, but it was a source of unending delight if only because it offered people—journalists in particular—the fun of making fun of it. It was described as an explosion in a shingles factory, rush hour in the subway, a dynamited suit of Japanese armor, and an academic painting of an artichoke, among many other things.[19] Puzzled as people were, New Yorkers understood immediately that the painting was more about its title and what the audience made of it, less about what was on the canvas. Imagine if the painting were titled *Study No. 2* or *Untitled*. What would viewers have made of it if they were directed by the title to engage with the eye and not the mind? Duchamp was possibly the first Western artist to stipulate that a painting is incomplete without a viewer. The viewer's perception made the work into art. Later in life, Duchamp insisted more and more on this particular point—that the artist is only one element of the larger phenomenon of a work. The viewer is necessary to grasp it mentally and thus complete the work.

In 1966, Richter painted his own version of *Nude Descending a Staircase—Ema (Nude on a Staircase)* (figure 9.2). Unlike Duchamp's cubist obscuring of the subject to focus on the motion, Richter depicts the figure realistically. Though she is in motion, she appears static because she's painted head-on. The light that both emanates from and surrounds Ema (then his wife) emphasizes her grace with neither irony nor mockery. There is a quality to the painting that makes clear the artist is looking deliberately, without naivete. He creates a radiant illumination similar to that of paintings he admired, in particular Titian's *Annunciation*. (This served as a source of four Richter paintings in 1973.) He blurred the image in a final gesture of equivocating the boundary between the figure and her surroundings. She seems to be of one substance with her surroundings and emerging from within it at the same time. Richter's *Nude* tested whether or not beauty is still conceivable, even when art happens not in the eye but in the mind. The painting says it is.

DUCHAMP DISCOVERS HOW TO CAN CHANCE

For all the deserved notoriety of Duchamp's *Nude*, his two breakthroughs of 1913 and 1914 proved far more significant. They went far beyond the *Nude*'s offense against canons. The discoveries, first of art occasioned by chance and then art as a readymade, refuted the very idea that the creator's craftsmanship and intention are fundamental to art. Origins don't matter. There is no backstory to lend meaning, no lineage to provide context.

Duchamp was in a constant struggle to liberate himself from the weight of history, which is one reason he resolved never to repeat his own work: "I,

Figure 9.2

"What can art do?" Gerhard Richter asked. His encounter with contemporary Western art after he left East Germany led him to study Duchamp's work. Here he thinks through Duchamp's *Nude* by painting a nude that is not "visually indifferent" yet also engages the mind. Gerhard Richter, *Ema (Nude on a Staircase)*, 1966.

with my Cartesian mind, refused to accept anything, doubted everything. So, doubting everything, if I wanted to produce anything I had to find something that gave me no doubt because it didn't exist before. Having invented them there was no doubt about them, ever. All along, I had that search for what I had not thought of before. When I had done one *Nude Descending a Staircase* I would not do another one."[20]

By 1913, in fact, he moved away from the easel and oils altogether. "Can one make works that are not works of 'art'?" he asked.[21] One day, tinkering around in his studio, he took three pieces of sewing thread cut to a specific length (one meter) and held them above the canvas from a specific height (one meter) and let them drop. They landed in patterns determined by chance. He then affixed them on the canvas with glue and assembled the results into a piece he called *3 Standard Stoppages* (*3 Stoppages Etalon*, a version of which is called *Network of Stoppages*), the French word for "invisible mending" (figure 9.3). Duchamp commented: "In itself it was not an important work of art, but for me it opened the way—the way to escape from those traditional methods of expression long associated with art. I didn't realize at the time what I stumbled on. . . . For me the *Three Stoppages* was the first gesture liberating me from the past."[22] Ceding control of crucial aesthetic decisions to chance, he found a way to free himself from the deadening authority of the past. He succeeded in making art that was visually indifferent and purely contingent in origin—"canned chance."[23] It invoked no historical associations and depended on no specific context for meaning. It was only later, when Duchamp began to talk about his artistic trajectory and thus created his own narrative, that the work acquired context and meaning. So what started out as anti-historical in time acquired its own history as a pivot and point of origin in art history. It was Duchamp himself who made it so.

His second work that was not a work of art was the readymade. Duchamp discovered that he could take a utilitarian manufactured object, such as a snow shovel or hat rack, display it as a work of art, and give it a title that created a comical reversal of expectations, or peripeteia. It demanded the participation of viewers who bring associations and expectations to an ordinary household item to do a double-take when they discover that the

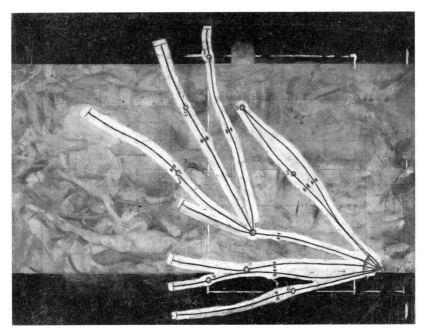

Figure 9.3

"Can one make works that are not works of 'art'?" Duchamp wondered. Following the creation of nonretinal art in the *Nude,* Duchamp experimented with chance. This became "the first gesture liberating me from the past" because it bore no reference to any previous work of art and demoted the role of artistic subjectivity. Marcel Duchamp, *Network of Stoppages,* 1914.

snow shovel is called *In Advance of the Broken Arm* and the hat rack is just that—*Hat Rack.*

The readymade began, as Duchamp liked to relate, rather innocently. He took a single bicycle wheel, set it upon a pedestal (a humble stool) in his studio, and gave it a twirl from time to time, to please himself. That was in 1913. He did not intend it as a readymade: "It was something I wanted to have in my room, the way one has a fireplace or pencil sharpener, except that it is not in any way useful. It's a pleasant device, pleasant because of the movements it made."[24] (Art critics point out that it was not only the first readymade, it was also the first mobile.) Duchamp never titled the wheel because he had not set out to create a readymade. Later, probably after he consecrated his first readymade, *In Advance of the Broken Arm* (a snow shovel), the bicycle wheel became in retrospect "the first one" and a museum-quality object (figure 9.4). Things happened like this—out of context, out of

Figure 9.4

Duchamp then went on to invent the readymade, inspired by a bicycle wheel he set up in his studio. He'd give it a spin from time to time to amuse himself. By declaring this to be art, he reiterated his conviction that art is an act of perception, not craft, happening in the mind, not the eye. Marcel Duchamp, *Bicycle Wheel*, 1951 (after lost original of 1913).

sequence, by chance. Once out of context, they lost all meaning and could be given a new meaning through a punning title. There could be no clearer proof that context creates meaning.

In 1917, Duchamp entered a piece called *Fountain* to an exhibition by the American Society of Independent Artists. It was a porcelain urinal. The submission was rejected, but *Fountain* was immortalized in a photograph by Alfred Stieglitz. The image circulated around the art world, and Duchamp achieved his goal. For Duchamp, readymades relied on "visual indifference, and, at the same time, on the total absence of good or bad taste."[25] In other words, the readymades would combine chance and the visual indifference of *Three Stoppages* with the intellectual frisson of the *Nude*.

Rich as these ideas were to Richter, he challenged Duchamp's hermetic and self-referential stance. In particular, he was put off by the "mystery-mongering" of such works as *Three Stoppages* and *The Large Glass*.[26] He created his own series of glass and mirror pieces to discover what glass could do on its own, so to speak, without Duchampian mystifications. His *4 Panes of Glass* of 1967 comprise four panels of clear glass, each measuring 196 by 106 centimeters, mounted on a metal frame and set at angles to each other (figure 9.5). The glass could both reflect the viewer in the room and make the reality of the room transparent.[27] They conflate the mimetic tradition of art as a window on the world and the modern tradition that says a picture is always a mirror. *4 Panes* tested whether a work of art reflects or reveals; it turns out to do both. By comparison, Duchamp's *Large Glass* is a work of solipsistic obscurantism—pure onanism. Duchamp, who frequently insisted that his focus was always on the erotic, would not have demurred.

Richter followed these works quickly with forays into abstraction and color field painting that he described as "pure retina painting."[28] In the following decades, he vigorously tested what of the European art tradition could be a source of regeneration in the twentieth century. He commented: "I see myself as the heir to an enormous, great, rich culture of painting, of an art in general, which we have lost, but which nevertheless is an obligation. In such a situation, it's difficult not to want to restore that culture, or—just as bad—simply to give up, to degenerate."[29]

Richter's quandary over what to paint dovetailed with his own need to see the reality that had been invisible to him in the GDR. He turned to painting two types of readymade images—photographs and earlier artists' works. Photographs served him as an entry point to reality. He was equally absorbed by painting in traditional genres, from landscape, still life, and portrait, to

Figure 9.5

Richter explores whether art is a depiction of the world or a mirror. Obliquely referring to the solipsistic mystifications of Duchamp's *Large Glass*, Richter answers this question by installing clear glass panes that both reveal reality (viewers see the world) and serve as a mirror (viewers see reflections of themselves in the world). Gerhard Richter, *4 Panes of Glass*, 1967.

color charts, color field painting, and abstract art. Over the course of his six-decade-long career, he has been mining these two veins, photographic records of reality and Western art traditions of genre and style. He revisits them over and over, switching seamlessly from one to the other. It is a rare practice that often bewilders art critics. They are looking for a consistent genre and style, a signature, a central concern, be it subject matter or use of media. Working in depth in a signature style is taken to be the sure sign of seriousness. They cannot find this in Richter's easy alteration of subject and style. He, on the other hand, says the variety they call out is "superficial."[30]

There is a clear consistency, beyond the loyalty he has to oil paints. It is his abiding concern "to try out what can be done with painting: how can I paint today, and above all what. Or, to put it differently: the continual attempt *to picture to myself what is going on.*"[31] There is no final answer to arrive at, as reality is intermediate. Instead, he explores the difference between apprehending reality—something that happens in the mind—and representing reality—something that art does. Still, there is a misapprehension, in the words of critic Arthur C. Danto, that Richter "evolved a kind of self-protective cool that enabled him and his viewers to experience historical reality as if at a distance. There is something unsettlingly mysterious about his art."[32] Mysterious, yes, but there is nothing cool about the work. There is no hint of irony, no matter how vivid his references to German Romantic art in his landscapes, how frankly affectless his color chart canvases, or how reverent the stained-glass panels he created for the restored Cologne cathedral. If anything is unsettling, it is the unabashed sincerity of his stated effort "to see the extent to which we need beauty—to see whether it's still conceivable today."[33] The world was still reeling from the facts of the Holocaust and the continued genocidal wars across the globe. People talked easily of "radical evil." Richter didn't shy away from acknowledging terrible things, but he was more interested in seeing if hope and faith could lead to radical good. Religion no longer had the power to guide people to a life of hope and faith. That was now the task for art.

Richter would not have moved to the West if he had contemplated giving up on the "enormous, great, rich culture of painting." He wanted to be free as an artist, and that meant embracing uncertainty: "Strange though this may sound, not knowing where one is going—being lost, being a loser—reveals the greatest possible faith and optimism, as against collective security and collective significance. *To believe, one must have lost God; to paint, one must have lost art.*"[34] To recover art, Richter was always removing the "I" of subjectivity from his art. This was in stark contrast to his contemporaries, the abstract expressionists, who vaunted subjectivity, and the Pop artists, who repudiated seriousness as such. Richter's objectivity is the moral core of his work. That's how it's possible to be lost and possess the greatest faith and optimism.

OCTOBER 18, 1977

Richter knew both that the present was obscured by the absence of the past and that the past was hiding in plain sight. He began to collect evidence—newspaper clippings, photos, postcards. Year after year, Richter amassed more images, archived them, pulled them out to study, arrange, and rearrange. These readymades spoke to him in their simplicity, candor, and lack of artistry: "Photography had to be more relevant to me than art history: it was an image of my, our, present-day reality. And I did not take it as a substitute for reality but as a crutch to help me to get to reality."[35] In the 1960s, family photos and newspaper clippings served him as unstylized representations of reality. He felt he could never achieve such objectivity on his own by painting, say, from nature. Instead, he copied the photo, and did so very quickly to avoid the mimetic frisson of photorealism that other artists aimed for. "When I painted from these banal, everyday photographs," he wrote, "I was really trying to bring out the quality—i.e., the message—of those photographs, and to show what gets overlooked, by definition, whenever we look at small photographs. People don't look on them as art; but as soon as they are transposed into art they take on a dignity of their own, and people take note of them. That was the trick, the concern I had in using those photographs."[36] (Think of how the enslaved girl Ashley's cloth sack takes on a dignity of its own when the historian Miles takes it up as a primary source.) Photos simplified things for Richter by obviating the artist's perceptual distortions that creep into all choices. The subject, angle, lighting, and point of view were all decided for him. He was not interested in expressing his own subjectivity or even the subjectivity of the objects or people he painted. To make room for the eye of the beholder, he had to remove the "I" of the painter. This is not a self-protective cool, simply the technique by which he makes "what is going on" legible. Technique does not make art: "What counts isn't being able to do a thing; it's seeing what it is. *Seeing is the decisive act, and ultimately it places the maker and the viewer on the same level.*"[37]

This long period of experiments in rendering reality visible culminated in his most famous, not to say notorious, photo-derived paintings. *October 18, 1977* is a series of fifteen black-and-white canvases about the spectacular deaths of Red Army Faction (RAF, aka the Baader-Meinhof gang) leaders. It centers on the day that the bodies of Andreas Baader, Gudrun Ensslin, and Jan-Carl Raspe were found dead in their cells by (apparent) suicide. Baader and Raspe shot themselves with pistols smuggled in for this purpose. Baader hid his in a phonograph player. (This phonograph was the subject of one canvas.) Ensslin hanged herself. The RAF were anti-capitalist terrorists responsible for a dramatic string of kidnappings, murders, extortions, and bombings of military, government, and industrial sites. The RAF kept West Germany on edge from their founding in 1970 until they declared themselves disbanded in 1998.

The first generation of RAF leaders was born and raised in postwar West Germany. They were the children of what Ensslin called "the Auschwitz generation." The RAF believed their elders to be so morally corrupt they could be resisted only with violence.[38] The revolutionaries were outraged that so many former Nazis escaped accountability for their crimes and instead found comfortable jobs in capitalist Germany. The self-proclaimed terrorists were inspired by contemporary Third World liberation movements to form guerrilla-style revolutionary cells. These bands aimed to disrupt "business as usual" by committing random or opportunistic acts of violence. Members including the founder, Ulrike Meinhof, were arrested in 1972 and confined to solitary confinement for as long as three years. Meinhof hanged herself in her cell the year before the October 1977 deaths.

Images of the crimes they committed, the victims they murdered, their arrests, their dead bodies, and mass gatherings on the day of their funeral were ubiquitous in the Western press. Richter had clipped these images and kept them in his archive, mulling over what he could do with them. He was in no rush. Time let memory sift the significant from the inconsequential. Richter did additional research in police files and in the end selected a handful of photos to paint (figure 9.6). His painting was undertaken with no political motives in mind. He professed no sympathy for the terrorists. He was struck by the incongruity of their actions and their reckless susceptibility to an all-devouring ideology. Richter said that it was weird, coming from the GDR, to see just how free the West was, only to witness the 1968 generation accusing the West of being fascist. What was the GDR, then, or the Soviet regime? He was "shocked to see how much support [the radicals] got, how powerful belief can be, conviction. Instantly, that is an interesting

Figure 9.6

Over his lifetime, Richter has amassed a large archive of images and photos from which he draws inspiration. Here he is in his studio working on the *October 18, 1977* series. The fifteen paintings were based on newspaper and police photographs. Behind him are two paintings of Red Army Faction leader Gudrun Ensslin, who hanged herself in her cell. Timm Rautert, *Gerhard Richter*, Köln, 1988.

word: it comes from the Latin 'con' (signifying completeness) and 'vincere' (to conquer)."[39] Richter came to feel grief and compassion for the radicals because they were fatally deluded by their conviction that change must come about through violence. The dead were young, pitiful victims of their own pitiless ideology. In their lives and self-inflicted deaths, they saw themselves as reproof against their parents and the cozy relationship between capitalism and former Nazis.

Most touching in the series are the four paintings of Ulrike Meinhof. The first painting is based on a photograph taken when she was much younger, in 1966. She looks over her shoulder directly into the camera, but her facial expression is tentative and hard to decipher (figure 9.7). It is a strange sensation to realize that at the time the photo was taken, she was a pacifist. Her future was open, and we, the viewers, know better than she what her fate was to be. The other three paintings are of her dead, laid out on the floor of her cell after she was taken down. The paintings are of different sizes but all taken from the same photograph, each a slightly different rendition of her head and upper torso. A dark gash across her neck, made by the rope, is clearly visible (figure 9.8).[40] The images possess the gravity of a death mask and the forensic indifference of crime scene documentation. The contrast between the life portrait and the death mask makes visible the price Ulrike and the country at large paid for the belief that violence can right the world. Life without hope is unbearable, but the certainty of false hope is always fatal. "Ideology means having laws and guidelines," Richter wrote in 1965, and "it means killing those who have different laws and guidelines."[41]

In conversation with the art historian and critic Robert Storr in April 2001, Richter recollects feeling strong opposition to the terrorists and to all ideologues. He thought that unlike the terrorists, he could exist without idealism and the illusions that sustain it. To do so would be more truthful. Later he came to see that his belief that he could live without illusions was itself an illusion. Idealism is simply necessary for life. On the other hand, big ideas and deep convictions contradict the notion of idealism because they mask a kind of despair. Richter tells Storr: "I remember the kind of worship around Malevich and others. I could never participate in that. I was never interested in that. I never shared any of those beliefs. For me the government

Figure 9.7

The *October* series depicts idealism and utopianism gone to murderous extremes. Richter said the paintings "provoke contradictions through their hopelessness and desolation; their lack of partisanship" (*Writings*, 204). Ulrike Meinhof was a pacifist when young, a journalist and mother of two, before starting the RAF. Richter takes pains to show her humanity, which caused considerable controversy. Gerhard Richter, *Youth Portrait*, 1988.

was the smaller evil because it believed the least. They were merely gangsters, of the sort that are always around in any period. *But those who were full of beliefs, they were dangerous.*"[42]

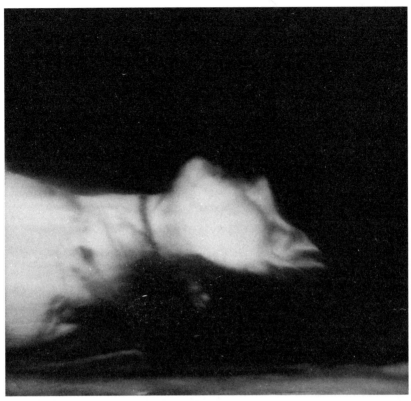

Figure 9.8
Growing disillusioned and impatient, Meinhof turned to terrorism to accelerate the destruction of corrupt capitalism. She was arrested in 1973 and hanged herself in prison three years later. This death portrait memorializes her transformation from idealist to terrorist. Richter's image engages the viewer in seeing what they are not prepared to see. Its objectivity makes her neither martyr nor devil. Gerhard Richter, *Dead*, 1988.

The *October* series was painted between May and December 1988 and exhibited the next year. The reception was decidedly mixed. Some people hailed the series as the return of history painting, something that many had concluded the horrors of the twentieth century made impossible. For Richter, this was an incoherent and confusing response. He saw the supposed political salience of the paintings as a distraction.[43] Others protested that it was morally objectionable to portray the terrorists and not their victims. Whose side was he on? This, too, struck the artist as nonsensical. When the

October series was bought by the Museum of Modern Art, the critic Hilton Kramer, joined by a posse of cultural commentators, vehemently censured the museum. But many artists, most notably Richard Serra, came to the defense of Richter and MoMA. Usually, Richter is not prescriptive about how his paintings are exhibited and sold, but in this case he insisted that the paintings remain together, not sold off as individual pieces and not reproduced for commercial purposes.

Why did he depict the humanity of the revolutionaries and ignore their victims? These images no longer spark that particular controversy because the event is so far in the past. Frankly, it would be naive to see the humanity of these ideological fanatics without seeing the conditions that created them, the spiritual strivings that were frustrated by Western capitalism. Richter's aversion to ideology as such rejects the assumption that there are simply perpetrators and victims, one entirely guilty and the other entirely innocent: "Our horror [on seeing atrocities and crime] feeds not only on the fear that it might affect ourselves but on the certainty that the same murderous cruelty operates and lies ready to act within each of us."[44]

October 18, 1977 completed his investigation of the power of ideology to hijack humanity's greatest asset—the ability to imagine and work toward a better world—and use that imagination to deliver death and destruction. Richter said that the completion of the cycle was a pivot point in his work: "I just wanted to put it on record that I perceive our only hope—or our one great hope—as residing in art. . . . *I was detecting something like hope in the very realization that this cruelty is present in everyone*—as if this very fact could be the starting-point of betterment, the key to the possibility of doing something."[45] He paints the gang members exactly as Chekhov had admonished artists to do: "as objective as a chemist; he must renounce ordinary subjectivity and understand that the dung heaps on the landscape play a venerable role, and the evil impulses are as much a part of life as the good ones."

HANDLING THE REMAINS

The *October 18, 1977* paintings have been interpreted in widely contradictory ways, which testifies to their success in representing the facts of the case with the minimal degree of artistic subjectivity. Richter notes that some viewers were surprised and baffled by the paintings because he had a reputation as "bourgeois," not a leftist.[46] By his own account, he was neither. The controversy surrounding the treatment of extant Nazi and Communist heritage continues without a clear resolution in sight. Should we bury the memories and unburden ourselves of the past, at the risk of repeating it? Or should we display the visible remains in public spaces and risk people misinterpreting and even glorifying it? Is it possible to disinfect the remains so they cannot spread the disease of murderous certainty?

In Berlin after 1989, several monumental buildings erected by the GDR were left without purpose and often without any possibility of reuse. The Palace of the Republic, home to the former East German parliament as well as a vast cultural event space, was built in 1973–1976. It was a spectacular exemplar of Socialist Realist modernism, and its preservation and reuse post-reunification had many advocates. True, it was riddled with asbestos, but abatement proceeded and it was declared safe. Nonetheless, the Bundestag voted to demolish the building and replace it with a reconstruction of the Berlin Palace that had occupied the site before the war. This, despite protests that demolishing the Palace of the Republic was an attempt to destroy the memory of the GDR, which would include the personal memories of many East Germans who spent happy hours there attending concerts, watching films, bowling, dancing, and dining.[47] What kind of harm does wiping out cultural memories, which are also deeply personal, do to a person's sense of self and self-worth? Given that it is nearly impossible to separate personal and collective memories attached to such prominent public spaces, how do we decide which takes priority—the innocent personal memory or the guilt-ridden collective memory?

How to handle the site of Hitler's bunker in Berlin posed a different set of questions. The bunker was destroyed during the war and the Soviets bulldozed what remained of the above-ground structure. After reunification, the site was cleared for construction of residential and commercial buildings. Crews uncovered further remains of the bunker. Debate began all over again about what to do with more evidence related to Hitler. No one came forward to argue for preserving it based on people's fond personal memories. Instead, the questions were about the site as a public monument. There was concern that "a memorial could become a shrine for neo-Nazis, but to erase it altogether might signal forgetting or denial. In the end, the bunker was reburied just as it was. The mayor said, perhaps in another fifty years people would be able to decide what to do. To remember or forget—which is healthier? To demolish it or to fence it off? To dig it up, or leave it lie in the ground?"[48]

The passage of half a century will certainly change perspectives on the past. But given the current controversies over monuments to the Confederacy that dot the American landscape and were largely erected many decades after the Civil War, it is naive to assume that the passage of five decades makes it easier to decide about public monuments that continue to be a source of pride to some and profound pain to others. The passage of time determines the consequence and thus meaning of any given action or actor. From the rich brew of chance and consequence, memory can distill critical moments of the past into an essence left, like a fine brandy, which becomes more potent and precious over time. In fifty years, the question will still be whether or not to destroy evidence of a troubled and charismatic past. People will still ask if the evidence itself has charisma and thereby poses a danger to the peace and stability of the living. In fifty years, people will still be fighting proxy battles over the future by debating how to use the past. Arguing that evidence needs to be preserved because people must "never forget" the crimes of the past mistakenly assumes that past events have an intrinsic and inviolable meaning that is stable over time. Memory is always dynamic, always a work in progress, always open to reinterpretation in light of the present day. It's very likely that a culture that cannot keep its memory open and labile becomes analogous to a person with autism, taking in every piece of new information and fitting it into an old fixed pattern. This inflexibility threatens the very survival of a culture in the long run, and in the twenty-first century, the long run is becoming very short.

Richter's objective approach to the past succeeds to a large extent in presenting evidence that neither glorifies nor vilifies it. We are habituated to photographs as images that are "true to life" because they capture a moment in time that becomes the past as soon as the images formed. When we form a single image of the past in an effort to remember, we contravene the fundamental nature of memory—that it is fluid, changing, compound. A single photo can stand in for and thus become what we know about the past. Richter largely avoids this trick of memory by blurring the images he makes. He claims one reason for this style is to "blur out the excess of unimportant information," leaving behind only the important and characteristic.[49] The final smudge, which he creates with a fine-hair brush, deliberately counters the impression that the image conveys an unambiguous reality. More to the point, it gives the viewer a sense of indeterminacy that photos usually lack because we think they represent things as they *really are*, frozen in time. In that sense, Richter's paintings behave more like a genuine memory than a snapshot. They make the image an approximation, whereas a photograph pins a moment in time, like a butterfly specimen fastened to a board, there for all to see, but lifeless. Further, blurring disarms the subconscious anxiety viewers bring to the ubiquity of images in contemporary culture. The anxiety is caused by a suspicion that the image will erase the memory, even of people we love.

The narrator of Sigrid Nunez's novel *The Friend* struggles to come to terms with the death of a close friend. She worries that writing about him risks not enhancing her memory of him but replacing the actual man with the recorded memory of the man, in the same way that "people whose memories of places they've traveled to are in fact only memories of the pictures they took there. In the end, writing and photography probably destroy more of the past than they ever preserve of it. So it could happen: by writing about someone lost—or even just talking too much about them—you might be burying them for good."[50] These are legitimate concerns, given what we know about how memories are formed. The brain holds astonishing quantities of information in long-term memory by generalizing specific examples and networking them into nodes of existing knowledge. It has to make something abstract out of something concrete. The very concreteness of Richter's photo-based paintings, especially their unaestheticized "banal" quality, brings the viewer back into the indeterminate temporal blur of reality. This way he captures what he calls the contradiction between "the human, temporal, real, logical side" of life that is "simultaneously so unreal, so incomprehensible and so atemporal."[51]

The false hopes of utopians and their nihilistic moral certainty led Europeans into an abyss, dragging the world with it into war after war. On what foundation can the inheritors of this legacy rebuild the world? What is to be considered sacred, absolute, and inviolable? Not nature. Richter painted landscapes, seascapes, cloudscapes, and still lifes that referred frankly to the German Romantic painting tradition exemplified by Caspar David Friedrich. Just before he began painting the *October* series, Richter recorded in his notebook that "my landscapes are not only beautiful or nostalgic, with a Romantic or classical suggestion of lost Paradises, but above all 'untruthful' (even if I did not always find a way of showing it); and by 'untruthful' I mean the glorifying way we look at Nature—Nature, which in all its forms is always against us, because it knows no meaning, no pity, no sympathy, because it knows nothing and is absolutely mindless: the total antithesis of ourselves, absolutely inhuman."[52] Even in light of the war-time atrocities perpetrated by the Axis (and the Allies as well), Richter felt "Nature is so inhuman that it is not even criminal. It is everything that we must basically overcome and reject—because, for all our superabundant horrendousness, cruelty and vileness, we are still capable of producing a spark of hope, which is coeval with us, and which we can also call love (this has nothing to do with unconscious, bestial, mammalian nurturing behavior). Nature has none of this. Its stupidity is absolute."[53] There's no meaning in the world without the consciousness that can create a moral order that acknowledges human suffering. This consciousness, made visible through art, endows the world with meaning.

"Art is the highest form of hope," and hope is the "pure realization of religious feeling."[54] Only through art can hope in the form of beauty become accessible to us amid the ugliness we create and the brutal indifference of nature to human suffering. Richter viewed the world as objectively as a scientist, creating a buffer between his subjectivity and the world he was picturing. This was necessary in order for him to "picture to [himself] what is going on." Some critics fault him for precisely this absence of subjectivity in his work; it makes his work either too cool or simply out of sync with the times, they claim.[55] His work makes no identifiable argument. It presents the facts of the case that hide in plain sight. It transposes banal images of daily life into a medium that commands attention. This objectivity achieves Richter's aim, which is to engage the viewer in the making of the art and the meaning of the art.

It is notable that one of the challenges that the *October* series posed to Richter's contemporaries was that it made them see things they were not prepared to see. They were not prepared to see the tortured humanity of the terrorists presented simply as such—neither glorified nor condemned. Instead, the paintings had an elusive objectivity which meant that people had to make sense of the facts on their own terms. Even Richter's abstract art, absent of identifiable content, is an exploration of what art can do as a form of picturing the world. Once we see the world in all its radical reality, we see that the world is in us and we are in the world. This knowledge cannot be gained quickly or painlessly, as Dostoevsky cautioned, but it is necessary.

10 THE FREE AND INDISPENSABLE WORK

BEYOND AUTONOMY

Picturing to ourselves what is going on, seeing the facts of the case clearly—this is the sense of reality that eludes us. Given how much information is pushed our way, it's hardly surprising that it's difficult to distinguish fact from fiction. The deliberate spread of disinformation about our shared past must be recognized for what it is—identity theft. Without authentic origins, people must make do with a damaged sense of identity. The less people are able to perceive the fakery, the more disoriented and vulnerable they become, uncertain who they are and what they have to defend. There are political regimes that like their citizens to have a damaged sense of identity. It is easier to turn them from citizens into subjects.

One American famous for his uncanny sense of reality, Abraham Lincoln, described this dilemma in his 1858 "House Divided" speech: "If we could first know *where* we are, and *whither* we are tending, we could better judge *what* to do, and *how* to do it." Now as then, Americans are confused about the nature of the times and the scope of our own agency to act in the world. In retrospect, we admire Lincoln's ability to sense where the Union was and whither it was tending. Yet despite all the warnings he and others sounded, and all the chances to step away from armed conflict that appeared, the Union broke apart. There were irreconcilable disagreements about what liberty looked like in rhetoric and reality. We are fascinated by Lincoln's ability to navigate a path through the war to armistice. But in the midst of civil war, his contemporaries and even supporters questioned his judgment.

They were deeply affected by how much blood was spilled and how uncertain the future was, month to month and week to week. Today Americans are divided by what we want and also, it appears, by what we value. We disagree even about where we are and if we live in a country governed by a legitimately elected administration. Some part of the population fears a coming civil war, and another part is armed and ready, eager to start the battle.[1]

In more stable times, the fact that people don't necessarily agree on social, cultural, or political ideas is not only normal, it is healthy. People see the world through different belief systems—a scientific worldview, a religious faith, or a political ideology—but at least they're looking at the same world. In that sense, we can say that they share a sense of reality. They know where they are. They may disagree about exactly where they should go, but whatever they mutually decide, they agree on how to get there: they will rely on the law and the public and private institutions that support civic society. But today, we can't agree on Lincoln's *where, whither, what,* and *how*. The spread of disinformation on the internet, the growth of conspiracy theories, and political loyalty pledged to a single individual rather than the rule of law have all accelerated the nation's departure from reality. Even if a majority of citizens—a shockingly small majority, but a majority nonetheless—believe in the rule of law and reject conspiracy theories, the divisions between those who do and do not is so great that the body politic is being pulled apart at the joints. Americans have relied on the separation of powers, free and fair elections, and a disinterested judiciary system to protect their rights. Today some people are shocked that the effectiveness of these institutions has eroded so quickly and are baffled about how to restore them. Other Americans have lost so much trust in these institutions that they see them not as protectors of their rights, but as violators. They call them the Deep State and are intent on dismantling them. The disinformation wielded by their media is designed to confuse people about precisely what it is they have to defend. This is a dangerous point of inflection: trust, once lost, takes more than a lifetime to regain.

Ironically, though, it was Russia's invasion of Ukraine in 2022 that has reminded people in the West what they have to defend and shown them the true cost of defending democracy. Within the first week of Russia's invasion of Ukraine, not only were Western expectations of Ukraine's weakness and Russia's mighty military proven wrong; people were also thunderstruck by the price Ukrainians are so willing to pay for their democracy. Putin was not alone in miscalculating that the Ukrainians didn't have a spirit of nationhood within them. He miscalculated that the West was so weak that it wouldn't rally to defend the principle of democracy, and that Europeans would prefer to stay safely at home with uninterrupted access to Russia's natural resources. Putin made himself over in the mold of a strong-man leader, but he is still a poor statesman and paranoid politician. He is proof that those without a sense of reality can be a threat to themselves and the world. Like Trump, he believes that having power is license to make one's own reality and impose it on the world.

At the end of a life spent largely in exile abroad, the Russian socialist Alexander Herzen (1812–1870) wrote:

> At all periods, man seeks his autonomy, his liberty and, though pulled along by necessity, *he does not wish to act except according to his own will*; he does not wish to be a passive gravedigger of the past or an unconscious midwife of the future; he considers history as his free and indispensable work. He believes in his liberty as he believes in the existence of the external world as it presents itself to him because he trusts his eyes, and because, without that confidence, he could not take a step. Moral liberty is thus a psychological or, if one wishes, an anthropological reality.[2]

Like Herzen, Dostoevsky insisted on the psychological necessity of freedom and the dire cost paid by individuals and society for stifling it. In the context of Russia's repressive regimes, insistence on the inviolable autonomy of the individual made sense. But in the West today, overweighting the importance of individual autonomy as constituent to freedom is a major obstacle to the urgent collective actions necessary for survival. Whether it's prizing individual liberty above public health ("This is America and I'll do what I want"), or putting national sovereignty above global cooperation to mitigate climate change—taken to extremes, autonomy is nihilistic, capable of destroying the self and the world. As individuals we cannot live with literal autonomy. As a species, it is unimaginable. But if the desire for individual autonomy is taken as faith in the world itself, as Herzen sees it, it creates a bond between the vital sense of reality and moral liberty. It means acknowledging that things could happen differently than they appear to have happened, and neither past nor future is predetermined. It allows us freedom of choice and it makes us responsible for our choices. We are in the world and the world is in us.

Our agency is limited in closed theories of history, sometimes severely, as in Marxism-Leninism. This is also the case if we take for granted that history moves forward, always improving compared to the past. America's identity crisis is in part a result of a self-confident belief in the March of Progress. That trust has effectively blinded citizens to the failures of both Republican and Democratic administrations to pursue liberty and justice for all. These failures led to a marked erosion of trust in the government institutions that had been created with the express purpose of promoting and enforcing justice. The American identity is deeply connected with technological progress because we believe technology promotes life, liberty, and the pursuit of happiness. But looked at more closely, trust in the power of technology seems to have tempted citizens to become free riders. The problems of self-governance may be too complex for us to grasp—but not to worry, experts are on the case, and they can solve the complicated problems we face in a technology-intensive political economy. After all, they've given us our cars, our computers, and our consumer goods delivered to our front door, all by means that are too complicated for the average person to understand. Things will always turn out well, a person might conclude, whether or not I work to make them happen. My single vote can't change things, so why bother voting? Instead, I will tend my own garden and not cause trouble. That will be my contribution.

The temptation to free-ride is exacerbated by Americans' faith in their own essential goodness. The psychologist Jennifer Richeson writes that "since the nation's founding, its prevailing cultural sensibility has been optimistic, future-oriented, sure of itself, and convinced of America's inherent goodness."[3] As a people and nation, Americans hold fast to their innocence, as if believing in good makes them good. The tragedy of history belongs to the Old World. Americans can be confident that even without their full participation in democracy as citizens, social, material, and even moral progress will continue. Much to our surprise, it hasn't. Richeson suggests the belief in our inherent goodness, coupled with faith in progress as intrinsic to history itself, leads to the assumption that racial progress will continue as it has before. Regression isn't possible, in this view, just temporary setbacks from time to time. The price of holding on to our innocence and not seeing, let alone taking responsibility for, unequal access to legal justice, social services, health care, economic opportunities and benefits, safe housing, and food security, whether provided by the government or the markets, is severely straining Americans' commitment to democratic governance. Public sector investment shrinks as the private sector expands. The political and economic instabilities of the twenty-first century have coincided with the weighting of marketplace freedom over social equality. The resulting imbalance between liberty and equality is deepening injustices long overlooked and now actively jeopardizes domestic tranquility.

When a gunman slew nine worshippers gathered for Bible study at the Emanuel A.M.E. Church in Charleston, South Carolina, in 2015, President Barack Obama decried the act and declared, "This is not who we are." He may or may not have used that language to exhort Americans to be their better selves. But whatever he meant, he resorted to the language of America's essential innocence. This, despite centuries of white Americans' violence against Black Americans. When white supremacists marched across the University of Virginia grounds in 2017 to confront protesters decrying Confederate statues, leading to the death of a woman protesting the march, Donald Trump remarked that there were good people on both sides. In his own bizarre way, he, too, was affirming the essential innocence of Americans. Why not be frank with us and acknowledge that there is evil among us as well as good? If the truth cannot be spoken by people in power, how can people trust them? The truth can often outrage people, but it is an effective antidote to poisonous lies. (Think of Representative Liz Cheney narrating the facts of the January 6, 2021, coup attempt during congressional hearings.)

Paradoxically, though, if Americans, or any people, are essentially innocent, then by definition they have no moral agency. To be innocent is to be free of guilt and without responsibility for what has happened and what will happen. On the other hand, to be free is to be burdened with the choice between acting for good or ill and assuming responsibility for that choice. This is the awful truth that D-503 first hears from a poet who tells him the true story of how the One State all began. In the beginning, a man and a woman were given a choice: "happiness without freedom or freedom without happiness; a third choice wasn't given." These hapless two, Adam and Eve, chose freedom. And what happened? "Understandably, for centuries, they longed for fetters. For fetters—you understand? This was the cause of world sorrow. For centuries! Until we figured out how to return to happiness again."[4] Forever innocent, without guilt, without responsibility, without freedom.

Present-day arguments over who is responsible for righting ancestral wrongs risk reducing that particular moral challenge to a debate about fixed origins. It encourages a tendency to shade the world in white and black, us and them, good and evil. There are multiple origins and multiple pivot points in the nation's history, strands that braid together to unite the states into one country. The expectation that a nation populated by immigrants, politically ascendant over the Indigenous populations, could or should be monocultural is incoherent. In any multiethnic country, there will always be significant groups counted as lesser than others. Because they have been raised to believe that their rights are equal to the majority's, they will agitate until they're treated equally under the law, if not in all other ways. In a mobile, nonauthoritarian country, those groups will change places over time. Their stories will be inscribed in history as they determine it to be, not as others do.

History isn't a moving sidewalk that carries people from point A to B to C, and so on, until time ends. Americans don't embrace a Marxist view of the best possible future and how to get there from here. They trust free markets as the means to freedom in all things. That said, if the United States had been less attached to the idea of progress and more attuned to the need to be resilient and adaptable, it might have avoided the worst consequences of a political economy based on the extraction and irreversible depletion of natural resources. It would have defined progress as increasing resilience, stability, and the close social bonds that are key to adaptation. This is not to argue that we are biologically determined; it is to say that when we have a sense of what we can control and what we cannot, we can flourish in a world prey to chance.

BEYOND ESSENTIALISM

Gerhard Richter's *October* paintings were criticized for their supposed sympathy with the people who perpetrated terrorism. Richter denied this was his intent. He believed it was his attempt to show the terrorists' humanity that provoked the censors and accusers. If there is anything that reveals the inner humanity of a person, it is their mortality. Particularly in the Western art tradition, death and decay are invoked as reminders that humans are not gods. The ubiquitous depiction of Christ crucified, suffering so visibly and even grotesquely, was powerful precisely because people knew that Jesus was God and chose to suffer as a human to free them of sin and guilt. Death demonstrated his dual nature as human and divine, son of man and son of God. (The resurrection demonstrated he was divine.) Richter depicts the Baader-Meinhof members not as martyrs for a great cause but as victims of a conviction that their ideology, "having laws and guidelines . . . , means killing those who have different laws and guidelines."[5] Life in the East taught him that no one can be innocent and that "the same murderous cruelty operates and lies ready to act within each of us."[6]

Why do humans have such a contradictory nature? Is it genetic? Can biology tell us anything about our moral nature? The anthropologist Richard Wrangham looks at our closest relatives, chimpanzees and bonobos, to ask why only humans, among all known species, are aggressive and homicidal while also being peaceable and cooperative. He argues that we are inheritors of the chimpanzee's aggression and the bonobo's sociability.[7] When in the wrong hands, biology can be given too much weight, which tempts people into a deterministic essentialism. (This is not the case with Wrangham.) In the last century, its ugliest form was eugenics. In the twenty-first century, it will be engineering humans to maximize some traits and minimize others. It's safe to say that these technologies will attract the attention of people who want to fight demographic trends that threaten the loss of their political dominance. Whatever ethnic or racial elite wishes to protect their privileges will turn to biological engineering in order to not just control the present but to design a future friendly to them and their kind. This is not inevitable, however, because other humans can stop them.

We create technologies and tools to extend our abilities to shape our external environment and our inner world. Our own agency is visible in the technologies we develop and use. We dedicate far too little attention to think through the ethical uses of technology, as if somehow it were something outside of us or, at best, something someone else with a face and a name created and is held responsible for—Mark Zuckerberg or Steve Jobs or Jeff Bezos. How we create and disseminate our own histories is already profoundly affected by new technologies because they expand the possibilities of people to tell their own histories, record their own voices, and expand access to these resources. We have committed ourselves almost completely to creating digital records, but we are failing to preserve them. We have neither the technology nor the institutional investments and knowledge to manage massive amounts of digital data over decades and beyond. The past will be inaccessible because we failed to preserve it. The result is that it will be even easier to fake the past.

It's evident now that a shared past can be fabricated to manipulate people into sacrificing their every drop of blood at the altar of a shared future. Why not a shared sense of the present reality? All of its elements are ready to hand. We can provide equal access to records of the past. We can use a historical framework that naturalizes uncertainty and unpredictability at the same time that it clarifies when and how human actions have made a difference. We asked if the values by which Americans define themselves—liberty and equality—are obsolete because they are legacies of a different time and place, or if they are invalid because they have been ignored or violated. But values are human-created things that coevolve with us; their meanings can't be fixed in the past or pegged to some ultimate future. We make and remake them in our own image. They are forever new because we and the world are forever new. Values don't mean what they once did and don't become obsolete by themselves. They only fade into oblivion when we stop remaking them in our own image.

Ultimately, moral orders arise from what is held sacred, inviolable, and infinite in value.[8] Each culture constitutes its own moral universe that informs the laws, customs, and political economies of the society. Moral values vary across time and place, but such variation does not amount to moral relativity; it is a recognition that each culture and each community develops a belief system that promotes stability and survival within very specific historical and physical circumstances. Each community sets its own values and defines relationships between individual and society. The tale of origins that links the present with the past creates a continuity that ensures beliefs and practices pass from one generation to another. For all that people point to the threats of increased chauvinism and racial strife, today's reactions against globalization should be understood as attempts to reorient people to critical social bonds and values of a local scale, not global. This makes the challenge of acting globally and collectively extremely difficult. Perhaps only an authoritarian society that forces such uniformity on its population will succeed in enforcing the draconian political and economic changes necessary to adapt in the twenty-first century. If so, democracies will be greatly disadvantaged because survival will come at the cost of liberty.

The inconvenient truth is that freedom must include the freedom to choose our own values. This results in pluralism of values and a diverse understanding of what we hold sacred. The plurality affords the resilience of the species and should be cherished at a time when natural- and human-caused stresses are pushing humanity to extremes. We should anticipate that some ways of being human will die off because they're no longer well suited to the stresses of the twenty-first century.

Whether we harmonize cultural and political differences or decide they are irreconcilable will be influenced by which history we define ourselves through—open or closed. Either way, we must reckon with long-standing contradictions between the theoretical value of individual rights and the reality of social injustice, between belief in freedom from oppression and belief in freedom to do as one wants. The lazy equivalence of material progress with moral progress turns a blind eye to glaring poverty. The public and pundits warn that these contradictions threaten democracy. But the only true threat to democracy would be to stop negotiating how to harmonize these contradictions; to do so would be allowing history as a source of self-knowledge to lose its integrity and become merely an instrument in a never-ending battle for the future. Lincoln said that the democratic decision-making process will never please all of the people all of the time, only some of the people some of the time. That's how you know the decisions conform to the will of the people. The challenge is to not solve the problem this way or that, but to keep working our way back to the center and holding it. Liberty and equality are not at odds, but lean on each other for their very existence. The equality of some cannot depend upon the inequality of others. The freedom of some cannot be supported by the lack of freedom of others. The present hazard lies not in extreme polarization of political views, but in cherishing our own virtue at the expense of other people.

Acknowledgments

I began writing this book in 2019, before COVID, before George Floyd's murder, before the November 2020 elections and attempted coup of January 6, 2021. Each event required that I rethink parts or all of the book. It was COVID that had the greatest influence on how the book took shape. Gone were the things that I normally rely on—access to libraries, ease of travel for research, even the usual gathering of friends and colleagues that would lead to serendipitous conversations. I submitted my text to the press in December 2021. Then on February 24, 2022, Putin invaded the sovereign nation of Ukraine. This would not have been possible had Russia reckoned with its past in the post-Soviet period. Instead, the ensuing bloodbath has been a dreadful demonstration of what happens when the past is outlawed and a fictional history is put in its place. It is extremely awkward, not to mention painful, for a historian to witness the entirely preventable continuation of past patterns unfold in real time. To paraphrase Dostoevsky, without historical reckoning, all is permitted. Americans' anguished and often violent reckoning with their past is far better than living with fake history.

My deepest intellectual debt is to the late professor Edward L. Keenan. Studying with him in the 1970s and 80s taught me a great deal about Russian, European, and Eurasian history. More than that, he shaped my understanding of history as the biggest and most beguiling database of human behaviors in all their variety, eccentricities, virtues, vices, and contradictions. In writing the book, I have also benefited greatly from conversations with historians and social scientists, many of whom I thank in my endnotes.

Special thanks go to Margaret Levi for her spirited smarts and for welcoming me into the rich intellectual environment nurtured at the Center for Advanced Study in the Behavioral Sciences at Stanford. Susan Schulten was a generous source of knowledge about America and its self-image. Long conversations with Victoria Rowe Holbrook, multiple time zones away in Istanbul, clarified what is at stake when we sit down to write. Such friends have done their best to keep me honest and bear no responsibility for any errors I commit here.

Writers write and publishers make books. I thank Chris Bourg, director of libraries at the Massachusetts Institute of Technology, for putting me in touch with Gita Manaktala, editorial director of the MIT Press. Gita is a very wise and sympathetic editor. She astutely helped me wrangle an unruly herd of ideas and sources into an argument. She urged me to engage the reader in thinking historically about the problems we have inherited and that are now our responsibility to bear. In addition to Gita, I thank Suraiya Jetha, Ginny Crossman, Paula Woolley, Erin Hasley, and Paula Dragosh. Special thanks to Kathy Borgogno, who located the images I use in the book, cleared their rights, and was a joy to work with throughout.

Above all, I thank six readers: four anonymous scholars, Gita Manaktala, and David Rumsey. My Anonymous Four gave me generous feedback, homing in on the parts I knew were weak and offering solutions. Gita helped me cut through the Gordian knots I tied so tightly. David Rumsey's infectious curiosity prompted me to travel well outside my comfort zone and stay there.

Notes

EPIGRAPH

Raymond T. McNally, trans. and ed., *The Major Works of Peter Chaadaev: A Translation and Commentary* (Notre Dame, IN: University of Notre Dame Press, 1969), 200.

CHAPTER 1

1. The global consequences of this geopolitical drift is described by Shivshankar Menon in "Nobody Wants the Current World Order," *Foreign Affairs*, August 3, 2022, https://www.foreignaffairs.com/world/nobody-wants-current-world-order?mod=djemCapitalJournal Daybreak.

2. I use the word "Americans" in this book as a shortcut to refer to people living in the United States, not all North and South Americans as such. For the sake of brevity, I use "American" as an adjective to refer to the United States.

3. Madeleine Albright, interview with Matt Lauer on *The Today Show*, NBC-TV, February 19, 1998, https://1997-2001.state.gov/statements/1998/980219a.html.

4. The terms of this debate are refuted by the historian Matthew Karp, who warns that in the context of historical origins, both religious and biological analogies must be used with great care. These analogies confuse the sacred and the profane and treat historical change as deterministic. Matthew Karp, "History as End," *Harper's Magazine*, July 2021, https://harpers.org/archive/2021/07/history-as-end-politics-of-the-past-matthew-karp/.

5. Leszek Kołakowski, "The Idolatry of Politics," Jefferson Lecture in the Humanities (May 7, 1986), http://hdl.handle.net/11215/3767.

6. Leo Tolstoy, "A Few Words Apropos of the Book *War and Peace*," in *War and Peace*, trans. Richard Pevear and Larissa Volokhonsky (New York: Alfred A. Knopf, 2011), 1219.

7. Vladimir Putin, "On the Historical Unity of Russians and Ukrainians," July 12, 2021, http://en.kremlin.ru/events/president/news/66181.

8. Sergei Lavrov, quoted in Peter Granitz, "High-Level Talks between Russia and Ukraine End with No Breakthrough," NPR.org, March 10, 2022, https://www.npr.org/2022/03 /10/1085677908/high-level-talks-between-russia-and-ukraine-begin?utm_source=npr _newsletter&utm_medium=email&utm_content=20220310&utm_term=6419016&utm _campaign=news&utm_id=5029400&orgid=151&utm_att1=50.

9. Quoted in Daniel T. Rodgers, *As a City on a Hill: The Story of America's Most Famous Lay Sermon* (Princeton, NJ: Princeton University Press, 2018), 249.

10. In the words of Czesław Miłosz: "Quite contrary to the predictions of Marx, this is the basic issue of the twentieth century. Instead of the withering away of the state, the state, like a crab, has eaten up all the substance of society." Czesław Miłosz and Nathan Gardels, "An Interview with Czesław Miłosz," *New York Review*, February 27, 1986, https://www.nybooks.com /articles/1986/02/27/an-interview-with-czeslaw-milosz/.

11. Frank Kermode calls world history "the imposition of a plot on time." Frank Kermode, *The Sense of an Ending: Studies in the Theory of Fiction with a New Epilogue* (New York: Oxford University Press, 2000), 43.

12. Kermode, *Sense*, 5, 17.

13. Simone Weil, quoted in "The Importance of Simone Weil," by Czesław Miłosz, in his *Emperor of the Earth: Modes of Eccentric Vision* (Berkeley: University of California Press, 1977), 91.

14. James Baldwin, "The White Man's Guilt," in *Baldwin: Collected Essays*, ed. Toni Morrison (New York: Library of America, 1998), 722–723.

CHAPTER 2

1. Anil Seth, *Being You: A New Science of Consciousness* (New York: Dutton, 2021), 199–200. Seth explains: "We perceive ourselves as stable over time in part because of a self-fulfilling prior expectation that our physiological condition is restricted to a particular range, and in part because of the self-fulfilling prior expectation that this condition does not change. In other words, effective physiological regulation may depend on systematically *mis*perceiving the body's internal state as being more stable than it really is, and is changing less than it really does. . . . Across every aspect of being a self, we perceive ourselves as stable over time because we perceive ourselves in order to control ourselves, not in order to know ourselves."

2. Anton Chekhov, letter to F. D. Batyushkov, December 15, 1897 [O. S.], *Polnoe sobranie sochinenii i pisem v tridtsati tomakh*, vol. 7 (Moscow: Gosudarstvennoe izdal'delstvo khu-dozhestvennoi literatury, 1944–1951), 123. My translation. O[ld] S[tyle] refers to the Julian calendar used by Russia until they adopted the Gregorian calendar in January 1918. The Russian Orthodox Church continues to use the Julian calendar.

3. The quotation is taken from a summary of a talk Gawande gave at Harvard University:

Ideas about aging and death changed dramatically in the past century, [Gawande] noted. Life expectancy in the early 1900s was just 47, a reflection of the fact that health threats loomed at every stage of life. Old age was not seen as something that increased your risk of dying, as it is today, but rather as a measure of good fortune.

Psychologists have shown that if you can reasonably expect to live another 20 years, you behave as if you're immortal, Gawande said. One consequence is that most of us don't give enough thought to what is most precious to us.

Alvin Powell, "Gawande Confronts the Inevitable," *The Harvard Gazette*, September 7, 2018, https://news.harvard.edu/gazette/story/2018/09/surgeon-author-atul-gawande -confronts-his-imperfections-in-hds-talk/.

4. Anton Chekhov, *Anton Chekhov's Selected Stories*, Norton Critical Edition, ed. and sel. by Cathy Popkin, trans. Michael Henry Heim (New York: W. W. Norton & Company, 2014), 521.

5. Chekhov, letter to Maria Kiselyova, January 14, 1887, in Chekhov, *Selected Stories*, 518.

6. Chekhov, letter to Alexei Suvorin, May 30, 1888, in *Anton Chekhov's Life and Thought: Selected Letters and Commentary*, ed. and annotated by Simon Karlinsky, trans. Michael Henry Heim (Evanston, IL: Northwestern University Press, 1973), 104.

7. Chekhov, "The Lady with the Little Dog," in Chekhov, *Selected Stories*, 421 (italics added).

8. Chekhov, "Lady," 421.

9. Chekhov, "Lady," 427.

10. Eric R. Kandel, *In Search of Memory: The Emergence of a New Science of Mind* (New York: W. W. Norton & Company, 2006), 59.

11. Santiago Ramón y Cajal, *Recollections of My Life*, trans. E. Horne Craigie with Juan Cano (Cambridge, MA: MIT Press, 1989), 459 (italics added).

12. Eric Kandel notes that "it was not until 1955 that Cajal's intuitions were borne out conclusively" when Sanford Palay and George Palade used an electron microscope to confirm the existence of that small gap between cells, the synaptic cleft. Kandel, *In Search*, 69.

13. Nathaniel J. Mandelberg and Richard Tsien, "Weakening Synapse to Cull Memories," *Science* 363, no. 6422 (January 12, 2019): 31–32.

14. Leor Zmigrod and Amit Goldenberg, "Cognition and Emotion in Extreme Political Action: Individual Differences and Dynamic Interactions," *Current Directions in Psychological Science* (December 29, 2020), https://doi.org/10.31234/osf.io/w3hj6.

15. Stanislaw Ulam, *Adventures of a Mathematician* (Berkeley: University of California Press, 1976), 181 (italics added).

16. Ulam, *Adventures*, 13.

17. Ulam, *Adventures*, 13–14.

18. Norman Macrae, *John von Neumann: The Scientific Genius Who Pioneered the Modern Computer, Game Theory, Nuclear Deterrence, and Much More* (New York: American Mathematical Society, 1999), 378.

19. Marina von Neumann Whitman, *The Martian's Daughter: A Memoir* (Ann Arbor: University of Michigan Press, 2012), 3.

20. Eugene Wigner, *The Recollections of Eugene P. Wigner: As Told to Andrew Szanton* (New York: Basic Books, 2003), 277.

21. Ulam, *Adventures*, 244.

22. Friedrich Nietzsche, *Human, All-Too-Human*, trans. and ed. Walter Kaufmann (New York: The Modern Library, 1992), 149.

23. This account is taken from Daniel T. Rodgers, *As a City on a Hill: The Story of America's Most Famous Lay Sermon* (Princeton, NJ: Princeton University Press, 2018). He points out that the sermon retreated into desuetude for generations. It resurfaced from time to time, but most memorably during the presidency of Ronald Reagan. Thanks to Susan Schulten for this and many other references about American tropes.

24. "The traditional Christian understanding of the inner self saw it as the site of original sin: we are full of evil desires that lead us to contravene God's law; external social rules, set by the Universal Church, lead us to suppress these desires. Rousseau followed Luther, but flipped the latter's valuation: the inner self is good or at least has the potential for being good; it is the surrounding moral rules that are bad." Francis Fukuyama, *Identity: The Demand for Dignity and the Politics of Resentment* (New York: Farrar, Straus and Giroux, 2018), 53.

25. This Twitter exchange was an early harbinger of claims that public health precautions—mask-wearing in particular—trampled on people's liberty. Rebecca L. Spang, "When Restaurants Close, Americans Lose Much More Than a Meal," *The Conversation*, March 20, 2020, https://theconversation.com/when-restaurants-close-americans-lose-much-more-than-a-meal-134196.

26. From an interview with James Baldwin, *Paris Review* 91 (Spring 1984). Quoted in Joshua Jelly-Shapiro, *Island People: The Caribbean and the World* (New York: Alfred A. Knopf, 2016), 3.

27. Joseph Henrich, *The Secret of Our Success: How Culture Is Driving Human Evolution, Domesticating Our Species, and Making Us Smarter* (Princeton, NJ: Princeton University Press, 2016), 325.

28. Macrae, *John von Neumann*, 171.

29. Cristian Candia et al., "The Universal Decay of Collective Memory and Attention," *Nature Human Behaviour* 3, no. 1 (January 2019): 82–91, https://doi.org/10.1038/s41562-018-0474-5.

30. Nadezhda Mandelstam, *Hope against Hope: A Memoir*, trans. Max Hayward (New York: Athenaeum, 1979), 347.

31. Sanam Yar and Jonah Engel Bromwich, "Tales from the Teenage Cancel Culture," *New York Times*, October 31, 2019, https://www.nytimes.com/2019/10/31/style/cancel-culture.html.

32. Jason Burke, "Laser Technology Shines Light on South African 'Lost City' of Kweneng," *The Guardian*, January 8, 2019, https://www.theguardian.com/cities/2019/jan/08/laser -technology-shines-light-on-south-african-lost-city-of-kweneng; John Giblin, "Meet the 800-Year-Old Golden Rhinoceros That Challenged Apartheid South Africa," *The Guardian*, September 16, 2016, https://theconversation.com/meet-the-800-year-old-golden-rhinoc eros-that-challenged-apartheid-south-africa-64093.

33. Giblin, "Meet the 800-Year-Old Rhinoceros."

34. Burke, "Laser Technology."

35. Robert Hass, "Chekhov's Anger," in *What Light Can Do: Essays on Art, Imagination, and the Natural World* (New York: Ecco Press, 2012), 18.

36. Quoted in Hass, "Chekhov's Anger," 18.

37. Anton Chekhov, *Uncle Vanya*, in *The Plays of Anton Chekhov*, trans. Paul Schmidt (New York: Harper Perennial, 1997), 236.

38. Isaiah Berlin, "The Role of the Intelligentsia," in *The Power of Ideas*, ed. Henry Hardy (Princeton, NJ: Princeton University Press, 2000), 126.

39. Chekhov, "The Student," in Chekhov, *Selected Stories*, 290–291.

40. Chekhov, "The Student," 293.

CHAPTER 3

1. Leszek Kołakowski, "On Collective Identity," in *Is God Happy? Selected Essays*, trans. Agnieszka Kołakowska (New York: Basic Books, 2013), 255.

2. Kołakowski, "Collective," 253.

3. "Schizophrenia is an illness in which the affected individual frequently feels that their sensations, emotions, and even actions are not their own. Because experiences seem to not come from oneself, they are usually attributed to someone or something else. Awareness of self is so fundamental to human experience that you may consider it to be inevitable and automatic. It may seem superfluous to put the adjective 'subjective' before experience, because all experience is subjective, but this absence in schizophrenia provides a stark illumination of the phenomenon." Veronica O'Keane, *A Sense of Self: Memory, the Brain, and Who We Are* (New York: W. W. Norton & Company, 2021), 137.

4. Kołakowski, "Collective," 255.

5. Kate Taylor, "Denying a Professor Tenure, Harvard Sparks a Debate over Ethnic Studies," *New York Times*, January 2, 2020, last updated October 14, 2021, https://www.nytimes .com/2020/01/02/us/harvard-latinos-diversity-debate.html.

6. He published *Poor Folk*, "The Double," and "Mr. Prokharchin" in 1846; "The Landlady" in 1847; and "A Weak Heart," "Polzunkov," "Honest Thief," "A Christmas Tree and a Wedding," and "White Nights" in 1848.

7. Joseph Frank, *Dostoevsky: The Years of Ordeal, 1850–1859* (Princeton, NJ: Princeton University Press, 1982), 51, 55; hereafter cited as *Years of Ordeal*. The following interpretation relies chiefly on the work of Frank, who wrote the five-volume definitive biography of Dostoevsky. While some details have been contested and nuances added to his body of work, Frank's volumes are still the most fruitful source for close readings of Dostoevsky's work in light of the life and times documented here.

8. He would later describe that moment in an anecdote in *The Idiot*.

9. In Semipalatinsk, today known as Semey, in Kirghizstan. Under these terms, the civil rights that were stripped away when he was found guilty were restored by virtue of military service. This allowed him to return to European Russia (i.e., west of the Urals) and live in St. Petersburg. This condition alone made his subsequent literary career possible. It has since come to light that Emperor Nicholas I had stage managed the entire drama, down to the smallest detail—the peasant garb, white hoods, the military troops, the drum beats, etc. The monarch was alarmed by the political turmoil of 1848 in Europe. As Frank notes, "Nicholas carefully orchestrated the scenario on this occasion to produce the maximum impact on the unsuspecting victims of his regal solicitude. And Dostoevsky thus underwent the extraordinary emotional adventure of believing himself to have been only a few moments away from certain death, and then of being miraculously resurrected from the grave." Frank, *Years of Ordeal*, 51.

10. Joseph Frank, *Lectures on Dostoevsky*, ed. Marina Brodskaya and Marguerite Frank (Princeton, NJ: Princeton University Press, 2020), 54.

11. In prison Dostoevsky began experiencing his first attacks of what would later be diagnosed as epilepsy. He describes those moments as epiphanies as well, precisely like the moment of mystic terror when he thought he was going to die. He felt a blissful sense of cosmic unity seconds before his convulsions began. After that, he would lapse into a state of torpor and often deep depression.

12. Joseph Frank, *Dostoevsky: The Stir of Liberation, 1860–1865* (Princeton, NJ: Princeton University Press, 1986), 345.

13. Typical of the time, the book appeared serially, first in *Time* (*Vremia*), then in *Epoch* (*Epokha*), which Dostoevsky founded and owned with his brother Mikhail.

14. Frank, *Years of Ordeal*, 8–9.

15. Fyodor Dostoyevsky, quoted in David McDuff, translator's introduction to Fyodor Dostoyevsky, *The House of the Dead*, trans. by David McDuff (London: Penguin Books, 1985), 7.

16. McDuff, translator's introduction, 14.

17. Maxime Leroy, cited in Frank, *Years of Ordeal*, 91–92.

18. Fyodor Dostoevsky, *Notes from a Dead House*, trans. Richard Pevear and Larissa Volokhonsky (New York: Vintage Classics, 2015), 11. Hereafter cited as DH. There have been many translations of this book over the years, and it is remarkable how much they differ from one another. I have chosen to use this translation to cite from the text, in part because it is readily

available to readers in English. However, the title they choose to use is literal and does not convey the text's focus on the dead rather than the house. Therefore, in the text I use *House of the Dead* when referring to the book.

19. From a letter to Natalya Fonvizina, quoted in Frank, *Years of Ordeal*, 76.

20. DH, 92–93.

21. DH, 28.

22. DH, 75–76.

23. DH, 18.

24. DH, 79 (italics in the original).

25. DH, 21–22.

26. DH, 111.

27. DH, 53.

28. DH, 300.

29. DH, 300.

30. DH, 301.

31. DH, 302.

32. DH, 303 (italics added).

33. DH, 303.

34. DH, 303–304. The convicts were given distinctive haircuts to denote their status as criminals; usually half their head was shaved.

35. DH, 228.

36. DH, 297–298.

37. Hegel, quoted in László F. Földényi, *Dostoevsky Reads Hegel in Siberia and Bursts into Tears*, trans. Ottilie Mulzet (New Haven, CT: Yale University Press, 2020), 21.

38. The Riverbends Channel, "James Baldwin v. William F. Buckley Jr. Debate (1965)," YouTube video, posted October 27, 2012, https://www.youtube.com/watch?v=oFeoS41xe7w.

39. DH, 3 (italics added).

40. Fyodor Dostoevsky, *Notes from Underground*, trans. and ed. Michael R. Katz (New York: W. W. Norton & Company, 2001), 15. Hereafter *Notes*.

41. Dostoevsky, *Notes*, 95 (italics added).

42. Dostoevsky, *Notes*, 15.

43. These opening lines are notoriously difficult to translate, even among all the difficulties encountered in translating Dostoevsky. I am using Katz's translation. In his introduction he

discusses the many ways these sentences have been rendered into English and how each falls short, including his own. Michael R. Katz, introduction to *Notes*, xiii–xiv.

44. Dostoevsky, *Notes*, 3.

45. O'Keane, *Sense of Self*, 158.

46. Note that the word *podpol'e* means "cellar," or "mouse hole."

47. Dostoevsky, *Notes*, 89.

48. Dostoevsky, *Notes*, 90 (italics in the original).

49. Dostoevsky, *Notes*, 91 (italics in the original).

50. Dostoevsky, *Notes*, 18 (italics in the original).

51. Dostoevsky, *Notes*, 27.

52. Dostoevsky, *Notes*, 96. This is from a letter to his brother Mikhail, written on March 26, 1864.

53. Dostoevsky, *Notes*, 11 (italics added).

54. Leszek Kołakowski, "The Priest and the Jester: Reflections on the Theological Heritage of Contemporary Thought," in *The Two Eyes of Spinoza and Other Essays on Philosophers*, trans. Agnieszka Kołakowska (South Bend, IN: St. Augustine's Press, 2004), 247.

55. Anton Chekhov, *Anton Chekhov's Life and Thought: Selected Letters and Commentary*, ed. and annotated by Simon Karlinsky, trans. Michael Henry Heim (Evanston, IL: Northwestern University Press, 1973), 331n1.

56. For an insightful perspective on the changing interpretations of Dostoevsky, see Czesław Miłosz, "Dostoevsky and Swedenborg," in *Emperor of the Earth: Modes of Eccentric Vision* (Berkeley: University of California Press, 1977), 120–143.

57. DH, 197.

CHAPTER 4

1. For details of the war's casualties broken down by country, see Government Communication Office, Republic of Slovenia, "World War 1 Casualties," accessed January 6, 2023, http://www.100letprve.si/en/world_war_1/casualties/index.html. Data from *Brill's Encyclopedia of the First World War* (Leiden: Brill, 2012).

2. There were many elites throughout the empire who were not ethnically Russian but were assimilated in various ways in the imperial culture. Usually, they were required to speak and teach in Russian, but allowed to practice the religion of their choice. Here I lump them together under the term "Russian" if they were part of the imperial upper classes.

3. Joseph Frank, *Lectures on Dostoevsky*, ed. Marina Brodskaya and Marguerite Frank (Princeton, NJ: Princeton University Press, 2020), 81.

4. For translations of all eight letters, as well as background about Chaadaev, the composition of the letters, and the convoluted history of publication, see *The Major Works of Peter Chaadaev: A Translation and Commentary*, trans. and ed. Raymond T. McNally (Notre Dame, IN: University of Notre Dame Press, 1969); hereafter referred to as *Chaadaev*.

5. *Chaadaev*, 30 (italics added).

6. *Chaadaev*, 42.

7. *Chaadaev*, 27.

8. Ivan Kireevsky, "On the Nature of European Culture and on Its Relationship to Russian Culture: Letter to Count E. E. Komorovsky," in *On Spiritual Unity: A Slavophile Reader*, trans. and ed. Boris Jakim and Robert Byrd (Hudson, NY: Lindisfarne Books, 1998), 189 (italics added).

9. Raymond T. McNally, "An Analysis of Chaadaev's Major Ideas on History," in *Chaadaev*, 13.

10. Peter Chaadaev, "Apologia of a Madman," in *Chaadaev*, 213–214 (italics added).

11. Joseph Henrich, *The WEIRDest People in the World: How the West Became Psychologically Peculiar and Particularly Prosperous* (New York: Farrar, Straus & Giroux, 2020), 461.

12. Kireevsky, "On the Nature," 189.

13. Kireevsky, "On the Nature," 219. This was the title of the tsar. Before Ivan III (1440–1505), the territory of present-day Russia was ruled by a number of related princes, each with their own principality, and the Hanseatic League city states of Novgorod and Pskov. Ivan III conquered or otherwise annexed them to become the Grand Prince of Moscow and thenceforth the title of Grand Prince, later Tsar, and then Emperor listed all the principalities subdued by Muscovites. It got to be quite a long list as his successors conquered more lands.

14. Kireevsky, "On the Nature," 218.

15. *Chaadaev*, 32.

16. *Chaadaev*, 215, 216.

17. Kazimir Malevich, "From Cubism and Futurism to Suprematism: The New Realism in Painting (1915)," accessed January 6, 2023, https://suprematism.co.uk/suprematism-manifesto.

18. Marinetti was snubbed by the futurists when he came to Russia in February 1914.

19. Aleksei Kruchenykh, *Victory over the Sun*, trans. Evgeny Steiner, in *A Victory over the Sun Album*, comp. Patricia Railing (Forrest Rowe, East Sussex: Artists Bookworks, 2009), 85.

20. Kruchenykh, *Victory*, 15.

21. Malevich to Matyushin, September 13, 1915. Cited in Margarita Tupitsyn and the MNCARS Editorial Activities, eds., *Russian Dada, 1914–1924* (Cambridge, MA: MIT Press, 2018), 61.

22. Alexandra Shatskikh, *Black Square: Malevich and the Origin of Suprematism*, trans. Marion Schwartz (New Haven, CT: Yale University Press, 2012), 44–45.

23. Malevich to Matyushin, in W. A. L. Beeren and J. M. Joosten, eds., *Kazimir Malevich, 1878–1935* (Amsterdam: Stedelijk Museum, 1988), 70.

24. Beeren and Joosten, *Kazimir Malevich*, 109.

25. Beeren and Joosten, *Kazimir Malevich*, 111.

26. On fevralism as the developmental stage of Suprematism, see Shatskikh, *Black Square*, 3–33.

27. Quoted in Achim Borchardt-Hume, ed., *Malevich* (London: Tate Publishing, 2014), 153.

28. Sergei Eisenstein, quoted in Borchardt-Hume, *Malevich*, 150, 152.

CHAPTER 5

1. Karl Marx and Friedrich Engels, *Manifesto of the Communist Party*, 18, https://www.marxists.org/archive/marx/works/download/pdf/Manifesto.pdf. The translation into Russian was by Mikhail Bakunin. Another translation appeared in 1882, done by Georgi Plekhanov, the leading Marxist of his generation.

2. Marx and Engels, *Manifesto*, 23 (italics added).

3. Leszek Kołakowski, *The Main Currents of Marxism: The Founders; The Golden Age; The Breakdown*, trans. P. S. Falla (New York: W. W. Norton & Company, 2005), 338.

4. Aleksander Wat, *My Century*, ed. and trans. Richard Lourie (New York: New York Review of Books, 1977), 21.

5. Kołakowski, *Main Currents*, 148 (italics added).

6. Wat, *My Century*, 17.

7. The legal scholar Kenji Yoshino argues: "In practice, I expect the liberty paradigm to protect the authentic self better than the equality paradigm. While it need not do so, the equality paradigm is prone to essentializing the identities it protects." Kenji Yoshino, *Covering: The Hidden Assault on Our Civil Rights* (New York: Random House, 2006), 191.

8. George Orwell, *Homage to Catalonia* (New York: Mariner Books, 2015), 87–88.

9. Kołakowski, *Main Currents*, 773.

10. Catherine Cooke and Evgeny Kovtun, eds., *The Great Utopia: The Russian and Soviet Avant-Garde, 1915–1932* (New York: Guggenheim Museum, 1992), 1, 22.

11. Quoted in Robert Service, *Lenin: A Biography* (London: Pan Books, 2000), 228.

12. V. I. Lenin, *The State and Revolution*, trans. Robert Service (London: Penguin Books, 1992), 92.

13. Fellow socialists Plekhanov, Potresov, and Zasulich accepted the notion that capitalism was necessary. Lenin split from them, and what was once a united party of Socialist Democrats became the Bolsheviks and Mensheviks.

14. Isaiah Berlin, "Russian Populism," *Russian Thinkers* (London: Penguin Classics, 1978), 241.

15. Lenin, *The State and Revolution*, 21.

16. *Revelations from the Russian Archives: A Report from the Library of Congress* (Washington, DC: Library of Congress, 1993) (italics in the original). This letter, so revealing about Lenin, was inaccessible until 1991, when it was featured in an exhibition at the Library of Congress.

17. Lenin, *The State and Revolution*, 82 (italics in the original).

18. Anton Chekhov, *Uncle Vanya*, in *The Plays of Anton Chekhov*, trans. Paul Schmidt (New York: Harper Perennial, 1997), 253.

19. Lesley Chamberlain, *Motherland: A Philosophical History of Russia* (New York: Rookery Press, 2004), 229.

20. Leszek Kołakowski, "The Marxist Roots of Stalinism," in *Is God Happy? Selected Essays*, trans. Agnieszka Kołakowska (New York: Basic Books, 2013), 96.

21. Kołakowski, *Main Currents*, 1210.

22. "Vladimir Putin Accuses Lenin of Placing a 'Time Bomb' under Russia," *The Guardian*, January 25, 2016, https://www.theguardian.com/world/2016/jan/25/vladmir-putin-accuses-lenin-of-placing-a-time-bomb-under-russia.

23. Andrei Soldatov and Irina Borogan, "Putin's New Police State: In the Shadow of War, the FSB Embraces Stalin's Methods," *Foreign Affairs*, July 27, 2022, https://www.foreignaffairs.com/russian-federation/putins-new-police-state.

CHAPTER 6

1. Stephane Audoin-Rouzeau and Annette Becker, *14–18: Understanding the Great War*, trans. Catherine Temerson (New York: Hill and Wang, 2002), 159 (italics added).

2. Quoted in Alison McQueen, *Political Realism in Apocalyptic Times* (Cambridge, UK: Cambridge University Press, 2018), 173. Thanks to Josiah Ober for bringing this book to my attention.

3. Andrew Preston, *American Foreign Relations: A Very Short Introduction* (Oxford: Oxford University Press, 2019), 4. Preston provides a valuable synopsis of American foreign relations, including some cautionary notes about the term "isolationist."

4. Daniel T. Rodgers, *Age of Fracture* (Cambridge, MA: Belknap Press, 2011), 251.

5. Andrzej Walicki, *Marxism and the Leap to the Kingdom of Freedom: The Rise and Fall of the Communist Utopia* (Stanford, CA: Stanford University Press, 1995), 352–353.

6. Leon Trotsky, *Literature and Revolution*, ed. William Keach and trans. Rose Strunsky (Chicago: Haymarket Books, 2005), 207.

7. Yevgeny Zamyatin, *We*, trans. Natasha Randall (New York: The Modern Library, 2006), 23.

8. Zamyatin, *We*, 31.

9. Zamyatin, *We*, 83.

10. Zamyatin, *We*, 120–121.

11. Zamyatin, *We*, 124.

12. Zamyatin, *We*, 55; the "Gas Bell Jar" was an instrument of torture.

13. Zamyatin, *We*, 153.

14. For Zamyatin's account of the publication history, see his letter of resignation from the All-Russian Writers Union, in Zamyatin, *A Soviet Heretic: Essays by Yevgeny Zamyatin*, ed. and trans. Mirra Ginsburg (Chicago: University of Chicago Press, 1970), 301–304.

15. Among those who left were Ivan Bunin, Vasily Kandinsky, Vladimir Nabokov, Nikolai Berdyaev, Alexandra Ekster, and Natalia Goncharova.

16. Zamyatin, *Soviet Heretic*, 305.

17. Zamyatin, *We*, 60.

18. Maria Gough, "Architecture as Such," in Achim Borchardt-Hume, *Malevich* (London: Tate Publishing, 2014), 162.

19. Aleksander Wat, *My Century*, ed. and trans. Richard Lourie (New York: New York Review of Books, 1977), 25.

20. Kazimir Malevich, "From Cubism to Futurism to Suprematism: The New Realism in Painting," in *K. S. Malevich: Essays on Art, 1915–1928*, 2nd ed., ed. Troels Andersen (Copenhagen: Borgen, 1971), col.1, 19.

21. See Richard Stites, *Revolutionary Dreams: Utopian Vision and Experimental Life in the Russian Revolution* (New York: Oxford University Press, 1989).

22. Jeanne D'Andrea, ed., *Kazimir Malevich, 1878–1932* (Los Angeles, CA: Armand Hammer Museum of Art and Cultural Center, 1990), viii–ix.

23. Tatyana Tolstaya, "The Square," trans. Anya Migdal, *New Yorker*, June 12, 2015, https://www.newyorker.com/culture/cultural-comment/the-square.

24. Zamyatin, *Soviet Heretic*, 301.

CHAPTER 7

1. Tim McDaniel, *The Agony of the Russian Idea* (Princeton, NJ: Princeton University Press, 1996), 8.

2. Chekhov, letter to Alexei Suvorin, May 30, 1888, in *Anton Chekhov's Life and Thought: Selected Letters and Commentary*, ed. and annotated by Simon Karlinsky, trans. Michael Henry Heim (Evanston, IL: Northwestern University Press, 1973), 104.

3. Wolfgang Schivelbusch, *The Culture of Defeat: On National Trauma, Mourning, and Recovery*, trans. Jefferson Chase (New York: Picador, 2001).

4. Nadezhda Mandelstam, *Hope Abandoned: A Memoir*, trans. Max Hayward (London: Harville Press, 1973), 11.

5. In *Stolen Air: Selected Poems of Osip Mandelstam*, sel. and trans. Christian Wiman (New York: Ecco Press, 2012), 42.

6. Osip died in a transit camp near Vladivostok.

7. Nadezhda Mandelstam, *Hope against Hope: A Memoir*, trans. Max Hayward (New York: Athenaeum, 1970), 159.

8. This is the central argument of Beth Holmgren's book, *Women's Works in Stalin's Time: On Lidiia Chukovskaia and Nadezhda Mandelstam* (Bloomington: Indiana University Press, 1993).

9. Mandelstam, *Hope against Hope*, 285.

10. Mandelstam, *Hope against Hope*, 48.

11. Mandelstam, *Hope Abandoned*, 158–159.

12. Mandelstam, *Hope Abandoned*, 159.

13. Mandelstam, *Hope against Hope*, 287.

14. Mandelstam, *Hope against Hope*, 289.

15. Frank Kermode, *The Sense of an Ending: Studies in the Theory of Fiction with a New Epilogue* (New York: Oxford University Press, 2000), 17.

16. Mandelstam, *Hope against Hope*, 329.

17. *Chaadaev*, 214.

18. Andrew Curry, "Nazi Massacre Unearthed in Poland 'Was Really a Horror,'" *Science* 373 (August 20, 2021): 839–840.

19. Tiya Miles, *All That She Carried: The Journey of Ashley's Sack, a Black Family Keepsake* (New York: Random House, 2021).

20. Mandelstam, *Hope against Hope*, 115.

21. Mandelstam, *Hope against Hope*, 54.

22. Mandelstam, *Hope against Hope*, 43.

23. From "At the Top of My Voice," an unfinished poem by Vladimir Mayakovsky written in 1930, the year he took his own life.

24. Clive James, "Bitter Seeds: Solzhenitsyn," in *Cultural Cohesion: The Essential Essays, 1968–2002* (New York: W. W. Norton & Company, 2003), 219 (italics added).

25. James, "Bitter Seeds," 215.

26. V. I. Lenin, *The State and Revolution*, trans. Robert Service (London: Penguin Books, 1992), 21.

27. Woodrow Wilson, quoted in Daniel T. Rodgers, *As a City on a Hill: The Story of America's Most Famous Lay Sermon* (Princeton, NJ: Princeton University Press, 2018), 183–184. Wilson said Americans "are chosen, and prominently chosen, to show the way to the nations of the world

how they shall walk in the paths of liberty." This destiny was not volitional, but created "by the hand of God."

28. The historian Wolfgang Schivelbusch has studied how national cultures deal with humiliating defeats. He argues that Woodrow Wilson, the first Southern president since the Civil War, brought the myth of the Lost Cause with him to the Oval Office. Specifically, the notion that the South was beaten militarily but had won a moral victory infused his foreign policy with the spirit of crusade. See Schivelbusch, *Culture of Defeat*.

29. Sigmund Freud, *Civilization and Its Discontents*, trans. and ed. James Strachey (New York: W. W. Norton & Company, 1961), 97n6.

CHAPTER 8

1. Nadezhda Mandelstam, *Hope Abandoned: A Memoir*, trans. Max Hayward (London: Harville Press, 1973), 178.

2. Simone Weil, *Gravity and Grace*, trans. Emma Crawford and Mario von der Ruhr (London and New York: Routledge, 1999), 108.

3. See Peter Wohlleben, *The Hidden Life of Trees: What They Feel, How They Communicate— Discoveries from a Secret World* (Vancouver/Berkeley: Greystone Books, 2016); and Suzanne Simard, *Finding the Mother Tree: Discovering the Wisdom of the Forest* (New York: Alfred A. Knopf, 2021).

4. On recent research into the production of lactase, the enzyme that makes milk digestible, see Carl Zimmer, "Early Europeans Could Not Tolerate Milk but Drank It Anyway, Study Finds," *New York Times*, July 28, 2022, https://www.nytimes.com/2022/07/27/science/early -europeans-milk-tolerance.html?searchResultPosition=1.

5. Witness the title of Mead's 1928 study, *Coming of Age in Samoa: A Psychological Study of Primitive Youth for Western Civilization*.

6. This evidence is detailed in Ian Ona Johnson, *The Faustian Bargain: The Soviet-German Partnership and the Origins of the Second World War* (New York: Oxford University Press, 2021).

7. On the proliferation of monuments to the war in Kaliningrad, see Thomas Grove, "In Putin's Standoff with Navalny, Many Russians Put Faith in President," *Wall Street Journal*, August 20, 2021, https://www.wsj.com/articles/in-putins-standoff-with-navalny-many-rus sians-put-faith-in-president-11618912333?st=nibkehz55ed1nxn&reflink=article_email _share.

8. Gerry Shih, "China's Library Officials Are Burning Books That Diverge from Communist Party Ideology," *Washington Post*, December 9, 2019, https://www.washingtonpost.com /world/asia_pacific/in-china-library-officials-burn-books-that-diverge-from-communist -party-ideology/2019/12/09/5563ee46-1a43-11ea-977a-15a6710ed6da_story.html.

9. Steven Lee Myers, "Shutting Down Historical Debate, China Makes It a Crime to Mock Heroes," *New York Times*, November 15, 2021, https://www.nytimes.com/2021/11/02/world /asia/china-slander-law.html?searchResultPosition=2.

10. Chris Buckley, "To Steer China's Future, Xi Is Rewriting Its Past," *New York Times*, November 7, 2021, https://www.nytimes.com/2021/11/07/world/asia/china-xi-jinping.html?smid=em-share; Linda Lew, "New Chinese Textbook That Says Cultural Revolution Brought 'Disaster' on Country Stirs Debate about Historical Memory," *South China Morning Post*, September 6, 2020, https://www.scmp.com/news/china/politics/article/3100389/new-chinese-textbook-says-cultural-revolution-brought-disaster.

11. Mandelstam, *Hope Abandoned*, 7.

12. Vladimir Putin, "On the Historical Unity of Russians and Ukrainians," July 12, 2021, http://en.kremlin.ru/events/president/news/66181.

13. Ivan Nechepurenko, "Joseph Brodsky Slept Here. The Great Poet's Cranky Neighbor Couldn't Care Less," *New York Times*, September 12, 2021, https://www.nytimes.com/2021/09/12/world/europe/joseph-brodsky-museum-russia.html.

14. Andrea Palasciano, "Life in Exile: Children of the Gulag Fight to Return Home," *ArtDaily*, October 16, 2021, https://artdaily.cc/news/132095/Life-in-exile--children-of-the-Gulag-fight-to-return-home#.YWrT7BrMIQc.

15. The talk was published as Isaiah Berlin, "The Pursuit of the Ideal," in *The Crooked Timber of Humanity: Chapters in the History of Ideas*, ed. Henry Hardy (New York: Alfred A. Knopf, 1991), 14–15.

CHAPTER 9

1. "World War II Casualties by Country 2022," *World Population Review*, accessed November 16, 2022, https://worldpopulationreview.com/country-rankings/world-war-two-casualties-by-country.

2. Wolfgang Schivelbusch, *Culture of Defeat: On National Trauma, Mourning, and Recovery*, trans. Jefferson Chase (New York: Picador, 2001), 230.

3. Anna Funder, *Stasiland: Stories from Behind the Berlin Wall* (New York: Harper Perennial, 2002), 161.

4. "Language can express only what language enables it to express. How to depict reality.
    "Language is the only language of consciousness. 'What one cannot say, one does not know.'
    "That is why all theory is absolutely circumscribed, almost unusable, but always dangerous." Gerhard Richter, *Writings 1961–2007*, ed. Dietmar Elger and Hans-Ulrich Obrist (New York: Distributed Art Publishers, 2009), 216.

5. For a meticulously documented assessment of what Germans did and did not know during and after the war, see Mary Fulbrook, *Reckonings: Legacies of Nazi Persecution and the Quest for Justice* (Oxford: Oxford University Press, 2018).

6. Gerhard Richter, *The Daily Practice of Painting: Writings and Interviews 1962–1993*, ed. Hans-Ulrich Obrist and trans. David Britt (Cambridge, MA: MIT Press, in association with Anthony d'Offay Gallery London, 1995), 13.

7. Richter, *Daily Practice*, 182.

8. Richter, *Daily Practice*, 13.

9. Richter dates the time he saw the exhibition to 1963. Richter, *Daily Practice*, 137. Dietmar Elger, Richter's biographer and director of the Gerhard Richter Archive, notes the exhibition of Duchamp's exhibition of readymades in Krefeld happened in 1965. Dietrich Elger, *Gerhard Richter, a Life in Painting*, trans. Elizabeth M. Solaro (Chicago: University of Chicago Press, 2009), 104.

10. Note from 1982, when Richter was fifty. Richter, *Writings*, 128.

11. Richter, *Writings*, 169 (italics in the original).

12. Quoted in Calvin Tomkins, *Duchamp: A Biography* (New York: Museum of Modern Art, 1996), 10–11 (italics added).

13. Quoted in Tomkins, *Duchamp*, 149 (italics added).

14. Calvin Tomkins, *Marcel Duchamp: The Afternoon Interviews* (Brooklyn, NY: Badlands Unlimited, 2013), 8–9.

15. Janis Mink gives a different version of the story. The cubists who organized the show found his work too dynamic and too futurist, and that muddied their attempt to define cubism in contrast to all other "isms." So Duchamp ended up exhibiting the *Nude* for the first time in Paris in 1912, at the Section d'Or, a show organized by his close friend Francis Picabia. That's where he met Apollinaire. Janis Mink, *Duchamp, 1887–1968: Art as Anti-Art* (Cologne: Taschen, 2016), 20.

16. Tomkins, *Afternoon Interviews*, 71

17. Tomkins, *Afternoon Interviews*, 16–17.

18. Pierre Cabanne, *Dialogues with Marcel Duchamp*, trans. Ron Padgett (New York: Da Capo Press, 1971), 31.

19. Milton W. Brown, *The Story of the Armory Show* (Washington, DC: Joseph H. Hirshhorn Foundation, 1963), 109–110.

20. Quoted in Tomkins, *Afternoon Interviews*, 64.

21. Marcel Duchamp, *The Writings of Marcel Duchamp*, ed. Michel Sanouillet and Elmer Peterson (New York: Da Capo Press, 1973), 74.

22. Quoted in Tomkins, *Duchamp*, 128.

23. Duchamp, *Writings*, 33. His notation reads: "If a thread one meter long falls from a height one meter straight on to a horizontal plane twisting *as it pleases* and creates a new image of the unit of length."

24. It's noteworthy that both Duchamp and Malevich created breakthrough pieces but didn't realize until several years later what they had done. In 1913 Duchamp spun the wheel and after a few years declared it to be a readymade. Because he cared about the historical record,

he claimed its priority based on putting it in the studio in 1913. By the same token, Malevich painted the *Black Square* in 1915 but, equally concerned about the art historical record, claimed that he had painted it in 1913 as part of the scenery for *Victory over the Sun*.

25. Quoted in Tomkins, *Duchamp*, 154.

26. Richter, *Daily Practice*, 225.

27. Mark Godfrey and Nicholas Sirota, eds., *Panorama: A Retrospective*, expanded ed. (London: Tate Publishing, 2016), 23.

28. Quoted in Hans-Ulrich Obrist, *The Richter Interviews* (London: HENI Publishing, 2019), 139.

29. Quoted in Armin Zweite, *Gerhard Richter: Life and Work; In Painting, Thinking Is Painting* (New York: Prestel Publishing, 2020), 7.

30. Richter, *Writings*, 253.

31. Richter, *Writings*, 96 (italics added).

32. Arthur C. Danto, "Gerhard Richter," in *Unnatural Wonders: Essays from the Gap between Art and Life* (New York: Farrar, Straus and Giroux, 2005), 181.

33. Richter, *Writings*, 81.

34. Richter, *Writings*, 15 (italics added).

35. Richter, *Writings*, 64.

36. Richter, *Daily Practice*, 117.

37. Richter, *Writings*, 257 (italics added).

38. Zweite, *Gerhard Richter*, 330.

39. Quoted in Obrist, *Richter Interviews*, 159.

40. The catalogue raisonée of the painting refers to the "dark deep line left by the noose," while Robert Storr refers to this line as "the rope still visible around her neck." See the notes on *Tote* (Dead, 1988), on Gerhard Richter's website, https://www.gerhard-richter.com/en/art/paintings/photo-paintings/baader-meinhof-56/dead-7689/?&categoryid=56&p=1&sp=32.

    Storr speaks on the cycle in a 2012 video on the artist's website; see https://www.gerhard-richter.com/en/videos/works/18-october-1977-79.

41. Richter, *Writings*, 34–35.

42. Quoted in Robert Storr, *Gerhard Richter: 40 Years of Painting* (New York: Museum of Modern Art, 2002), 307–308 (italics added).

43. Richter, *Writings*, 213.

44. Richter, *Writings*, 159.

45. Richter, *Writings*, 159–160 (italics added).

46. See Arthaus Musik, "Gerhard Richter: 40 Years of Painting | Documentary: Gerald Fox" (2003), YouTube, November 23, 2020, https://www.youtube.com/watch?v=FE5EMVR7SWE.

47. "Berlin's Palace of the Republic Faces Wrecking Ball," *DW*, January 20, 2016, https://www.dw.com/en/berlins-palace-of-the-republic-faces-wrecking-ball/a-1862424.

48. Funder, *Stasiland*, 51–52.

49. Richter, *Daily Practice*, 37.

50. Sigrid Nunez, *The Friend* (New York: Riverhead Books, 2018), 210.

51. Richter, *Writings*, 46.

52. Richter, *Writings*, 158.

53. Richter, *Daily Practice*, 124.

54. Richter, *Daily Practice*, 100.

55. See Jed Perl's comments in "Gerhard Richter: 40 Years of Painting | Documentary: Gerald Fox," https://www.youtube.com/watch?v=FE5EMVR7SWE.

CHAPTER 10

1. According to a recent survey led by Garen Wintemute of University of California, Davis, "one in five Americans believes violence motivated by political reasons is—at least sometimes—justified. Nearly half expect a civil war, and many [about 40%] say they would trade democracy for a strong leader." In Rodrigo Pérez Ortega, "Half of Americans Anticipate a US Civil War Soon, Survey Finds," *Science*, July 19, 2022, https://www.science.org/content/article/half-of-americans-anticipate-a-us-civil-war-soon-survey-finds.

2. Quoted in Joseph Frank, *Dostoevsky: The Stir of Liberation, 1860–1865* (Princeton, NJ: Princeton University Press, 1986), 327 (italics in the original).

3. Jennifer A. Richeson, "Americans Are Determined to Believe in Black Progress," *The Atlantic*, September 2020, https://www.theatlantic.com/magazine/archive/2020/09/the-mythology-of-racial-progress/614173/.

4. Yevgeny Zamyatin, *We*, trans. Natasha Randall (New York: The Modern Library, 2006), 55.

5. Gerhard Richter, *Writings 1961–2007*, ed. Dietmar Elger and Hans-Ulrich Obrist (New York: Distributed Art Publishers, 2009), 34–35.

6. Richter, *Writings*, 59.

7. Richard Wrangham, *The Goodness Paradox: The Strange Relationship between Virtue and Violence in Human Evolution* (New York: Pantheon Books, 2019).

8. Jonathan Haidt, *The Righteous Mind: Why Good People Are Divided by Politics and Religion* (New York: Vintage Books, 2012), 193.

Bibliography

Alterman, Eric. "The Decline of Historical Thinking." *New Yorker*, February 4, 2019. https://www.newyorker.com/news/news-desk/the-decline-of-historical-thinking.

Anderson, Elizabeth. "What Is the Point of Equality?" *Ethics* 109, no. 2 (January 1999): 287–337. https://doi.org/10.1086/233897.

Appiah, Kwame Anthony. *The Lies That Bind: Rethinking Identity; Creed, Country, Color, Class, Culture.* New York: Liveright Publishing, 2018.

Audoin-Rouzeau, Stephane, and Annette Becker. *14–18: Understanding the Great War.* Translated by Catherine Temerson. New York: Hill and Wang, 2002.

Baldwin, James. "The White Man's Guilt." In *Baldwin: Collected Essays,* edited by Toni Morrison, 722–727. New York: Library of America, 1998.

Barron, Stephanie, and Maurice Tuchman, eds. *The Avant-Garde in Russia, 1910–1930: New Perspectives.* Los Angeles, CA: Los Angeles County Museum of Art, 1980. Exhibition catalog.

Beeren, W. A. L., and J. M. Joosten, eds. *Kazimir Malevich, 1878–1935.* Amsterdam: Stedelijk Museum, 1988. Exhibition catalog.

Berger, Kevin. "How We'll Forget John Lennon." *Nautilus*, January 10, 2019. http://nautil.us/issue/68/context/how-well-forget-john-lennon.

Berlin, Isaiah. "The Pursuit of the Ideal." In *The Crooked Timber of Humanity: Chapters in the History of Ideas,* edited by Henry Hardy, 14–15. New York: Alfred A. Knopf, 1991.

Berlin, Isaiah. "The Role of the Intelligentsia." In *The Power of Ideas,* edited by Henry Hardy. Princeton, NJ: Princeton University Press, 2000.

Berlin, Isaiah. *Russian Thinkers.* London: Penguin Classics, 1978.

Berlin, Isaiah. "Soviet Russian Culture." In *The Soviet Mind: Russian Culture under Communism,* edited by Henry Hardy, 130–165. Washington, DC: Brookings Institution Press, 2011.

"Berlin's Palace of the Republic Faces Wrecking Ball." *DW*, January 20, 2016. https://www.dw.com/en/berlins-palace-of-the-republic-faces-wrecking-ball/a-1862424.

Blight, David W. *Race and Reunion: The Civil War in American Memory*. Cambridge, MA: Belknap Press, 2001.

Borchardt-Hume, Achim, ed. *Malevich*. London: Tate Publishing, 2014. Exhibition catalog.

Brown, Milton W. *The Story of the Armory Show*. Washington, DC: Joseph H. Hirshhorn Foundation, 1963.

Buckley, Chris. "To Steer China's Future, Xi Is Rewriting Its Past." *New York Times*, November 7, 2021. https://www.nytimes.com/2021/11/07/world/asia/china-xi-jinping.html?smid=em-share.

Burke, Jason. "Laser Technology Shines Light on South African 'Lost City' of Kweneng." *The Guardian*, January 8, 2019. https://www.theguardian.com/cities/2019/jan/08/laser-technology -shines-light-on-south-african-lost-city-of-kweneng.

Cabanne, Pierre. *Dialogues with Marcel Duchamp*. Translated by Ron Padgett. New York: Da Capo Press, 1971.

Candia, Cristian, C. Jara-Figueroa, Carlos Rodriguez-Sickert, Albert-László Barabási, and Cesar A. Hidalgo. "The Universal Decay of Collective Memory and Attention." *Nature Human Behaviour* 3, no. 1 (January 2019): 82–91. https://doi.org/10.1038/s41562-018-0474-5.

Chamberlain, Lesley. *Lenin's Private War: The Voyage of the Philosophy Steamer and the Exile of the Intelligentsia*. New York: St. Martin's Press, 2006.

Chamberlain, Lesley. *Motherland: A Philosophical History of Russia*. New York: Rookery Press, 2004.

Chekhov, Anton. *Anton Chekhov's Life and Thought: Selected Letters and Commentary*. Edited and annotated by Simon Karlinsky. Translated by Michael Henry Heim. Evanston, IL: Northwestern University Press, 1973.

Chekhov, Anton. *Anton Chekhov's Selected Stories*. A Norton Critical Edition. Edited and selected by Cathy Popkin. Translated by Michael Henry Heim. New York: W. W. Norton & Company, 2014.

Chekhov, Anton. *Uncle Vanya*. In *The Plays of Anton Chekhov*, translated by Paul Schmidt, 207–255. New York: Harper Perennial, 1997.

Churchwell, Sarah. *Behold, America: The Entangled History of "America First" and "the American Dream."* New York: Basic Books, 2018.

Clark, T. J. *Farewell to an Idea: Episodes from a History of Modernism*. New Haven, CT: Yale University Press, 1999.

Cohen, Erin J. *Imagining the Unimaginable: World War, Modern Art, and the Politics of Public Culture in Russia, 1914–1917*. Lincoln: University of Nebraska Press, 2008.

Cooke, Catherine, and Evgeny Kovtun, eds. *The Great Utopia: The Russian and Soviet Avant-Garde, 1915–1932*. New York: Guggenheim Museum, 1992.

Curry, Andrew. "Nazi Massacre Unearthed in Poland 'Was Really a Horror.'" *Science* 373 (August 20, 2021): 839–840.

D'Andrea, Jeanne, ed. *Kazimir Malevich, 1878–1932*. Los Angeles, CA: Armand Hammer Museum of Art and Cultural Center, 1990. Exhibition catalog.

Danto, Arthur C. "Gerhard Richter." In *Unnatural Wonders: Essays from the Gap between Art and Life*, 180–187. New York: Farrar, Straus and Giroux, 2005.

Daston, Lorraine. *Against Nature*. Cambridge, MA: MIT Press, 2019.

Delsol, Chantal. *The Unlearned Lessons of the Twentieth Century: An Essay on Late Modernity*. Translated by Robin Dick. Wilmington, DE: ISI Books, 2006.

Dickerman, Leah. *Inventing Abstraction, 1910–1925: How a Radical Idea Changed Modern Art*. New York: Museum of Modern Art, 2013. Exhibition catalog.

Dostoevsky, Fyodor. *Notes from a Dead House*. Translated by Richard Pevear and Larissa Volokhonsky. New York: Vintage Classics, 2015.

Dostoevsky, Fyodor. *Notes from Underground*. Translated and edited by Michael R. Katz. New York: W. W. Norton & Company, 2001.

Dostoyevsky, Fyodor. *The House of the Dead*. Translated by David McDuff. London: Penguin Books, 1985.

Duchamp, Marcel. *The Writings of Marcel Duchamp*. Edited by Michel Sanouillet and Elmer Peterson. New York: Da Capo Press, 1973.

Eichenbaum, Boris. "The Theory of the 'Formal Method.'" In *Russian Formalist Criticism: Four Essays*, translated by Lee T. Lemon and Marion J. Reis, 99–139. Lincoln: University of Nebraska Press, 1965.

Eksteins, Modris. *Rites of Spring: The Great War and the Birth of the Modern Age*. Boston: Mariner Books, 1989.

Elger, Dietrich. *Gerhard Richter, a Life in Painting*. Translated by Elizabeth M. Solaro. Chicago: University of Chicago Press, 2009.

Everdell, William R. *The First Moderns*. Chicago: Chicago University Press, 1997.

Finkel, Eli J., Christopher A. Bail, Mina Cikara, Peter H. Ditto, Shanto Iyengar, Samara Klar, Lilliana Mason, Mary C. McGrath, Brendan Nyhan, David G. Rand, Linda J. Skitka, Joshua A. Tucker, Jay J. Van Bavel, Cynthia S. Wang, and James N. Druckman. "Political Sectarianism in America." *Science* 370, no. 6516 (October 30, 2020): 533–536.

Fisher, Max. "In a Race to Shape the Future, History Is Under New Pressure." *New York Times*, January 5, 2022. https://www.nytimes.com/2022/01/05/world/history-revisionism-nationalism.html?smid=em-share.

Földényi, László F. *Dostoevsky Reads Hegel in Siberia and Bursts into Tears*. Translated by Ottilie Mulzet. New Haven, CT: Yale University Press, 2020.

Foner, Eric. *The Story of American Freedom*. New York: W. W. Norton, 1998.

Foner, Eric. *Who Owns History? Rethinking the Past in a Changing World*. New York: Hill and Wang, 2002.

Frank, Joseph. *Dostoevsky: The Mantle of the Prophet, 1871–1881*. Princeton, NJ: Princeton University Press, 2003.

Frank, Joseph. *Dostoevsky: The Miraculous Years, 1865–1871*. Princeton, NJ: Princeton University Press, 1996.

Frank, Joseph. *Dostoevsky: The Seeds of Revolt, 1821–1849*. Princeton, NJ: Princeton University Press, 1976.

Frank, Joseph. *Dostoevsky: The Stir of Liberation, 1860–1865*. Princeton, NJ: Princeton University Press, 1986.

Frank, Joseph. *Dostoevsky: The Years of Ordeal, 1850–1859*. Princeton, NJ: Princeton University Press, 1982.

Frank, Joseph. *Lectures on Dostoevsky*. Edited by Marina Brodskaya and Marguerite Frank. Princeton, NJ: Princeton University Press, 2020.

Frank, Joseph. *Through the Russian Prism: Essays on Literature and Culture*. Princeton, NJ: Princeton University Press, 1990.

Freud, Sigmund. *Civilization and Its Discontents*. Translated and edited by James Strachey. New York: W. W. Norton & Company, 1961.

Fukuyama, Francis. *Identity: The Demand for Dignity and the Politics of Resentment*. New York: Farrar, Straus and Giroux, 2018.

Fulbrook, Mary. *Reckonings: Legacies of Nazi Persecution and the Quest for Justice*. Oxford: Oxford University Press, 2018.

Funder, Anna. *Stasiland: Stories from Behind the Berlin Wall*. New York: Harper Perennial, 2002.

Furet, François. *The Passing of an Illusion: The Idea of Communism in the Twentieth Century*. Translated by Deborah Furet. Chicago: University of Chicago Press, 1999.

Gerwarth, Robert. *The Vanquished: Why the First World War Failed to End*. New York: Farrar, Straus and Giroux, 2016.

Ghosh, Amitav. *The Great Derangement: Climate Change and the Unthinkable*. Chicago: University of Chicago Press, 2016.

Giblin, John. "Meet the 800-Year-Old Golden Rhinoceros That Challenged Apartheid South Africa." *The Guardian*, September 16, 2016. https://theconversation.com/meet-the-800-year-old -golden-rhinoceros-that-challenged-apartheid-south-africa-64093.

Gleason, Abbott. *European and Muscovite: Ivan Kireevsky and the Origins of Slavophilism*. Cambridge, MA: Harvard University Press, 1972.

Godfrey, Mark, and Nicholas Sirota, eds. *Panorama: A Retrospective*. Expanded ed. London: Tate Publishing, 2016. Exhibition catalog.

Graham, Loren. *Lysenko's Ghost: Epigenetics and Russia*. Cambridge, MA: Harvard University Press, 2016.

Gray, John. *Black Mass: Apocalyptic Religion and the Death of Utopia*. New York: Farrar, Straus and Giroux, 2007.

Grove, Thomas. "In Putin's Standoff with Navalny, Many Russians Put Faith in President." *Wall Street Journal*, August 20, 2021. https://www.wsj.com/articles/in-putins-standoff-with-navalny -many-russians-put-faith-in-president-11618912333?st=nibkehz55ed1nxn&reflink=article _email_share.

Grzymala-Busse, Anna. "Time Will Tell? Temporality and the Analysis of Causal Mechanisms and Processes." *Comparative Political Studies* 44, no. 9 (September 2011): 1267–1297.

Guerman, Mikhail, compiler and introduction. *Art of the October Revolution*. Translated by W. Freeman, D. Saunders, and C. Binns. New York: Harry N. Abrams, 1979.

Haidt, Jonathan. *The Righteous Mind: Why Good People Are Divided by Politics and Religion*. New York: Vintage Books, 2012.

Hannah-Jones, Nikole, Caitlin Roper, Ilena Silverman, and Jake Silverstein. *The 1619 Project: A New Origin Story*. New York: One Word, 2021.

Harari, G. M., S. R. Müller, C. Stachl, R. Wang, W. Wang, M. Bühner, P. J. Rentfrow, A. T. Campbell, and S. D. Gosling. "Sensing Sociability: Individual Differences in Young Adults' Conversation, Calling, Texting, and App Use Behaviors in Daily Life." *Journal of Personality and Social Psychology* (May 20, 2019). Advance online publication. http://dx.doi.org/10.1037/pspp0000245.

Hass, Robert. "Chekhov's Anger." In *What Light Can Do: Essays on Art, Imagination, and the Natural World*, 14–31. New York: Ecco Press, 2012.

Henrich, Joseph. *The Secret of Our Success: How Culture Is Driving Human Evolution, Domesticating Our Species, and Making Us Smarter*. Princeton, NJ: Princeton University Press, 2016.

Henrich, Joseph. *The WEIRDest People in the World: How the West Became Psychologically Peculiar and Particularly Prosperous*. New York: Farrar, Straus & Giroux, 2020.

Holmgren, Beth. *Women's Works in Stalin's Time: On Lidiia Chukovskaia and Nadezhda Mandelstam*. Bloomington: Indiana University Press, 1993.

Hustvedt, Siri. "A Woman in the Men's Room: When Will the Art World Recognize the Real Artist behind Duchamp's Fountain?" *The Guardian*, March 29, 2019. https://www.theguardian.com /books/2019/mar/29/marcel-duchamp-fountain-women-art-history.

Illies, Florian. *1913: The Year before the Storm*. Translated by Shaun Whiteside and Jamie Lee Searle. Brooklyn, NY: Melville House, 2013.

James, Clive. "Bitter Seeds: Solzhenitsyn." In *Cultural Cohesion: The Essential Essays, 1968–2002*, 214–226. New York: W. W. Norton & Company, 2003.

Jelly-Shapiro, Joshua. *Island People: The Caribbean and the World*. New York: Alfred A. Knopf, 2016.

Johnson, Ian Ona. *The Faustian Bargain: The Soviet-German Partnership and the Origins of the Second World War*. New York: Oxford University Press, 2021.

Joselit, David. *Infinite Regress: Marcel Duchamp, 1910–1941*. Cambridge, MA: MIT Press, 1998.

Kandel, Eric R. *In Search of Memory: The Emergence of a New Science of Mind*. New York: W. W. Norton & Company, 2006.

Karp, Matthew. "History as End." *Harper's Magazine*, July 2021. https://harpers.org/archive/2021/07/history-as-end-politics-of-the-past-matthew-karp/.

Kermode, Frank. *The Genesis of Secrecy*. Cambridge, MA: Harvard University Press, 1979.

Kermode, Frank. *The Sense of an Ending: Studies in the Theory of Fiction with a New Epilogue*. New York: Oxford University Press, 2000.

Kershaw, Ian. *To Hell and Back: Europe, 1914–1949*. New York: Viking Press, 2015.

Kireevsky, Ivan. "On the Nature of European Culture and on Its Relationship to Russian Culture: Letter to Count E. E. Komorovsky." In *On Spiritual Unity: A Slavophile Reader*, translated and edited by Boris Jakim and Robert Byrd, 189–232. Hudson, NY: Lindisfarne Books, 1998.

Kołakowski, Leszek. *The Main Currents of Marxism: The Founders; The Golden Age; The Breakdown*. Translated by P. S. Falla. New York: W. W. Norton & Company, 2005.

Kołakowski, Leszek. "The Marxist Roots of Stalinism." In *Is God Happy? Selected Essays*, translated by Agnieszka Kołakowska, 92–114. New York: Basic Books, 2013.

Kołakowski, Leszek. "On Collective Identity." In *Is God Happy? Selected Essays*, translated by Agnieszka Kołakowska, 251–263. New York: Basic Books, 2013.

Kołakowski, Leszek. "The Priest and the Jester: Reflections on the Theological Heritage of Contemporary Thought." In *The Two Eyes of Spinoza and Other Essays on Philosophers*, translated by Agnieszka Kołakowska, 239–361. South Bend, IN: St. Augustine's Press, 2004.

Kruchenykh, Aleksei. *Victory over the Sun*. Translated by Evgeny Steiner. In *A Victory over the Sun Album*, compiled by Patricia Railing, 4–99. Forrest Rowe, East Sussex: Artists Bookworks, 2009.

Lampe, Angela, ed. *Chagall, Lissitzky, Malevich: The Russian Avant-Garde in Vitebsk, 1918–1922*. Paris: Centre Pompidou, 2018. Exhibition catalog.

Lenin, V. I. *The State and Revolution*. Translated by Robert Service. London: Penguin Books, 1992.

Lew, Linda. "New Chinese Textbook That Says Cultural Revolution Brought 'Disaster' on Country Stirs Debate about Historical Memory." *South China Morning Post*, September 6, 2020. https://www.scmp.com/news/china/politics/article/3100389/new-chinese-textbook-says-cultural-revolution-brought-disaster.

Lieven, Dominic. *The End of Tsarist Russia: The March to World War I and Revolution*. New York: Penguin Books, 2015.

Macrae, Norman. *John von Neumann: The Scientific Genius Who Pioneered the Modern Computer, Game Theory, Nuclear Deterrence, and Much More*. New York: American Mathematical Society, 1999.

Malcolm, Janet. *Reading Chekhov: A Critical Journey*. New York: Random House, 2001.

Malevich, Kazimir. "From Cubism to Futurism to Suprematism: The New Realism in Painting." In *K. S. Malevich: Essays on Art, 1915–1928*. 2nd ed. Edited by Troels Andersen. Copenhagen: Borgen, 1971.

Mandelberg, Nathaniel J., and Richard Tsien. "Weakening Synapse to Cull Memories." *Science* 363, no. 6422 (January 12, 2019): 31–32.

Mandelstam, Nadezhda. *Hope Abandoned: A Memoir*. Translated by Max Hayward. London: Harville Press, 1973.

Mandelstam, Nadezhda. *Hope against Hope: A Memoir*. Translated by Max Hayward. New York: Athenaeum, 1970.

Mandelstam, Osip. *Stolen Air: Selected Poems of Osip Mandelstam*. Selected and translated by Christian Wiman. New York: Ecco Press, 2012.

Margalit, Avishai. *The Ethics of Memory*. Cambridge, MA: Harvard University Press, 2002.

May, Henry F. *The End of American Innocence: A Study of the First Years of Our Own Time, 1912–1917*. New York: Alfred A. Knopf, 1959.

McDaniel, Tim. *The Agony of the Russian Idea*. Princeton, NJ: Princeton University Press, 1996.

McNally, Raymond T. *The Major Works of Peter Chaadaev: A Translation and Commentary*. Notre Dame, IN: University of Notre Dame Press, 1969.

McQueen, Alison. *Political Realism in Apocalyptic Times*. Cambridge, UK: Cambridge University Press, 2018.

Menon, Shivshankar. "Nobody Wants the Current World Order." *Foreign Affairs*, August 3, 2022. https://www.foreignaffairs.com/world/nobody-wants-current-world-order?mod=djemCapital JournalDaybreak.

Merrefield, Clark. "Political Sectarianism in America and Three Things Driving the 'Ascendance of Political Hatred.'" *The Journalist's Resource*, October 29, 2020. https://journalistsresource.org /politics-and-government/political-sectarianism-political-hatred/.

Miles, Tiya. *All That She Carried: The Journey of Ashley's Sack, a Black Family Keepsake*. New York: Random House, 2021.

Miłosz, Czesław. "Dostoevsky and Swedenborg." In *Emperor of the Earth: Modes of Eccentric Vision*, 120–143. Berkeley: University of California Press, 1977.

Miłosz, Czesław. "The Importance of Simone Weil." In *Emperor of the Earth: Modes of Eccentric Vision*, 85–98. Berkeley: University of California Press, 1977.

Miłosz, Czesław, and Nathan Gardels. "An Interview with Czesław Miłosz." *New York Review*, February 27, 1986. https://www.nybooks.com/articles/1986/02/27/an-interview-with-czeslaw -milosz/.

Mink, Janis. *Duchamp, 1887–1968: Art as Anti-Art*. Cologne: Taschen, 2016.

Mochkofsky, Graciela. "Why Lorgia García Peña Was Denied Tenure at Harvard." *New Yorker*, July 27, 2021. https://www.newyorker.com/news/annals-of-education/why-lorgia-garcia-pena -was-denied-tenure-at-harvard.

Murphy, Colleen. "How Nations Heal." In *Boston Review*, January 15, 2021. https://bostonreview .net/articles/colleen-murphy-transitional-justice/.

Myers, Steven Lee. "Shutting Down Historical Debate, China Makes It a Crime to Mock Heroes." *New York Times*, November 15, 2021. https://www.nytimes.com/2021/11/02/world/asia/china -slander-law.html?searchResultPosition=2.

Nechepurenko, Ivan. "Joseph Brodsky Slept Here. The Great Poet's Cranky Neighbor Couldn't Care Less." *New York Times*, September 12, 2021. https://www.nytimes.com/2021/09/12/world /europe/joseph-brodsky-museum-russia.html.

Neiman, Susan. *Learning from the Germans: Race and the Memory of Evil*. New York: Farrar, Straus and Giroux, 2019.

Newman, Eric A., Alfonso Araque, and Janet M. Dubinsky, eds. *The Beautiful Brain: The Drawings of Santiago Ramón y Cajal*. New York: Abrams, 2017.

Nietzsche, Friedrich. *Human, All-Too-Human*. Translated and edited by Walter Kaufmann. New York: The Modern Library, 1992.

Nietzsche, Friedrich. *On the Advantage and Disadvantage of History for Life*. Translated by Peter Preuss. Indianapolis, IN: Hackett Publishing, 1980.

Nisbet, Robert. *History of the Idea of Progress*. New York: Basic Books, 1980.

Nunez, Sigrid. *The Friend*. New York: Riverhead Books, 2018.

Obrist, Hans-Ulrich. *The Richter Interviews*. London: HENI Publishing, 2019.

O'Keane, Veronica. *A Sense of Self: Memory, the Brain, and Who We Are*. New York: W. W. Norton & Company, 2021.

Onyeador, Ivuoma N., Natalie M. Daumeyer, Julian M. Rucker, Ajua Duker, Michael W. Kraus, and Jennifer A. Richeson. "Disrupting Beliefs in Racial Progress: Reminders of Persistent Racism Alter Perceptions of Past, but Not Current, Racial Economic Equality." *Personality and Social Psychology Bulletin*, August 20, 2020. https://doi.org/10.1177/0146167220942625.

Orwell, George. *Homage to Catalonia*. New York: Mariner Books, 2015.

Palasciano, Andrea. "Life in Exile: Children of the Gulag Fight to Return Home." *ArtDaily*, January 17, 2021. https://artdaily.cc/news/132095/Life-in-exile--children-of-the-Gulag-fight-to-return -home.

Passmore, John. *The Perfectibility of Man*. New York: Charles Scribner's Sons, 1970.

Pérez Ortega, Rodrigo. "Half of Americans Anticipate a US Civil War Soon, Survey Finds." *Science*, July 19, 2022. https://www.science.org/content/article/half-of-americans-anticipate-a-us -civil-war-soon-survey-finds.

Powell, Alvin. "Gawande Confronts the Inevitable." *The Harvard Gazette*, September 7, 2018. https://news.harvard.edu/gazette/story/2018/09/surgeon-author-atul-gawande-confronts-his-imperfections-in-hds-talk/.

Pradeu, Thomas. *Philosophy of Immunology*. Cambridge, UK: Cambridge University Press, 2019.

Preston, Andrew. *American Foreign Relations: A Very Short Introduction*. Oxford: Oxford University Press, 2019.

Ramón y Cajal, Santiago. *Recollections of My Life*. Translated by E. Horne Craigie with Juan Cano. Cambridge, MA: MIT Press, 1989.

Rappaport, Helen. *Conspirator: Lenin in Exile*. New York: Basic Books, 2010.

Rasula, Jed. *Destruction Was My Beatrice: Dada and the Unmaking of the Twentieth Century*. New York: Basic Books, 2015.

Rees, Martin. *On the Future: Prospects for Humanity*. Princeton, NJ: Princeton University Press, 2018.

Revelations from the Russian Archives: A Report from the Library of Congress. Washington, DC: Library of Congress, 1993.

Richeson, Jennifer A. "Americans Are Determined to Believe in Black Progress." *The Atlantic*, September 2020. https://www.theatlantic.com/magazine/archive/2020/09/the-mythology-of-racial-progress/614173/.

Richter, Gerhard. *The Daily Practice of Painting: Writings and Interviews, 1962–1993*. Edited by Hans-Ulrich Obrist. Translated by David Britt. Cambridge, MA: MIT Press, in association with Anthony d'Offay Gallery London, 1995.

Richter, Gerhard. *Writings 1961–2007*. Edited by Dietmar Elger and Hans-Ulrich Obrist. New York: Distributed Art Publishers, 2009.

Ricoeur, Paul. *Memory, History, Forgetting*. Translated by Kathleen Blamey and David Pellauer. Chicago: University of Chicago Press, 2004.

Rieff, David. *In Praise of Forgetting: Historical Memory and Its Ironies*. New Haven, CT: Yale University Press, 2016.

Rodgers, Daniel T. *Age of Fracture*. Cambridge, MA: Belknap Press, 2011.

Rodgers, Daniel T. *As a City on a Hill: The Story of America's Most Famous Lay Sermon*. Princeton, NJ: Princeton University Press, 2018.

Rorty, Richard. *Achieving Our Country: Leftist Thought in Twentieth-Century America*. Cambridge, MA: Harvard University Press, 1998.

Schivelbusch, Wolfgang. *The Culture of Defeat: On National Trauma, Mourning, and Recovery*. Translated by Jefferson Chase. New York: Picador, 2001.

Schulz, Jonathan F., Duman Bahrami-Rad, Jonathan P. Beauchamp, and Joseph Henrich. "The Church, Intensive Kinship, and Global Psychological Variation." *Science* 366, no. 6466 (November 8, 2019). DOI: 10.1126/science.aau5141.

Service, Robert. *Lenin: A Biography*. London: Pan Books, 2000.

Seth, Anil. *Being You: A New Science of Consciousness*. New York: Dutton, 2021.

Shatskikh, Alexandra. *Black Square: Malevich and the Origin of Suprematism*. Translated by Marion Schwartz. New Haven, CT: Yale University Press, 2012.

Shih, Gerry. "China's Library Officials Are Burning Books That Diverge from Communist Party Ideology." *Washington Post*, December 9, 2019. https://www.washingtonpost.com/world/asia _pacific/in-china-library-officials-burn-books-that-diverge-from-communist-party-ideology /2019/12/09/5563ee46-1a43-11ea-977a-15a6710ed6da_story.html.

Shklovsky, Victor. "Art as Technique." In *Russian Formalist Criticism: Four Essays*, translated by Lee T. Lemon and Marion J. Reis, 3–24. Lincoln: University of Nebraska Press, 1965.

Simard, Suzanne. *Finding the Mother Tree: Discovering the Wisdom of the Forest*. New York: Alfred A. Knopf, 2021.

Sims, C. R., R. A. Jacobs, and D. C. Knill. "An Ideal Observer Analysis of Visual Working Memory." *Psychological Review* 119, no. 4 (July 2012). https://doi.org/10.1037/a0029856.

Soldatov, Andrei, and Irina Borogan. "Putin's New Police State: In the Shadow of War, the FSB Embraces Stalin's Methods." *Foreign Affairs*, July 27, 2022. https://www.foreignaffairs.com /russian-federation/putins-new-police-state.

Spang, Rebecca L. "When Restaurants Close, Americans Lose Much More Than a Meal." *The Conversation*, March 20, 2020. https://theconversation.com/when-restaurants-close-americans -lose-much-more-than-a-meal-134196.

Spinney, Laura. *Pale Rider: The Spanish Flu of 1918 and How It Changed the World*. New York: Public Affairs, 2017.

Spinney, Laura. "What Are COVID Archivists Keeping for Tomorrow's Historians?" *Nature* 588 (December 24/31, 2020). https://www.nature.com/articles/d41586-020-03554-0.

Stites, Richard. *Revolutionary Dreams: Utopian Vision and Experimental Life in the Russian Revolution*. New York: Oxford University Press, 1989.

Storr, Robert. *Gerhard Richter: 40 Years of Painting*. New York: Museum of Modern Art, 2002. Exhibition catalog.

Storr, Robert. *Gerhard Richter: Doubt and Belief in Painting*. New York: Museum of Modern Art, 2003.

Tates, Sophie, Karen Kelly, Bart Rutten, and Guert Imanse, eds. *Kazimir Malevich and the Russian Avant-Garde: Featuring Selections from the Khardzhiev and Costakis Collections*. Translated by Karen Kelly. Amsterdam: Stedelijk Museum, 2013. Exhibition catalog.

Taylor, Kate. "Denying a Professor Tenure, Harvard Sparks a Debate Over Ethnic Studies." *New York Times*, January 2, 2020. Updated October 14, 2021. https://www.nytimes.com/2020/01/02 /us/harvard-latinos-diversity-debate.html.

Tolstaya, Tatyana. "The Square." Translated by Anya Migdal. *New Yorker*, June 12, 2015. https://www.newyorker.com/culture/cultural-comment/the-square.

Tolstoy, Leo. "A Few Words Apropos of the Book *War and Peace*." In *War and Peace*. Translated by Richard Pevear and Larissa Volokhonsky. New York: Alfred A. Knopf, 2011.

Tomkins, Calvin. *Duchamp: A Biography*. New York: Museum of Modern Art, 1996.

Tomkins, Calvin. *Marcel Duchamp: The Afternoon Interviews*. Brooklyn, NY: Badlands Unlimited, 2013.

Trotsky, Leon. *Art and Revolution: Writings on Literature, Politics, and Culture*. Edited by Paul N. Siegel. New York: Pathfinder Press, 1970.

Trotsky, Leon. *Literature and Revolution*. Edited by William Keach. Translated by Rose Strunsky. Chicago: Haymarket Books, 2005.

Trudolyubov, Maxim. *The Tragedy of Property: Private Life, Ownership and the Russia State*. Translated by Arch Tait. Cambridge, UK: Polity Press, 2018.

Tucker, Robert C., ed. *The Lenin Anthology*. New York: W. W. Norton & Company, 1975.

Tupitsyn, Margarita, and the MNCARS Editorial Activities, eds. *Russian Dada, 1914–1924*. Cambridge, MA: MIT Press, 2018.

Ulam, Stanislaw. *Adventures of a Mathematician*. Berkeley: University of California Press, 1976.

Underwood, Emily. "A Sense of Self." *Science* 372, no. 6547 (June 11, 2021): 1142–1145.

Vakar, Irina A., and Tatiana M. Mikhienko, eds. *Kazimir Malevich: Letters and Documents; Memoirs and Criticism*. London: Tate Publishing, 2015.

"Vladimir Putin Accuses Lenin of Placing a 'Time Bomb' under Russia." *The Guardian*, January 25, 2016. https://www.theguardian.com/world/2016/jan/25/vladimir-putin-accuses-lenin-of-placing-a-time-bomb-under-russia.

Wade, Lizzie. "Unearthing the Reality of Slavery." *Science* 366, no. 6466 (November 8, 2019): 678–681.

Wagstaff, Sheena, and Benjamin H. D. Buchloh, eds. *Gerhard Richter: Painting after All*. New York: Metropolitan Museum of Art, 2020. Exhibition catalog.

Walicki, Andrzej. *Marxism and the Leap to the Kingdom of Freedom: The Rise and Fall of the Communist Utopia*. Stanford, CA: Stanford University Press, 1995.

Wat, Aleksander. *My Century*. Edited and translated by Richard Lourie. New York: New York Review of Books, 1977.

Weil, Simone. *Gravity and Grace*. Translated by Emma Crawford and Mario von der Ruhr. London and New York: Routledge, 1999.

Whitman, Marina von Neumann. *The Martian's Daughter: A Memoir*. Ann Arbor: University of Michigan Press, 2012.

Wigner, Eugene. *The Recollections of Eugene P. Wigner: As Told to Andrew Szanton*. New York: Basic Books, 2003.

Witham, Larry. *Picasso and the Chess Player: Pablo Picasso, Marcel Duchamp, and the Battle for the Soul of Modern Art*. Lebanon, NH: University Press of New England, 2013.

Wohlleben, Peter. *The Hidden Life of Trees: What They Feel, How They Communicate—Discoveries from a Secret World*. Vancouver/Berkeley: Greystone Books, 2016.

Wrangham, Richard. *The Goodness Paradox: The Strange Relationship between Virtue and Violence in Human Evolution*. New York: Pantheon Books, 2019.

Yar, Sanam, and Jonah Engel Bromwich. "Tales from the Teenage Cancel Culture." *New York Times*, October 31, 2019. https://www.nytimes.com/2019/10/31/style/cancel-culture.html.

Yoshino, Kenji. *Covering: The Hidden Assault on Our Civil Rights*. New York: Random House, 2006.

Zamyatin, Yevgeny. *A Soviet Heretic: Essays by Yevgeny Zamyatin*. Edited and translated by Mirra Ginsburg. Chicago: University of Chicago Press, 1970.

Zamyatin, Yevgeny. *We*. Translated by Natasha Randall. New York: The Modern Library, 2006.

Zimmer, Carl. "Early Europeans Could Not Tolerate Milk but Drank It Anyway, Study Finds." *New York Times*, July 28, 2022. https://www.nytimes.com/2022/07/27/science/early-europeans-milk-tolerance.html?searchResultPosition=1.

Zmigrod, Leor, and Amit Goldenberg. "Cognition and Emotion in Extreme Political Action: Differences and Dynamics." *Current Directions in Psychological Science* (December 29, 2020). https://doi.org/10.31234/osf.io/w3hj6.

Zweite, Armin. *Gerhard Richter: Life and Work; In Painting, Thinking Is Painting*. New York: Prestel Publishing, 2020.

Image Credits

Figure 2.1
Santiago Ramón y Cajal
Glial Cells Surrounding Pyramidal Neurons in the Human Hippocampus
© Instituto Cajal. Consejo Superior de Investigaciones Científicas (CSIC), Madrid.

Figure 2.2 (top)
Stalin and Yezhov before doctoring
Anonymous artist
Nikolai Yezhov with Stalin and Molotov at the Moscow-Volga Canal Embankment
Photo: HIP / Art Resource, NY

Figure 2.2 (bottom)
Stalin and Yezhov after doctoring
F. Kislov. Kliment Voroshilov, Vyacheslav Molotov, Stalin walking along the banks of the Moscow-Volga Canal, April 1937. Nikolai Yezhov has been removed from the original image. Part of the David King Collection. Purchased from David King by Tate Archive 2016.
Photo: Presented to Tate Archive by David King 2016 / © Tate, London / Art Resource, NY

Figure 4.1
Kazimir Malevich
Stage design for *Victory over the Sun*, 1913 (1915 version)
10.3 x 9 cm, pencil and India ink on paper, pasted on paper
Collection Stedelijk Museum Amsterdam

Figure 4.2
Kazimir Malevich
Black Square (Black Suprematist Square), 1915
Oil on linen, 79.5 x 79.5 cm
Tretyakov Gallery, Moscow, provided by Wikimedia Commons, PD

Figure 4.3
Kazimir Malevich
Black Square x-ray, 1915
Photographer Alexander Zemlianichenko
AP Images / Alexander Zemlianichenko

Figure 6.1
Kazimir Malevich
Woman with a Rake, 1928
Oil on canvas
Tretyakov Gallery
Photo: Tretyakov Gallery, provided by Wikimedia Commons, PD

Figure 9.1
Marcel Duchamp
Nude Descending a Staircase, No. 2, 1912
Oil on canvas, 147 x 89.2 cm
Philadelphia Museum of Art: The Louise and Walter Arensberg Collection, 1950, 1950-134-59 ©
    Association Marcel Duchamp /ADAGP, Paris / Artists Rights Society (ARS), New York 2022

Figure 9.2
Gerhard Richter
Ema (Nude on a Staircase) / Ema (Akt auf einer Treppe), 1966
Oil on canvas, 200 x 130 cm
© Gerhard Richter 2022 (0171)

Figure 9.3
Marcel Duchamp
Network of Stoppages / Réseaux des stoppages, 1914
Oil and pencil on canvas, 148.9 x 197.7 cm
The Museum of Modern Art, New York, NY. Abby Aldrich Rockefeller Fund and gift of Mrs.
    William Sisler. © Association Marcel Duchamp / ADAGP, Paris / Artists Rights Society
    (ARS), New York 2022
Photo: Digital Image © The Museum of Modern Art / Licensed by SCALA / Art Resource, NY

Figure 9.4
Marcel Duchamp
Roue de bicyclette / Bicycle Wheel, 1951 (third version, after lost original of 1913)
Metal wheel mounted on painted wood stool, 129.5 x 63.5 x 41.9 cm
The Museum of Modern Art, New York, NY, The Sidney and Harriet Janis Collection. © Asso-
    ciation Marcel Duchamp / ADAGP, Paris / Artists Rights Society (ARS), New York 2022
Photo: Digital Image © The Museum of Modern Art / Licensed by SCALA / Art Resource, NY

Figure 9.5
Gerhard Richter
4 Panes of Glass / 4 Glasscheiben, 1967
Glass and iron, four panels of glass in steel frames, each 190 x 100 cm
© Gerhard Richter 2022 (0170)

Figure 9.6
Timm Rautert
Gerhard Richter, Köln 1988
Gerhard Richter artwork © Gerhard Richter 2022

Figure 9.7
Gerhard Richter
Youth Portrait / Jugendbildnis, 1988
Oil on canvas, 67 x 62 cm
© Gerhard Richter 2022 (0171)

Figure 9.8
Gerhard Richter
Dead / Tote, 1988
Oil on canvas, 62 x 62 cm
© Gerhard Richter 2022 (0171)

Index

Page numbers followed by "f" indicate figures.

South Africa, 40

Soviet Union. *See also* Equality: Russia and; Secret police, Soviet; *specific Soviet leaders*
   compared with United States, 8
   dissolution (1991), 109
   Nadezhda Mandelstam and, 135–136, 149
   transformation of Russian Empire into, 113
   utopianism and, 9, 71, 114, 122f, 123
   World War II and, 155–156, 163, 188

Stalin, Joseph, 37f, 109, 119, 136, 137, 163
   descriptions and characterizations of, 35, 36
   de-Stalinization, 74, 104
   and his enemies, 35, 36, 37f, 38
   Lenin and, 101–102, 104, 109, 155
   Nikolai Yezhov and, 36, 37f, 38
   photographs of, 36, 37f, 38
   poems about, 134, 143
   post-Stalin era, 74, 104, 136, 144, 157–159
   totalitarianism and, 7, 35
   World War II and, 155, 163

"Stalin Epigram" (Mandelstam), 134

Stalinism and Marxism, 98

Storr, Robert, 184, 221n40

Stravinsky, Igor. See *Rite of Spring, The*

"Student, The" (Chekhov), 43–46, 132

Subjectivity, 209n3. *See also* Objectivity
   art and, 87, 176f (*see also* Nonobjective art)
      Gerhard Richter and, 165, 171, 181–182, 187–188, 191
   Chekhov on writers and, 17, 165, 187

Suprematism, Kazimir Malevich and, 86, 88–92, 114, 119–121, 122f, 123. See also *Black Square*

Tatin, Vladimir, 90

Taylor, F. W., 115

Technology, 12, 199–200

Teleology(ies). *See* Narratives

Terror, 144
   in Soviet Union, 104, 109, 113–114, 117–118, 124, 127, 138

Terrorists, 182
   Gerhard Richter and, 183, 184, 186, 186f, 192, 199
   Meinhof and, 186f
   Western democracies and, 31

Theory, Gerhard Richter and, 164–165

Tolstaya, Tatyana, 124–125

Tolstoy, Leo, 6, 52, 53, 60, 146

Tomkins, Calvin, 172

Totalitarianism, 108, 127, 138, 155
   Stalin and, 7, 35

Trotsky, Leon, 104, 114

Trump, Donald, 1, 8, 197

Ukraine, history, 9. *See also* Russian invasion of Ukraine (2022)

Ulam, Stanislaw, 26–29

Uncle Vanya (Chekhov), 41–42, 107

United States
   Civil War, 193–194
   compared with Russia, 8, 111
   equality and, 2–3, 6, 7, 11, 13, 31, 32, 49, 154, 200
   identity crisis, 2, 196
   modern history, 1–2

Utopia(s), 159, 160
   art and, 9, 122f, 185f
   dystopia and, 9, 160
   in *We* (Zamyatin), 114, 160

Utopian experiments, 3

Utopianism, 191
   Dostoevsky and, 50–54, 60, 69
   Soviet Union and, 9, 71, 114, 122f, 123

Utopian socialism, 50, 52–54

Utopian thinkers of nineteenth century, 72. *See also* Dostoevsky, Fyodor

Utopian vision of history, 9

Values, 153–154, 200, 201
   American, 2, 7, 11
   freedom to choose one's, 154, 201
   Marx on, 96